THE OTHER ELIZABETH TAYLOR

A Persephone Life
Published by Persephone Books Ltd 2009

© Nicola Beauman

Typeset in ITC Baskerville by Keystroke,
High Street, Tettenhall, Wolverhampton

Printed and bound in Germany by
GGP Media GmbH, Poessneck
on Munken Premium (FSC approved)

978 1906462109

Persephone Books Ltd
59 Lamb's Conduit Street
London WC1N 3NB
020 7242 9292

www.persephonebooks.co.uk

THE OTHER ELIZABETH TAYLOR

by

NICOLA BEAUMAN

PERSEPHONE BOOKS
LONDON

CONTENTS

ILLUSTRATIONS

p 15 ET as a small child; with her mother and brother; with her father and brother; with a schoolfriend

p 16 Miss Sprules (on extreme left) with other teachers early 1900s; Lower IV Abbey School; Abbey School late 1920s (ET in top row fifth from the right)

p 45 ET's letter to Virginia Woolf 15 October 1932

p 46 map with Pigotts (the Coles' house at Naphill was at the bottom of the 'B' for Bucks); Rupert Brooke; Don Potter

p 71 cast of *Take Two from One,* the Naphill Players March 1934 (ET in front row, fourth from the right)

p 72 the weighing of the mayor 1935; ET's father-in-law; the Taylor sweet factory (all three © High Wycombe Public Library)

p 99 Ray Russell late 1930s

p 100 ET with short hair; ET with Joanna sitting by the Taylor car; ET with Joanna and Renny; Renny

p 129 one of ET's 1942 letters to Ray Russell, September 1942, written from Scarborough p 130 ET during the early 1940s

p 159 the first page of Chapter 15, ms. of *Never and Always*
p 160 ET by Basil Shackleton; *At Mrs Lippincote's* jacket; *At Mrs Lippincote's* reviews; *Palladian* jacket (both jackets by Ray Russell)

p 189 four book jackets
p 190 Maud Eaton (*later* Geddes) with her bicycle in Hampstead Garden Suburb; two photographs taken by Maud (one of an unknown child and one of Highgate Cemetery)

p 219 Katharine White; William Maxwell with his wife Emily; an envelope sent to *The New Yorker*; Blanche Knopf
p 220 Robert Liddell; Ivy Compton-Burnett; Elizabeth Bowen; Barbara Pym

p 259 ET in 1954 by Pearl Freeman
p 260 ET with Pamela Hansford Johnson 1 December 1954 at a Book Society party, © Getty Images

p 291 ET by Douglas Glass, © NPG
p 292 *A Game of Hide and Seek* reviews; ET by David Moore in 1957; ET by unknown photographer, © NPG; David Blakely

p 313 ET by Lotte Meitner-Graf 1957, © NPG
p 314 ET drawn by Rodrigo Moynihan early 1950s

p 343 map of Penn drawn by ET for Robert Liddell

ILLUSTRATIONS

p 344   1962 invitation

p 375   1971 newspaper picture by unknown photographer
p 376   ET by unknown photographer

Back of the front cover: Wantage Road, Oxford Road,
Burnhams and Crendon Street
Back of the back cover: Lower Grounds Cottage, Penn
Cottage, Five Ways Café and Grove's Barn

Most of the illustrations are in the Russell Papers; some are
in the Grant Papers or the High Wycombe Public Library or
were lent to the author by one of ET's friends; three are the
copyright of the National Portrait Gallery (NPG); the letter
to Virginia Woolf on p 45 is reproduced by permission of the
Society of Authors and the University of Sussex. The author
wishes to thank all the institutions and individuals who
allowed her to reproduce these pictures.

THE OTHER ELIZABETH TAYLOR

PREFACE

'A friend of mind worked in the Bodleian, and said there were bundles of letters there, with "burn immediately" on them. So *that* doesn't work.'[1] Elizabeth Taylor would have greatly disliked the idea of a biography and destroyed most of her papers in the last months before her death in 1975. She kept the original notebooks into which she copied the second draft of her novels. She kept letters of any obviously literary significance (from other writers, from her publisher). And of course she kept letters from her family. But an enormous amount was thrown away.

She professed to be, and wanted to be seen as, a very private person, and would have abhorred the biographer's intrusion into her personal life. She anticipated its horror in a 1969 short story called 'Sisters'. This is about Mrs Mason, who has led a life of impeccable respectability and few disappointments, 'nothing much more than an unexpected shower of rain, or a tough cutlet, or the girl at the hairdresser's getting her rinse wrong.' Then she is visited by someone writing the biography of her rackety sister. 'He had small, even teeth . . . They glinted, like his spectacles, the buttons on his jacket and the signet ring on his hand'; as he tries to tease out revelations he settles back in his chair 'clasping his ladylike hands'.

However: 'During all the years of public interest, Mrs Mason had kept her silence, and lately had been able to bask indeed, in the neglect which had fallen upon her sister, as it falls upon most great writers at some period after their death';[2] although she gives little away to the biographer, she feels shaken and exposed. A 1972 reviewer of the collection in which this story appeared wrote that it 'suggests the kind of betrayal and violation described by Henry James in *The Aspern Papers*.'[3]

Indeed it does, and it was to fend off this violation that Elizabeth threw so much away. She wanted to preserve the reputation built up over the thirty years from 1945 (her first novel) until her death: the Home Counties wife of the sweet manufacturer to whom nothing much, 'thank heavens', ever happens, who managed *out of her imagination* to write her heartfelt, emotionally charged novels about anguish, loneliness and despair. But because they were written in an outwardly 'lending library' style, and because the reputation was successfully maintained during the thirty years of her writing life, the *persona* adversely affected the books. It did not become her books – it is easy to see that underneath the respectable exterior lies a writer who was concealing much of herself from the reading public – but affected her readers' perception of her.

After Elizabeth's death all her remaining papers were sold to the University of Tulsa; she had also insisted that her correspondence with the writer Robert Liddell, which had been a long, extremely intimate one, should be destroyed, and this he apparently respected. But many would agree with the critic John Carey when he expressed the wish that the

letters 'had fallen into less scrupulous hands', adding that
Robert Liddell's account (in his book about Elizabeth and Ivy
Compton-Burnett) of 'the pleasures he has no intention of
sharing with us strikes an unfortunately prim and possessive
note.'[4] Hilary Spurling, Ivy Compton-Burnett's biographer,
who saw the letters relating to her, also thought that the
destruction of the letters meant Elizabeth 'will not now have
the reputation she otherwise surely would have had as a great
letter-writer.'[5] But Robert insisted that 'her chief wish was that
nothing should survive that could hurt anyone about whom
she had been funny – and very funny she was'[6] and that he
had to respect her wishes.

However, in 1936 when she was 23, Elizabeth had met Ray
Russell, a young man of her own age who was a fellow
member of the High Wycombe branch of the Communist
Party. They fell in love. And as important as their affair, over
the next twelve years, during four of which Ray was a prisoner
of war in Austria and Elizabeth was a young mother at
home in High Wycombe, she wrote him letters, some of the
most remarkable letters of the twentieth century. What she
did not realise, or we have to assume she did not realise, was
that the letters still exist. It is these letters that allow us to
see her development as a person and as a writer.

So the question has accompanied the writer of this biography throughout the long haul – is the intrusion justified?
The answer has to be that it is, and for the following reason:
modern literary biography throws light on the work and
leads the reader to a deeper understanding of it. A selective
chronicle of the writer's life might be pleasant but it would be

completely irrelevant to the twenty-first century. As anyone reading this book knows and understands, for the last forty years literary biography as a genre has been, above all things, an attempt to be accurate. To leave out the truth, if it can be established as truth, is simply not possible.

Not possible, and also disastrous for Elizabeth's reputation. She was one of the most important English novelists writing in the middle years of the last century; and yet has not been considered as such. A literary biography that describes her influences, her milieu, her working methods, how her work was received, can only enhance the way her twelve novels and four volumes of short stories are perceived; and the discovery of five hundred extraordinary letters, an unpublished novel and several unpublished short stories is part of this process. However, during the years I was at work on this material, I began to realise that there were aspects of Elizabeth's life I did not want to make public while her widower John was alive. Two years ago he died and so I decided to publish my book, and have written what I hope is an honest, but ultimately compassionate biography. It is a book that Elizabeth would have preferred not to be written – but I hope she would not have resented it. It is after all true, or as true as I have been able to make it.

PROLOGUE

*I have had a rather uneventful life, thank God. [But] another,
more eventful world intrudes from time to time in the form
of fan letters to the other Elizabeth Taylor. Men write to me
and ask for a picture of me in my bikini. My husband
thinks I should send one and shake them, but I have not got
a bikini.*[1]

Over Christmas 1944 a film was shown on British cinema
screens – *National Velvet* starring a twelve-year-old actress
called Elizabeth Taylor; her one previous role had been
Helen in *Jane Eyre* the year before. A month later, in the New
Year of 1945, a young woman of 32 sent a novel to a London
agent. It was not the first novel she had written, far from
it, and the agent had not been able to place the previous
one, but the publication of several short stories and the
agent's kindness had made her at least more optimistic than
despairing. The novel, *At Mrs Lippincote's*, is about a young
wife in wartime; her name is Julia and she is married to
Roddy; she has a son called Oliver. It is sharp, funny, angry,
perceptive.

When the novel was published in the autumn of that year
it was the beginning of a writing career that would last thirty

years; and *At Mrs Lippincote's* appearance in print brought to an end well over fifteen years of writing without being published. The young writer was called Elizabeth Taylor.

So what's in a name? If the newly-published novelist, who was born Betty Coles and became, on her marriage in 1936, Elizabeth Taylor, had realised how extraordinarily famous her namesake was to become she might have used a different name. But no one could have predicted that Elizabeth Taylor the actress would become not only one of the most famous actresses in the world but one of the most famous women in the world. Elizabeth Taylor the novelist did not realise this would happen, how could she? We do not know if she went to *National Velvet*, although her eight-year-old son and five of his friends went in October. The film that had far greater significance for her was *Brief Encounter*, which was premiered in November and shown in British cinemas in the early spring of the following year.

She wrote a few years later to her friend Barbara Pym:

I hate my name. I was buying a hat this afternoon . . . and when I signed the cheque the assistant said nastily: 'I think you must have been first with that name.' I said morosely: 'Years and years first.' She consoled me by saying: 'Well, I think *you* have more character. Although I shouldn't say it of one of my customers, the other one is very empty-headed.' This will show you what a grand shop I was in – no groves of dress material, such as you once described. Hardly anything at all.[2]

CHAPTER ONE

READING 1912–30

Even when I was a child I wouldn't ask for what I desperately wanted, however near my grasp it was & no matter how my mother would have loved to grant my wish. A curious longing to protect the nature & depth of my desires, cageyness. [1]

Betty Coles was born on 3 July 1912, at the house at 71 Wantage Road, Reading where she lived until she was two. It was a pleasant unexciting road, tree-lined, with well-kept semi-detached houses and an air of only mild prosperity; at the back of the gardens was the Huntley and Palmer sports ground; in the street the horse and cart delivered coal and groceries and children played hopscotch or, in nearby Prospect Park, 'were bowling hoops around the boarded-up bandstand where the Temperance Brass Band played on summer Sunday evenings'.[2] At the end of the street shops lined the main road into the centre of Reading; 'the watery light . . . hung colourless above the railway-bridge and behind the grey and yellow brick terraces.'[3]

Betty's parents registered her birth two weeks later and called her Dorothy Betty; later she disowned, indeed expunged Dorothy, and we do not know if she was called by that name when she was small and adopted Betty later, or if she was always called by her second name. Nor do we know whether, when she came to use Elizabeth in the early 1930s and disowned Betty, she had any regrets about having abandoned a name that could so easily have been turned into the connotation-rich Dorothea. But then young women were not normally given names like Dorothea (or even Celia or Gwendolen or Miriam) in England during the first years of the last century; the other girls at school with Betty Coles were called Daphne, Kathleen, Joan, Nancy, Audrey, Mary (how lucky that she was the one who became a nun), Brenda, Peggy, Ina. . . .

Yet Betty, in its turn, came to be as much of a burden as Dorothy: it is a world away, for example, from Betsy, the name of Harriet's daughter in the 1951 A *Game of Hide and Seek* ('"I have a daughter of fifteen," she said. "It is hard to believe," he said with weary sarcasm'[4]). However, her sensitive awareness of everything a name stood for (how she must have wished, later on, that she had simply been called Elizabeth as the future Queen would be in 1926), of the nuances of Dorothy and Betty compared with Betsy and Elizabeth, would be less important in her work than one might think. When she became the sophisticated dissector *par excellence* of English middle-class, and not quite middle-class, life, she was at first peculiarly cavalier about names, for example using a variant of her own name (Beth, Liz, Betsy, Betty and Liz)[5] five times; calling one of the characters in her first (published) book Mr Taylor, even though she was by then married and herself called Taylor;[6] and giving another, the child of seven, her father's name Oliver, although this was also her brother's first name and the name of the boy to whom she had once been the governess (Oliver Knox). A progression from one name to another – Dorothy/Betty/ Elizabeth/Liz – may have shaken her sense of identity, or at least her sense of what's in a name; or perhaps sharing her name with the most famous film star in the world meant that names in general mattered to her less than they would to most people. But by the time she wrote her last book, she fully understood their symbolic importance: 'The little girls on Campden Hill were called Dora and Isobel, because the names seemed to set a fashion of fashionable quaintness;* and had importance for Maggie', whose name was really Margaret 'and even, though few people knew, Margaret Rose at that'.[7] 'Such writing does more to establish milieu than pages of solemn exposition,'[8] the Australian critic Robin Grove would write one day, quoting this passage.

On Betty's mother's side, the side that mattered to her, her grandfather was called Harry – Harry Fewtrell.** The surname is romantic and Betty would cling to its overtones: 'Thank Christ I am half French by birth and wholly French by inclination.'[9] She believed, or hoped, that Fewtrell had been 'perverted by time and migration from the French "de Futral" or something like that,'[10] and was pleased that 'in my

---

* The repetition of the word 'fashion' in this, Elizabeth's posthumously published novel, would certainly have been edited out by her if she had been able to write her usual second draft.
** 1854–1944

mother's family there were a great many Jean-Jacques – also Jean Baptiste'.[11] On the other hand, she was 'never interested in people's ancestors, nothing further back than parents can I bear';[12] she meant in novels, but it applied to herself, so she just clung rather vaguely to the concept of her Norman ancestry without ever finding out about it. But the being French by inclination has some truth in it: how happy she would have been if, somehow, she had escaped and become French. They love her books in France, despite it being almost impossible to translate all her nuances of language.

Like his father before him, Harry had been a carriage-trimmer and heraldic painter (doing crests and decorations); he was also a 'jobbing artist', painting exterior views of pubs to sell to the landlord, and advertising scenes that were used in railway carriages by the Great Western Railway. Harry married Rosa Taylor Mulcock* (her mother's name was Taylor) in 1881 when she was 19 and he was 27, he being from Reading and she from Abingdon. Rosa's father, also Harry, was a carriage-builder and indeed we can assume he was initially his son-in-law's employer. Harry and Rosa ran a newsagent's shop in Reading, at 263 Oxford Road. Then, after the First World War, they emigrated to British Columbia and one of their sons took over the business; Betty would remember her mother standing in a long dress of peacock-blue arranging ivy in a vase, 'crying because her mother and father had gone away for ever'[13] (and she never saw them again).

* 1861–1950.

In Canada, Harry, by then in his late sixties, became a full-time and rather successful painter of countryside scenes. 'He is the only one of my relations I have loved. Since I was 8, our friendship has been carried on by letters and very often one learns more about people that way,'[14] his favourite grand-daughter would write. It was not only because he wrote a good letter that she loved Harry, it was because of his painting. She considered that she too was a painter, but one who happened not to be able to draw. 'I always see things very much in pictures,' she would often tell interviewers. 'I can't paint, but I see scenes as clearly as if I'd painted a picture.'[15] In her letters she would frequently compare the art of painting with the art of writing and, when she had money, buy pictures; and in seven out of her twelve novels she would portray writers and/or painters and explore the contrasts and similarities in their work.[16]

Harry's family (he had eight children, of whom one died and one was adopted) grew up in the house in Oxford Road, and it was from here in September 1911, in the Wesleyan chapel along the road, that his 21-year-old daughter Elsie, an apprentice dressmaker and also an accomplished pianist, was married to a local boy. Oliver Coles, her husband, who was 26, was the son of a railwayman called William Frank Coles who had died some years before, leaving Emily, his widow, to bring up four sons; since Oliver was rather an unusual name (taken perhaps from *Oliver Twist*) his parents may have hoped, or anticipated, that he would better himself and not be destined for the railways (and indeed he became an inspector for Sun Insurance).

Betty, who was born nine months after her parents' marriage, spent her babyhood at Wantage Road, first at 71 and then at 95. This is where the three of them were living when, just after Christmas 1914, Oliver went off to Bedford to join the Argyll and Sutherland Highlanders as a private. The following May he went to France, to Festubert near Neuve Chapelle, but was not sent to the firing line because of heart disease (the result of rheumatic fever when he was 14) and in fact spent most of his six weeks in France on sick leave. He came back to England in June and spent the summer in various convalescent homes before going up to Edinburgh in September. Here Elsie and Betty joined him. 'I remember quite well living in Edinburgh as a child, but only in a few pictures . . . I see 2 distinct cities – the one, vast, rose-crowned I saw as a child, & the other, awfully municipal & full of chain-stores & lacking in magic which I saw when I went back there when grown-up.'[17]

Oliver was discharged from the army for good in the spring of 1916, on a disablement pension, and a month later Elsie had another baby. He was called Oliver Campbell but always known as Campbell, perhaps as a tribute to his father's newly acquired Scottish connections; his harelip unfortunately resulted in a speech impediment which would mean a lot of worry for the whole family. Betty, who was in bed on Armistice Day '(wars come & go, I am always ill in bed), got out & peeped through the curtains at children below with flags'.[18] By now the Coles had moved in to a house in Reading just along from the Sun Insurance office: this was 257 Oxford Road, three houses away from the Fewtrells' newsagent's shop and very near Oliver's mother, two of his brothers, his aunt Louisa at 159 and one of Elsie's brothers, Ernest, in Waterloo Road. They were near their families; yet the house hardly represented a step up socially, indeed it signified the kind of radical belt-tightening necessary after four years of a private's wages. But even though Oliver soon re-established himself as an insurance inspector, he and Elsie remained in Oxford Road for the next twelve years.

Betty would first become conscious of its social significance when she went to the Abbey School at the age of eleven. Here she realised that the girls from better-off families lived in the kind of wide tree-lined avenues in which she had been born, or even in turreted and balconied houses on the river; whereas her home was on a main artery road. In fact it was the road to Oxford, running west from Reading, and was lined with houses and shops (Home and Colonial, the International Stores, Lipton's, the kind of shops that had marble counters, rice and semolina displayed in open hessian sacks, big slabs of butter, fish and meat pastes in jars, broken biscuits sold in bulk), cyclists and the occasional motor-car going by, the railway bridge a few yards away and trams stopping outside. Cassandra in *Palladian* (1946), who is looking at the view from her bedroom window for the last time – both her parents have died – remembers ever after:

The sound of the shop-doors opening and shutting across the road (the continual *ping* of one doorbell after another), the paper-boy yelling in the gutter, the trams like absurd and angry monsters roaring under the railway bridge. She smelt the sooty garden below, the dusty privet, full of old mauve and white tram tickets, could see a line of trucks shunted across the bridge . . .'[19]

Betty's early life was bound up in that of her mother: Elsie Coles and her daughter were especially close, even though 'kisses were not part of anything between us'.[20] 'I was born when she was only a girl and as I grew up she was still young. I suppose I lived in the shadow of her loveliness and gaiety and kindness. But I was content to do so. She was not like my mother. She was always my comrade.'[21] (The word was here deliberately used in the Communist Party sense since, at the time she wrote this, Betty was a staunch CP supporter.)

Oliver Coles, however, was rarely mentioned. He and Betty may have been temperamentally unlike; or, just as likely, Oliver's experiences in France may have caused lingering depression, the kind of depression that is expressed in sullenness and bad temper. 'I remember the long evenings in summer,' Betty would write in a piece about childhood, 'lying restlessly in bed . . . I would creep softly across to the window and lean out, dreaming . . . to be brought back with utter shock, by the stern voice in the room behind me.' This would not have been Elsie, nor would she have shouted '"Shut the door after you. Must you always be told?"' since she well understood Betty's fear of going upstairs to be 'alone with spectres and the prospect of nightmares.'[22] Significantly, it was Oliver not Elsie who 'always gave us a small dose of Epsom salts first thing on Christmas morning, as he seemed to think it would help us with the rich food we were to eat.'[23]

There is also the rather unappealing detail, from a Fewtrell cousin, that 'Oliver kept you in your place',[24] and there may well be a similarity with Liz's father in *A Wreath of Roses* (1949): 'When she was a child, her father was a bit heavy-handed with her. One of those dry, domineering men . . . Not brutality. But talk, endless discussions about what would become of her character . . . Disapproval is deadly poison, though.'[25] For whatever reason, the adult Betty would write one day, 'I prefer to be a stranger to him – I do not really care for my father'[26] and

in all honesty, it is really only my mother's family which claims my heart. My father's stock is boring & dull to me. Such worthy, solid good working-class people, going to Chapel, being sober & doing their duty. Entirely admirable. I like better the French rabble – the wild, the kind, the outré, the beautiful.[27]

Elsie was devoted and kind but 'so easily fatigued'.[28] Nor can she have spent a great deal of time being wild or outrée with her daughter. She had a family to look after (for a year she even looked after her eight-year-old nephew because her brother had polio), a house to run (the Coles had a maid called Ethel but not all the time), and she was conscientiously active in neighbourhood life – when she died the local paper for the area where the Coles then lived said that she was 'an untiring and zealous worker in all village interests, and was closely identified with the work of the village hall and women's institute.'[29] There is a sense that she was almost neurotically preoccupied with domesticity, for example, she spent hours in the ground-floor front parlour, 'a noisy room from the street and the trams,'[30] at her sewing-machine. When, in the 1961 short story 'Girl Reading', Etta goes to stay with a friend from school, leaving her mother to her half tin of sardines and 'the dark and narrow hall with its smell of umbrellas and furniture polish', Etta asks what she has being doing: '"Oh, the usual," her mother said brightly. "I am just turning the collars and cuffs of your winter blouses."'[31] And in an earlier story, 'intolerable pictures broke through – her mother at the sink; her mother ironing; her mother standing between the lace curtains staring out at the dreary street with a wounded look in her eyes.'[32]

Fifty years later a schoolfriend of Betty's would comment that 'as far as I know Betty had rather less opportunity than many of us for academic encouragement at home.'[33] This was another way of saying that Oliver and Elsie were not in their daughter's league – she was isolated by her intelligence, and although deeply fond of her mother, and dependent on her, Elsie and Betty had little in common intellectually. Loneliness was the reason why she learnt to be so self-contained and was a solitary reader at a precociously young age. 'The first of my reading was Beatrix Potter . . . After that came two characters in a coloured primer – Fan and Ned – and then the Bruin Boys in *Rainbow*,'[34] still read by seven-year-old Oliver in *At Mrs Lippincote's* twenty years later.

'Hallo, old man. . . . Had a good day?'
'Yes. Thank you.'

'What are you reading now?'

'*Rainbow.*'

'Is *that* still going? Good God, not that vile girl, Bonnie Bluebell, still?'

Oliver nodded, looking with more interest than usual at his father.[35]

Betty's first 'proper' book was *Alice in Wonderland*: trying to read it was 'an extraordinary experience of dropping and floundering, of growing and diminishing.'[36] Later, she claimed, she moved on to *Crime and Punishment* 'which so alarmed me as a child (a rather fat child in socks reading – almost eating – my way through Dostoevsky, picking up my comic – *Rainbow* – with my cheeks still wet from *Tess*).'[37] She also 'read the E Nesbit Bastable stories over and over'[38] (and continued to do so as an adult). But as well as reading she was writing, 'as far back as she can remember' (an interviewer would observe one day) 'she was writing – at first to keep herself company, as a little girl. These early efforts consisted of "plays with three lines in a scene" and she once wrote a play based on *The Decameron*. At school she wrote "very sad" novels under her desk.' [39] Alas, nothing has survived.

Betty realised quite early that she lived in a dullish provincial town – it was not that she longed for Moscow but that she knew that Moscow existed. Even then, Reading consisted of miles and miles of comfortable but potentially stultifying terraces and semi-detached houses, and whenever she described it in her novels it was not with nostalgia. Like Oliver, perhaps, she was not especially appalled by all the gables and spotted laurels of the other houses. He had never found himself in congenial surroundings and now looked at it all as if it were a description in a book, which bored him, but which he was not compelled to read. In this way, he walked with indifference down the wide pavement where a tree or two grew at the kerb, examined little notices at tradesmen's entrances, saw several crocuses on rockeries of clinkers and the sour hard earth in shrubberies. Who has not walked in a madness of oppression down such roads?[40]*

And the main character in her 1957 novel *Angel* walks along streets that were 'grey and gritty . . . [She] passed the Prison, with its plum-coloured brick and dagger-like slits of windows . . . At the back of the Prison were a little park and some public gardens . . . This hateful town! thought Angel.'[41] Betty, on the other hand, 'was happy at home and happy at school, and very happy indeed in the dusty, old-fashioned public library'[42] where, she claimed, her real education took place ('my second home was Reading Public Library' [43]).

When Betty was six she was sent to a little school in Tilehurst Road called Leopold House, one of hundreds of similar schools in England taking in about thirty children at a time and gently trying to start them off in English and

---

* This last sentence would exercise some literary critics as being an example of a perhaps illegitimate use of the authorial voice.

Maths, as well as team games and sport on a big lawn surrounded by rhododendrons; seeing the sign up announcing the name of the school he was to go to, Oliver in *At Mrs Lippincote's* thinks that he had 'no idea what Montessori Methods might be, but hoped that Eleanor would see to it that it was not some foreign system of torture or coercion.'[44]

During her first two years at Leopold House, Betty was inseparable from her friend Alan. On Saturdays they would go to Woolworth's to buy comic versions of Victor Hugo, Jules Verne and Wilkie Collins, then read them on the tram home while they munched cherries and spat the stones overboard. 'It was a pleasant friendship. It began playing soldiers (his father was an officer or major, mine a private) on his dining-room floor. His father made him superior. "The king is reviewing *my* troops," he used to say. "Jesus is reviewing *mine*," I replied primly.'[45] Then Alan went to Africa with his parents. His departure cannot have been long after her grandfather's, and Betty, abandoned twice over, retreated more than ever into books, bicycling or getting the tram to the library. Yet, despite being a 'great reader', she was not a lonely, introverted child. She remembered her childhood as being very happy, with the house in Reading full of other people's children. It was

> always our house where the children congregated, where we acted our plays & had our gangs. On wet afternoons we played football in the hall, or took the large feather bed from the spare room & put it at the foot of the attic stairs & cast ourselves down upon it

from great heights or climbed on to the kitchen roof & pelted one another with unripe grapes off the vine. My mother would sit at the the sewing-machine stitching ballet frocks for all my friends. Then she would play the piano for us for hours and there were always delightful things to eat. [46]

In September 1923, when she was just 11, dressed in the uniform bottle-green pleated gym tunic, Betty arrived at the Abbey School. It was the best girls' school in Reading and we have no idea why Oliver and Elsie decided to send her there, except that a Sun Insurance Inspector would have wanted the best for his children and Betty, in any case, had already turned out to be exceedingly clever. Socially it must have been an appalling leap: Betty could not help but notice the contrasts between her life in the Oxford Road and the life of her schoolfriends, yet might not have been a novelist if she had not been removed from her milieu and sent to the Abbey – it is always the outsider who is the closest observer. By going to the Abbey she moved out of her class, hence some of her rootlessness, her restlessness. That same removal from her milieu must also have affected her relationship with her family. One senses a hint of auto-biography in the description in *Angel* of Mrs Deverell going down to serve in the shop after tea: 'It was an unspoken assumption that there would be no advantage gained from sending Angel to a private school if she was to demean herself behind the counter when she returned. So she sat upstairs on her own.'[47]

There had been an Abbey House school in Reading, housed in the old Abbey gatehouse, in the eighteenth century: Jane Austen and her sister Cassandra were there for a time ('I like having gone to the same school as Jane Austen and Miss Mitford. It gives me a proud feeling'[48]), as was Mrs Sherwood who wrote *The Fairchild Family* (1818), required reading for every middle-class Victorian child. Long after this school closed a High School was started in the 1860s in quite another part of Reading, and this was attended by Mary Russell Mitford, author of *Our Village*, and best known nowadays for having been the breeder of Elizabeth Barrett Browning's dog Flush. In 1913, the Church Schools Company bought land in Kendrick Road, put up new buildings and transferred Reading High School here. It was renamed the Abbey School because, wrote the headmistress:

> We felt that it was a pious duty to revive the memory of the School which was honoured by the presence of such distinguished pupils . . . whose reverence for true scholarship and learning enabled them to paint for us in clear and forcible English pictures of the ways and manners, and, above all, the people of the time in which they lived.[49]

Betty would be part of this tradition.

Parents who wished their daughters to have the social status that being an AS girl bestowed, accepted unquestioningly that it was 'run on Christian lines, with high moral and ethical values as part of everyday life.'[50] Betty, however, was a lifelong and unquestioning atheist, even though 'everyone in this school is extremely holy. Clergymen's daughters have a vested interest in religion. I have a sneaking feeling they even get into this school cheap. I daresay if I said this aloud I'd be expelled.'[51] Apart from the chapel, there were gardens, playing fields surrounded by poplars, tennis courts and a swimming pool; the school buildings were red brick and undistinguished, cheerful or depressing depending on your temperament.

> Once, passing through the school hall which smelt of furniture-polish, was hung with brass-rubbings and shields, and in whose parquet, grand-piano, mirrors, the bitterly white sky outside was reflected, Miss Bell found Betsy rather mopish, standing beneath the green baize notice-board, her hands on a radiator. From all the rooms near-by came the authoritative, raised voices of women teaching. . . .
>
> One of the prefects, eyeing her aloofly, came into the hall, took up a great brass bell and swung it to and fro. In the classrooms, desk-lids banged, the authoritative voices were raised above scuffling confusion, then one door after another was thrown open.[52]

Typically, instead of running the school on lines that suit girls (fewer exams, more private research, less emphasis on competitive sports and loyalty to one's House, greater emphasis on the kind of literature girls read for pleasure – Charlotte Brontë – rather than as a duty – Walter Scott), it was run as though it was a boys' school. Betty was bad at games, and this was something that marred the schooldays of any girl who attended schools like the Abbey, Cheltenham, Wycombe Abbey or St Paul's, where there seemed to be absolutely no interest in or even awareness of the truth that most pupils' futures would be dictated by their emotional lives not by their prowess at sport; to say ruefully that someone was only 'fairly sporty', as was Betty, was to pity them. During games lessons she would hover on the edge of the hockey or cricket field, making daisy chains, longing and longing to be set free. Once, however, Cassandra in *Palladian* (1946) 'standing at the edge of the circle for a penalty corner, had had the ball rebound from her stick into the goal. Little girls had capered at the touch-line, mistresses had clapped their fur-backed gloves together and she had walked to the centre feeling a hypocrite for the first time in her life.'[53]

The Headmistress of the Abbey, Miss Musson, was 'very much Newnham in the Nineties and *always* wore a grey coat and skirt, full-length, and a severe white shirt and stiff collar and tie. She rode a push-bike and had pince-nez which she jerked on a gold chain from an attachment on her lapel.'[54] The History mistress was a Mrs Sacret, who was unusual because she was a widow and had two daughters at the school; she was an excellent teacher, apparently took no pleasure in being intimidating and often talked in endearingly disjointed sentences about domestic matters exactly like Mrs Turner, the headmistress in *Palladian* ('"Cups of tea . . . Sanatogen . . . Benger's . . . Change your damp stockings." Even the spirit attended to, but with a domestic helpfulness.

"I *do* think you'd feel ever so much more comfortable in yourself if you would come to church.'"[55]) Like Mrs Turner her hair was eternally 'collapsing on her shoulder and dropping tortoiseshell pins into her lap.'[56] One former pupil thought that Mrs Sacret was one of the kindest people she had ever known, and remembered easy, friendly parties 'where one was regaled generally with cold tongue and doughnuts. Lots of the people who went there were musical and there was lots of singing – particularly Schubert – and hilarious and really funny charades. It was worth going to the Abbey to have known Mrs Sacret.'[57] Betty too remembered Mrs Sacret as 'the only good person I have ever met'[58] and said, accepting ruefully that she took her mother for granted, 'my real mother is Mrs Sacret'.[59]*

The other important influence was Miss Sprules, who taught English and about whom her pupils had wildly differing opinions. She was described in the official history of the school as someone who had the gift of inspiring and holding the love of the girls, whose 'understanding and high standards'[60] made her an integral part of school life; and one of her pupils wrote robustly that 'much of Betty's literary achievement would have been due to her inspired teaching.'[61] But another remembered that Miss Sprules 'always shuffled along, eyes cast down in gloom. . . . She was a picture of misery with a quavery, querulous voice. . . . She killed every

---

* Mrs Sacret was alleged to be the sister of the writer Helen Waddell (1889–1965) but the author has not been able to confirm this.

author, making the girls underline parts of speech in poetry and explain classical allusions.'[62] She disapproved of original work, squashed any hint of creativity and wanted her girls unthinkingly to revere nineteenth-century writers such as Scott and Tennyson. 'She would set essay subjects or sometimes "poems" and then read them aloud and make all our attempts completely absurd and her band of good little "yes girls" would snigger at the appropriate places. I wonder anyone ever had the courage to write after that experience,' wrote Suzanne Hale in 1978. Miss Sprules was in fact a petty tyrant who could have found no other outlet than in a girls' school. 'Poor lady, nowadays she would undoubtedly be recognised as a gross psychological problem but she was nonetheless an extraordinarily cultured person, very well informed and a voracious reader.'

Betty suffered with the rest. But since she had innate talent and had learnt not to expose herself, Miss Sprules's appalling régime was a good training ground: a writer, must, after all, have a basic resilience and it was perhaps Miss Sprules who gave Betty a thicker skin than she might have had otherwise. 'If you were tough enough to survive Miss Sprules you were well-equipped for original writing. Betty clearly had the toughness as well as her great natural gifts.'[63] She was also forced to read literature she might otherwise have ignored (during every holidays the girls had to read a classic and then were examined on it), to write a good précis (an extremely useful skill that went on being taught in schools until the 1960s but, mysteriously, not after that) and to learn poetry off by heart of the *In Memoriam*, 'Mariana', *The Faerie Queene*,

Wordsworth variety; this would make girls who did not have much subsequent education appear more literary than in fact they were. But the net result was that 'the English reading to me at school was terrible indeed – a dreaded business of *The Talisman* and *Ivanhoe* and *Hereward the Wake*. . . . Outside school-reading came the Brontës, their lives and their works linked vividly together for me.'[64]

Every year a groan went up when Betty won the form-prize for English Literature, yet she still resisted being in thrall to Miss Sprules. 'My impression,' her friend Daphne Day would write in 1978, 'was that she was hurt that her star pupil did not confide in her, or ask her advice – although Betty must have owed her quite a lot.'[65] She did owe her a lot. But she could never forget – who would? – that 'the English mistress many times attacked her about the work she did or the essays she wrote and didn't believe the work was her own, and poor Betty, on a number of occasions, was reduced to tears.'[66] Angel, twenty-five years later, does not cry: 'She was questioned by Miss Dawson when the other girls had gone home. She doesn't believe I wrote it, she thought, glancing with contempt at the flustered little woman with the slipping pince-nez and the bird's-nest hair. Who does she think wrote it if I didn't?'[67] Even on Betty's last day at school she and Miss Sprules had a row in the science lab (rather oddly). She never told Daphne and Peggy, Joan and Natalie, what it was about, but one can imagine – Miss Sprules wanted her to agree to some kind of further education or career. One can imagine Betty saying she wanted to write and this being cursed as presumptuous, arrogant and generally immodest.

But despite everything, the wonderfully expressive simplicity of Betty's prose style was much influenced for the good by Miss Sprules's edicts. She was very firm about correct grammar and disliked the use of latinate words. 'I remember her insistence on "begin" rather than "commence" or "start".'[68] 'Once she gently chided an essayist for using the word expectorate. "It's such a very unpleasant thing to write about, why not use the word spit and get it over quickly."'[69] As Betty said later on:

> At school I handed in long and florid essays with great pride. These were returned hectic with corrections, stripped bare. This, and being taught Greek, stumbling through Homer and some of the plays, was the best training I could have had. I am still inhibited about certain rules of style I was taught then. When I break them, I feel I have been faithful to them for enough years to begin to take liberties.'[70]

Miss Sprules disapproved of similes, forcing her pupils to write with a pared-down conciseness alien to the normal eleven-year-old. Every time Betty 'did my essay in English and used some of the similes out of my novel. It seemed a pity to waste them'[71] they would have been crossed out, an early indicator that, just as a baby has to be tamed and civilised, so a writer has to balance what he or she wants to write against the suggestions, objections and criticisms of other people. Sophy in *Palladian* can write, 'so poor ill-fated Mary looked up yet once again into the tumultous vacuity of the star-canopied empyrean and the muffled oars beat sonorously upon the turgid surface of the lake;'[72] but her adult creator, who put much of her eleven-year-old self into Sophy, cannot write like that any longer. 'That "vast vacuity" stuff I lifted whole out of an essay I wrote at that age – full of such flamboyant and bizarre words'[73] – words she would also use again in *Angel*. When asked by her teacher what 'into the vast vacuity of the empyrean' means Angel replies straightaway, 'the highest heavens'[74] – obviously a phrase straight from the lips of Miss Sprules (via Milton, although Angel's teacher thinks it is Pater).

Apart from English and History, there was Mathematics and there was Greek. The former Betty could never manage ('Hatred flowed between me and the Maths mistress'[75]) and, unbelievable as it now seems, if a pupil failed at Maths then he or she failed the entire School Certificate and was debarred from any form of higher education, which was what happened to Betty. Yet what she loved best of all, un-affectedly and deeply, was Greek.

> We went to see the *Antigone* in Greek, but although we were well primed beforehand you can't follow it like that without a crib. Peggy made rather a good joke. She leant across and whispered, 'This is all Greek to me'. I thought we should die of laughing.[76]

One of the reasons she would retain affectionate memories of the Abbey was that, in true boys' school tradition, all the girls learnt the rudiments of Latin and one or two, most unusually, made a start on 'what Elizabeth Barrett Browning called "Ladies' Greek – without any accents".' [77]

This made Betty very happy, and she worshipped the Greek mistress 'for once in my life' purely for her intellect. 'The greatest bliss to sit and listen to her reading Homer. I was streets ahead of the others – had special lessons alone with her in a sunny little room in a tower with jasmine round the windows and a plaster-cast of Julius Caesar on the book-shelves.' [78] And she described a rather shy, dowdy Girtonian called Miss Jagger who could not keep order in Latin lessons and in the end was sacked, but was a lasting influence: 'My emotional and intellectual life is bounded by [her]. Everything stands or falls by what she says,' [79] Betty would write. Miss Jagger would reappear as Miss Bell* in *A Game of Hide and Seek*, where, for Betsy, life 'unfolded wonderfully from one Greek lesson to another' and 'some drama in the language itself held her – some heightened quality which she recognised as belonging to her own life; in the very sounds of the words voices wailed, lied, vowed constancy, vowed revenge, adored immoderately, accepted defeat with stubborn scorn.' [80] Learning Greek gave Betsy, and Betty, confidence and set them apart; they believed, like Julia in *At Mrs Lippincote's*, that 'learning Greek at school is like storing honey against the winter.' [81]

---

* Miss Bell was also partly modelled on Sylvia Benton, who replaced Miss Jagger; she was to teach modern Greek to Elizabeth's friend Robert Liddell in the 1950s and was also an archaeologist: in Miss Bell's bed-sitting room 'lumps of stone from the Excavations at Cnossus . . . lay about on the hearthrug for Betsy to look at' (p 185).

As well as Greek lessons, what Betty remembered with happiness about her schooldays was bicycling home for lunch with Elsie, going to tea with Peggy Morris or Josephine Bales, Girl Guide meetings and the annual camping expedition at Mapledurham, and family holidays in France or in the Buckinghamshire countryside. Occasionally she was taken to London. She would write when she was 35, 'everything about publishing has always been wonderful to me since I was a small child breathing all over the windows in Henrietta Street and watching parcels of books coming out, as some people watch brides coming out of church.'[82]

Most of all she loved long discussions during break with Daphne Day (in itself a name straight out of *Rainbow* or *Girl*) who, at school, was 'bookish and intellectual & wrote verse as girls do [and] is now [ten years later] fat, untidy, a tremendous cook, a real farmer's wife.'[83] Occasionally Betty professed some interest in games and apparently played hockey: just before leaving school in December 1929, she wrote something for the school magazine (until 1944 this would be the only piece she would ever have had printed). 'The famous International hockey player' Miss Pollard showed the girls a short film and gave a demonstration. 'The film was both instructive and amusing. . . . A great deal of help was given by the showing of each movement in slow motion, although some of the results were very grotesque.'[84]

For what continued to matter most was literature. 'Betty was thought very advanced,' Joanna Love would write, 'because she had a subscription to Boots Lending Library. If we cycled back from school together invariably we had to stop

at Boots Library for her to browse and change her books.'[85]
But she was not just reading, she was writing. To begin with
she wrote 'very long plays, I used to tell my mother about
them. I don't know how she kept a straight face.'[86] They had
'a dozen changes of scenery and huge casts. Terribly dramatic.'[87] She also wrote poetry and 'specialised in blank
verse, "so much easier."'[88] At the age of twelve she sent a love
poem to the editor of *Life and Letters* to be considered for
publication; when it was rejected by Desmond MacCarthy
he commented that it was '"very nice but a trifle stormy".
Since then I have tried not to be stormy.'[89] 'Before I was
sixteen I had finished my third novel. It had twenty-three
chapters and was called, ironically, Succession. But I could be
sure of only one thing – that I wanted to be a novelist.'[90]

At Leopold House Betty had often been in trouble, not
being especially naughty 'but where the others would become
docile & propitiating (common-sense) I became rough & rebel-
lious & got the whole packet, more than I really deserved.
And would never stoop to explaining.' [91] By the time she left
the Abbey, however, she had learnt how to propitiate and was
both self-effacing and 'no trouble to anybody',[92] in fact, in the
words of a contemporary,

> a very nice-looking, fair, pretty, and rather shy girl,
> but with a formidable gift for satire even then. She
> would stand silently by and one was aware that she
> was summing everything up and was not taken in by
> any sort of eyewash. When I read her books I recognise
> details of her early life, she seems to have stored

everything up and to have a phenomenal and I am sure uncomfortable memory.[93]

Some, however, remembered her as being 'I'm afraid to say not very nice – caustic and sardonic to girls younger than her, not a happy person.'[94] Others found her kind to everyone. Her friend Joan particularly remembered her comforting her when her dog was run over and killed and she felt that she could talk to Betty when no one else would do.[95] Yet, despite her fondness for someone like Joan, Betty never found anyone she could really confide in, a 'best friend': 'Though I was happy at school there was always the feeling that, like an iceberg, I was two-thirds submerged & only touching my friends with the top bit. They – with one or two exceptions – valued me on the strength of the top bit & did not know about the other & it was a little thwarting. I always longed for something a little more.'[96]

She received 99% for her School Certificate English paper, the highest mark anyone had ever received at the Abbey School (they did not give her 100% because, it was said, no one's handwriting is perfect). But her failure at Maths meant there was no question of any kind of further education of the kind that was to be undertaken by her contemporaries, who trained to be nurses, teachers or librarians, read Geography, became doctors and so on. Yet what if Betty's superb mark in English had allowed her to go to university and read it as a subject, or continue with the Greek that she enjoyed so much? She made the resolution that she would 'go on with Greek, & I will read the *Medea* & *Electra* & *Bacchae*

& Aristophanes & the *Rhesus* & the *Eumenides* & the *Oresteia*';
yet fifteen years later 'have read none of them & it would have
been better for me if I had.' [97] The system was such that Betty,
like Harriet in *A Game of Hide and Seek*, left school with no
idea of what she would do next: Vesey seemed so sure about
his future but '"there is nothing for me to do, as there is for
you. I wonder will happen to me . . ." Relief made him robust.
"Someone will marry you," he cruelly said.'[98] Betty herself
wrote in her diary:

> My last day at school. I shall never be so happy again.
> Miss B kissed me and said: 'Always be true to yourself.'
> I thought it was just doing that made me get into one
> row after another all these years. I shall never forget
> my Greek lessons and how they excited me and it was
> a great grief to take my books out of my desk for the
> last time. Everyone else knows what they are going to
> do, except me. I only want to write what I want to write.
> This evening I tried to read some of the Alcestis but it
> didn't seem the same. I feel as if my life is over, and I
> don't know what to do. Perhaps someone will marry me.

Yet she did not waver: 'It is Sunday. Deirdre was confirmed. I
made my beard for the play. I am writing another novel.'[99]
There is a certainty about a diary entry like this which (even
if touched up years later) still makes it clear that Betty as a
young girl was already completely determined to be a writer.
She was only 17 but it seemed to be a given. 'One always
assumed she was going to be a writer.'[100]

She officially left school in July 1930 although in fact her last day was six months earlier, just before Christmas 1929. In *Angel* the heroine, Angelica Deverell, or Angel, has been ill and refuses to return to school for the last few days of the Christmas term:

'As a matter of fact, mother, I am never going back to school again . . . I told [the doctor] I was wasting time at school and that I wanted to have a chance to write my novels . . .'

'But we have to give a term's notice. And besides that, you can't hang about here all day and every day.' Mrs Deverell's voice was full of dismay at the idea . . . 'You must have a *situation*. You must have something to fall back on. Writing stories won't butter many parsnips, I can tell you.'[101]

It was the beginning of 1930 and for the next few months Betty stayed at home, 'quite at a loss to know how to earn my living. I wanted to be a novelist, but it is not easy suddenly to be that at 17. I spent a year trying to write, despairing.'[102] For a while she learnt to type at a secretarial college ('Miserably, she bowed her head over the abominable hooks and dots of her shorthand, or touch-typed rows of percentage signs or fractions where should have been "Dear Sirs, We beg to confirm receipt of your esteemed order."'[103]) This was in the centre of Reading and, in the lunch hour, she sat 'in the churchyard by the Butts . . . The post office faced the churchyard and when Angel had posted her parcel she crossed the cobbled square and sat down on an iron seat among the graves.'[104] The parcel was the manuscript of a novel which she was sending to a publisher; Betty, like her invented writer Angel, was trudging with hers to the post office, hearing the sickening thump on the doormat when it winged its way back to her. 'Soon I knew the shame of taking from the postman a great parcel of rejected manuscripts. "Perhaps my next one will be some good" I wrote in my diary to console myself.'[105]

Then, in the early summer of 1930, the Coles family moved away from Reading to Naphill near High Wycombe, the place where they had often been on holiday. Sun Insurance had put Oliver in charge of a 'District'; he would have a car to drive about in and the family did not need to live in a town or near a station. Betty, who had no plans other than to stay at home writing novels, refused to go in the car with her family. She walked from Reading to High Wycombe and from there took a bus 'into Buckinghamshire', as Jane Austen might have written. It was where she would live for the rest of her life.

CHAPTER TWO

NAPHILL 1931−35

I find it difficult to talk about myself because I often feel I am only a mirror reflecting other people – real or unreal – always more blurred than the person I am talking to or about. And then – the lack of anything spectacular. Never even having 'run away'.[1]

Elizabeth Taylor would one day describe her first visits to Naphill in a late (1971) short story called 'Miss A and Miss M' about two schoolmistresses living for the summer at 'St Margaret's', a decaying mansion in large grounds where paying guests went for three or four weeks at a time. The narrator

> was a town child, and the holidays in the country had a sharp delight which made the waiting time of school term, of traffic, of leaflessness, the unreal part of my life. At Easter, and for weeks in the summer, sometimes even for a few snatched days in winter, we drove out there to stay – it wasn't far – for my mother loved the country, too, and in that place we had put down roots.

St Michael's, as the guest house was in fact called, was run by the Misses Lavinia ('Lavey') and Sylvia Smart, 'two elderly ladies who had come down in the world, bringing with them quantities of heavily riveted Crown Derby, and silver plate.'[2] In the bedrooms the wallpaper had a faint pattern of roses; oil lamps and candles lit all the rooms; the guests ate communally at a long table. Although the food was good there was no alcohol and a general air of asceticism; people were quiet, bookish and decent, and many returned every year so that they made friends and looked forward to seeing them again. Naphill became a synonym for idyll. 'Summer after summer through my early teens, the sun shone, bringing up the smell of thyme and marjoram from the earth.' Guests would set out from the house in aertex shirts, shorts and sandals, with sandwiches in their rucksacks and guidebooks in their pockets; on their return they would play croquet or help the kitchen staff by shelling peas or peeling potatoes; in the evenings after dinner there were charades, singing and solo whist, while Betty went on plodding through that holiday's Walter Scott – it was *Quentin Durward* in the short story – because there would be a test when she went back to school. Life at Naphill was very healthy and very innocent.

But it was not as innocent as it appeared. This is implied when the narrator in the story stays the night in the cottage in the grounds lived in by 'Miss A and Miss M'. She realises when she undresses how appalling were the things she wore underneath her dress – 'lock-knit petticoat, baggy school bloomers, vest with Cash's name tape, garters of stringy elastic tied in knots' and turns her back to put on her nightdress.

'I need not have bothered, for Miss Martin was there between us in a flash, standing before Miss Alliot with Ovaltine.' Not long afterwards Miss Alliot marries a much older man; Miss Martin takes her own life. (Elements of this story were based on the relationship between two teachers from Wycombe Abbey School who had a holiday cottage in the grounds of St Michael's.) What is conveyed in the story, and is referred to so many times throughout Elizabeth Taylor's work, directly or obliquely, is that love, for example the love the child narrator feels for Miss Alliot, is something that has to be gone through like measles. 'That was a time when one fell in love with who-ever was *there*,' the narrator remarks. 'In my adolescence the only males available to me for adoration were such as Shelley or Rupert Brooke . . . Miss Alliot was heaven-sent.'[3] She falls in love almost as if she were swallowing a pill or learning how to ride a bicycle. The point of the story is that her self-absorption ensures she has no interest in the relationship between the two schoolmistresses and it would have been beyond her imagining that they were lovers; but when one of them kills herself because she cannot live without the other – that is the moment the child grows up.

The person Betty chose to adore was most probably the son, or daughter, of one of the families who came to St Michael's. In 1956 she wrote to a friend living at St Peter's Square, Hammersmith: 'This is not by any means the first letter I have written to St Peter's Square. My girlhood's love lived at No. 12. Please blow a kiss to it when you are passing – if it is dark and no one is about.'[4] (This might have been the son of the Walter Repton Coyle and his wife Elizabeth

Alexandra Coyle who appear in the 1927 voting register for that address.)

It was because of holidays at St Michael's that Naphill came to seem something of a promised land; coupled with Elsie's claim to have seen a ghost on the landing at Oxford Road. So she, Oliver and the two children abandoned the trams and the railway bridge and the walks to the shops along dreary pavements and came to live in the part of Buckinghamshire where they had so often been as visitors. They rented (from the Disraeli estate) a thatched cottage, two farm labourers' houses knocked together, in Hughenden Road; it was called Burnhams, presumably because it faced Burnham Hill. From here they could bicycle the two miles to High Wycombe or get the bus; Oliver would depart in his new car to make very much the same round he had been making for the last twenty years apart, that is, from the war years. He had been allotted the Wycombe area, close to the Putney to Windsor district that had been covered by the playwright and novelist RC Sherriff and which he had only given up the year before, after his huge success with *Journey's End*. Sherriff, like Oliver,

> had to go round seeing clients who didn't answer letters or hadn't filled in forms correctly or were in trouble of various kinds over their insurances. I had to smooth over ruffled people who had made claims that weren't covered by their policies, and trace the ones who had moved and hadn't told us where they had gone to. I also had to keep in touch with our local

agents and try to pep up the ones who weren't doing enough business or were slack about sending in the money they had collected.[5]

Initially Betty stayed at home, reading and writing, 'filling up her six exercise-books with a trance-like devotion' which seemed to Angel's mother, and probably to Elsie, 'such a strange indulgence, peculiar, suspect. There had never been any of it in the family before.' When Angel's manuscript is returned 'she was filled with anger. They had dared to give no reasons, omitted all excuses, had sent no letter. She loathed them, whoever they were, with the utmost ferocity; as maniacal as a vain woman jilted.' [6] Like Angel, Betty had no doubt that the only thing she wanted to be was a novelist, but unlike Angel she sensed she had a long, private, apprenticeship ahead of her.

What she could do was read. From her surviving Commonplace Book, which she kept from about 1928–36, we know that she read Katherine Mansfield, Siegfried Sassoon, Yeats, Edward Thomas, *The Waves* (published in 1931), *To the Lighthouse*, *Persuasion*, DH Lawrence, Thomas Mann, Richard Church (who would review her appreciatively in fifteen years' time) and TS Eliot. Many of the copied-out extracts are of poetry, as is the way with commonplace books, and although Elizabeth was devoted to Austen and Forster she did not copy out any of the latter. She does not mention Mrs Gaskell or George Eliot or Dickens (whom she loathed). Once, as a schoolgirl, she wrote in her diary 'I adore Mary Webb'[7] but she outgrew her fast.

In 1932, Betty wrote a fan letter ('and was thrilled when she got an answer back'[8]):

Dear Miss Virginia Woolf,

May I tell you how grateful I am to you for *The Waves*. I have been reading your work since I was at school and it has always helped me to have an un-muddled attitude to life, to see the vividness and importance of every minute, the significance of every action.

The Waves was a tremendous adventure. I have just read it a second time. So rarely, in prose, is anyone so keenly appreciative of individual words. It is like a symphony. Suddenly the English language is translated into fluid music, like Greek . . .[9]*

Eventually, however, Elsie insisted on looking around for something for Betty to do, a '*situation*', and managed to find a job for her as a governess. She was to teach seven-year-old Oliver Knox. He was the son of the classical scholar Dillwyn Knox, one of the four Knox brothers (the others were Wilfred, an Anglo-Catholic priest, Ronald, a Roman Catholic priest and well-known writer, and 'Evoe', the writer and editor of *Punch*). Dillwyn was a friend of Maynard Keynes and Lytton Strachey at Cambridge, afterwards becoming a

* Virginia Woolf replied, but the letter was lost in a flood in the late 1940s.

Fellow of King's and working at the British Museum. He had been a cryptographer (deciphering codes) during the First World War and was again to be a code-breaker at Bletchley Park during the Second.[10]

Oliver was not quite seven at the end of 1930 and was to lend some of his temperament and his name to the character of seven-year-old Oliver Davenant in *At Mrs Lippincote's* as well as to Hilary in a 1955 short story called 'Poor Girl'. In this the governess, whose first pupil he is, reprimands him, to no effect, when he persists in calling her 'dear girl'. He

> was a flirtatious little boy. At seven years, he was alarmingly precocious, and sometimes she thought that he despised his childhood, regarding it as a waiting time which he used only as a rehearsal for adult life. He was already more sophisticated than his young governess and disturbed her with his air of dalliance.[11]

The precociousness was true to life, but Oliver Knox was a grave, self-contained, good-humoured little boy whom Betty enjoyed being with very much and who, like his namesake in *At Mrs Lippincote's*, was always charmingly irreverent, always conscious of the absurd but serious *au fond* ('he always said he would be a judge when he grew up, & I always felt he was practising on me,'[12] Elizabeth would write). The real Oliver grew up to work in the closing stages of the war at Bletchley, as his father had done, to read Classics at Cambridge, and then to be a successful and original copywriter: he worked first in a leading advertising agency and then independently, before retiring to Italy to go on with Classics and to write novels. Knowing these things about him it is not difficult to imagine his effect, even at the age of seven, on Betty. Presumably, too, even as a child he displayed the delight in life and the gift for friendship that were to be so evident throughout his life. Forty years after Betty had taught him, he remembered that she was

> unlike most grown-ups, a very slight figure; but walked decisively, if with the suggestion of a stoop, this being (as I now think) perhaps symbolic – her diffidence the thinnest of veils covering a decisiveness, a positiveness, even a detached sort of cruelty. I daresay this makes her sound too harsh; as a governess she was never harsh, but she was always definite, not finding it necessary to justify or explain.

He then went on to compare her to Attlee: the public perception of him was as someone who did not say much, who seemed innocuous, but then would sum everything up and get things done with great clarity and effectiveness.

At first Betty would walk the mile and a half 'down a steep road, across a cornfield, and through a beechwood'[13] to the Knoxes' 'freezing draughty house,'[14] Courns Wood at North Dean. Later she was also asked to teach two little girls called Alison Dearing and Alison Oakshott, as well as the Nuttgens children from North Dean, and would teach them at home at Burnhams, at a miniature kindergarten there. The children learnt French, Maths and Greek legends and danced barefoot on the lawn; and Elsie sewed dressing-up clothes for them and played the piano.

The Knox family showed Betty new possibilities. But near Courns Wood was another ménage of equal if not greater interest and this was the sculptor Eric Gill's house at Pigotts. It was on the summit of Pigotts Hill, and access to it (in those days) was by a very steep path just wide enough to take a car; at the top was a wide, open plateau with buildings ranged round a quadrangle. Gill had moved here in 1928 and lived in the red-brick farmhouse, 'the Big House', while grouped around were red-brick cottages and wooden huts, homes to the two Gill daughters and their husbands, as well as a chapel, a stone and engraving workshop and the building that housed the printing press. To Betty this was far removed not only from the polished corridors of the Abbey School and the orderly life of an insurance inspector, but also from the sensible home-cooked food and paraffin lamps of St Michael's. It was not just the people who were different from any she had met before, it was a new aesthetic experience. At Pigotts, such a short distance from the rectitude of High Wycombe, Gill had recreated the life he had led formerly in rural Wales.

In the courtyard 'where hens pecked between the paving-stones,'[15] there were two pigs in a pigsty, huge pieces of stone (the beginnings of an outsize Virgin and Child perhaps), piles of logs, sacks of stoneground flour, Gill himself always in a handwoven tunic with leather belt, thick woollen knee-socks and sandals; and the smell of woodsmoke and honeysuckle and, often overwhelmingly, of pigs. Indoors there was the mixed scent of ground coffee and beeswax polish, a large kitchen-living room with an open fireplace at one end and at the other a long table and huge dresser lined with pewter plates. All day long, the characteristic sound was the noise of hammer and chisel on stone. 'The outside world,' Betty would write in her novel *The Wedding Group* about 'Quayne'*/Pigotts, 'had jerry-built houses, plastic flowers, chemical fertilisers, materialism, and devitalised food. Beech woods on four sides protected Quayne';[16] even though in the surrounding Buckinghamshire countryside suburbia was encroaching: trees were felled, lanes turned into roads and fields became housing estates.

Soon after moving to Naphill, Betty went over to Pigotts: she may already have been there when she stayed at St Michael's; or the Knoxes may have taken her there (they occasionally went to tea, for example in December 1932);[17] or she met the younger members of the Gill household at The Gate, a pub in the village of Bryants Bottom, and was taken to Pigotts by them; or she simply visited with other friends from Naphill, for

the industriousness, the purposefulness, the central sense of holiness: all this deeply impressed the many visitors to Pigotts, visitors who came thronging up the hill on Sundays. People came to regards Pigotts

* The name would be taken from characters in Elizabeth Bowen's 1938 novel *The Death of the Heart.*

. . . as a place of refuge, a source of inspiration . . . it
seemed like a good deed in a terrifying world.[18]

Despite the powerful atmosphere of Roman Catholicism, to
which she was always so antipathetic, this was so for Betty.
Soon she was going to Pigotts to help in the workshop: 'Many
hours I used to spend in Eric Gill's works, sometimes helping
in such jobs as required no intelligence, or not much – sorting
type and cutting up papers. They did some lovely books.'[19]
For the rest of her life she considered Gill a friend more
than a mere acquaintance – he carved the house sign for her
new house in 1937, they went on exchanging Christmas
cards until he died in 1940, and she wrote in 1942, 'I always
think of that old sailor's diary that Eric Gill lent me – about
the girl whose "girlhoods were wore off"'.[20] Gill's most lasting
influence was on her handwriting which, after 1931, lost its
rounded girlishness and took on the flowing angularity
characteristic of italic script.

Then, much later, in 1965, rumours began that she had
been more than a mere acquaintance. Sir John Rothenstein,
the art historian, described in his autobiography an occasion
in late June 1930 when Gill displayed a sketchbook 'in which
he had made a series of nude drawings of a girl with a fine
figure who had assumed poses of startling impropriety.'
When asked who the girl was he had replied that she was
'the Deputy-Librarian at High Wycombe'.[21] Rothenstein recycled this anecdote in a letter to Gill's 1966 biographer
Robert Speaight. He referred to 'the exact drawing of a
certain feature' of a female model and added, 'I remember I

said weakly, to try to ease the embarrassment and tension, "Who was your model?" Gill replied, "Oh, she was the librarian at High Wycombe."'[22]

Betty was indeed a librarian from 1934–6, and because of the popular image of librarians there is something rather humorous in the idea of her sexual or non-sexual involvement with Eric Gill resting on whether she was Deputy-Librarian or librarian or whether indeed, as is most likely, it was some other young woman altogether. In any case, it is understandable that Gill's 1989 biographer, Fiona MacCarthy, was led to the conclusion that 'the model was almost certainly Elizabeth Coles, a neighbour of the Gills who had left the Abbey School in Reading that same summer.'[23] (However, confronted by Elizabeth's daughter, she agreed to change the text for the 1990 paperback edition, substituting: 'It was not, apparently, another young librarian, Elizabeth Coles, better known as the novelist Elizabeth Taylor.'[24])

Although Betty could have known the Gill household by June 1930, she had only lived in Naphill for a month, she was still only 17, she was not yet a librarian, and she could never be said to have had 'a fine figure' (she was always very small and thin as a young woman, once mentioning during the war that she weighed six and a half stone). And it seems extremely unlikely that she would have adopted a pose of 'startling impropriety': 'posed' yes, but nude no. However, it seems very possible that Betty did pose for Gill, and most people assumed that she did so; for example the current owner of Pigotts published a privately printed pamphlet about the surrounding area in 1993, and although he knew about the dispute over Elizabeth Taylor's involvement or non-involvement with Gill, he noted firmly that 'when young she was one of Gill's models'.[25] Yet two of the young men to whom she was to be close in the next few years, Don Potter and Ray Russell, both felt they would have known if Gill had drawn her. However, Betty herself was not to be blameless in inspiring further rumours. In her 1968 novel *The Wedding Group* Harry Bretton, the Gill figure, has a library of pornographic books: 'Some of my grandfather's books have to be seen to be believed,' says his granddaughter Cressy, and when told that her sister is pregnant by someone unknown, 'even thought with horror of her grandfather ... Incest, perhaps ... '[26]

Betty may have sat for Gill on one of his regular Friday life-drawing afternoons (there is one extant drawing of a girl that could have been her), but even if she did, he certainly did not seduce everyone – despite his biographer's assertion that 'few women ... resisted him'[27] – since, obviously, there had to be at least some element of reciprocation. Betty was soon to lose her virginity; but almost certainly not to a man thirty years older than herself, in the interval between a drawing being finished and the bell ringing for tea.

It is much more likely that it was Gill's personality and way of life that was seductive. He was after all one of the greatest sculptors in England and he lived in a quite unconventional and, in some respects, very enviable way. After Rothenstein's book was published in 1965, Elizabeth read it and decided to use Pigotts as the background to her next novel. In *The Wedding Group* she described Gill/Harry Bretton

Burnhams,
Naphill,
Nr. H. Wycombe,
Bucks.

October 15th 1932

Dear Miss Virginia Woolf,

May I tell you how grateful I
am to you for "The Waves." I have
been reading your work since
I was at school and it has
always helped me to have
an unmuddled attitude to life,
to see the vividness and importance
of every minute, the significance
of every action.

"The Waves" was a tremendous
adventure. I have just read it a
second time. So rarely, in prose,
is anyone so keenly appreciative
of individual words. It is like
a symphony. Suddenly the English

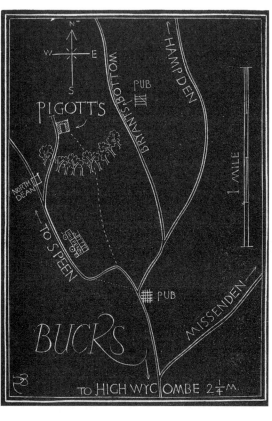

at Quayne as someone rather pathetically patriarchal (both men, real and fictional, were addressed as Master), smugly surrounded by female relations who hoed the vegetable garden, scrubbed potatoes and mended sheets. Significantly, it would turn out to be one of the weakest of her novels, which may have something to do with Elizabeth being unable to get the right tone: this needed to be a mixture of satire, sexual sophistication and an awareness that Gill/Harry was, despite his shortcomings, a great man. The typed copy of the manuscript still exists* and the first couple of pages are hugely corrected, far more scribbled-on than was usual with her typescripts. She seems to have found it particularly difficult to write the Pigotts/Quayne passages.

But there was someone who was part of the Gill entourage with whom Betty had a very close friendship indeed and this was the stone- and woodcarver Donald Potter. He had arrived at Pigotts in 1931 when he was 29. Although he started his working life in a munitions factory in the First World War, he became a protégé of Baden-Powell's and discovered his talent for woodcarving when he was asked to make the six-foot high totem poles used at scouting jamborees; in 1960 he would also carve the granite statue of Baden-Powell which can still be seen outside the Scout headquarters in Queen's Gate in Kensington.

What must have been intensely exciting for Betty was that, although Don had not been to art school or had any other formal training, he was now a woodcarver, and an excellent

* in the library of the University of Tulsa

one at that; he, we can be sure, encouraged her to feel that a university degree or any of the other formal qualifications being awarded to her Abbey School contemporaries were unnecessary for a writer. And he was endlessly kind. He always remembered that 'she had begun writing short stories and essays and seemed instinctively to know that she would be a writer. I well remember her sending work round to the various publishers and getting them returned with the usual refusal.'[28] Betty showed him what she was writing and was in fact mortified when, during the war, he came to see her and confessed that he had kept some of her work from ten years before: 'I blushed with vexation. I cannot bear to think of such things existing. I writhe inside when I consider their badness. Two years ago is bad enough – but *ten*!'[29] In addition, Don was ten years older, extremely handsome and he was '*there*', either at Pigotts or at his cottage – called, no one knew why, 'Slab Castle' – in the village of Speen less than a mile from Pigotts.

Don and Betty met at a village concert at North Dean Village Hall when there was a 'tableau' she had organised featuring Bluebeard, Humpty Dumpty, Little Red Riding Hood, Mary Queen of Scots being beheaded and so on. A tableau, or as Don called it, 'a show of waxworks', is in itself a good example of the innocent nature of entertainment in pre-television days; 'all I can remember is her being very serious and at the same time the whole thing being damn funny.'[30]

In 1997, I went to see the then 94-year-old Don Potter; he was still living at Bryanston in Dorset, where he had taught from 1940–84 and where he stayed until his death in 2004. I wrote in my notebook:

It was one of those visits which are awe-inspiring. You step inside and are knocked out by the amazing smell – a mixture of wood, woodsmoke, linseed oil and coffee. We sat by a wood-burning stove which was set on a stone plinth which DP said was designed by his old pupil Terence Conran. The house is full of Don's incredible woodcarvings – of which I like the abstract most – and he spends 'most of the time' in his studio (which was freezing!). The house is so beautiful, clean, sweet smelling, an art object in itself like Kettle's Yard. D built the kitchen which has a (navy blue) Rayburn (though he used a little electric stove to heat up the coffee – this smelt very nostalgic, I think had been percolated in the morning and had, I suppose, that indefinable 1960s smell of heated-up percolated coffee). He is totally active and vigorous with a shock of beautiful and thick long white hair. [31]

He and Betty 'were lovers for about two years', from about 1932–4 he told Gill's biographer in 1987;[32] he told the present writer that they 'were in love'[33] and said that theirs was a 'youthful love affair, which was a splendid happening while it lasted.'[34] He denied that they were lovers, although he did say that they

used to go to the Thames at Marlow on his motor-bike and swim with no clothes on. He was absolutely firm about that. They did not make love, just 'embraced'. Betty would sometimes go to his cottage and Donald would often go to Burnhams [the Coles' cottage] for Sunday night supper – to get a square meal since he had very little money.[35]

The swimming with no clothes on inspires a memorable image of uninhibited and idyllic 1930s scenes which, curiously, were perhaps less unusual, or less provocative, than they would be now. Also, this part of the Thames seems to have been associated in so many people's minds with unsophisticated and almost primitive pleasures. John Lehmann, who was the youngest of the Lehmann children at Bourne End, lyrically described expeditions round Marlow in his autobiography: at Winchbottom 'in spring the hedgerows and copses were covered in primroses, more abundantly than anywhere else in the surrounding county and before dusk we returned in triumph with our baskets filled with sheaves of the soft-petalled, deliciously scented little flowers . . . '[36] There was also bluebell-gathering in the woods of Hedsor; summer was the time for river picnics and river explorations; in September the Lehmanns went blackberry-picking across the river at Cockmarsh; and here, in the winter, everyone from the surrounding area came to skate.

Betty's parents were kind and hospitable to Don. She, he wrote, was a 'splendid [super was crossed out] girl, wise for her years and used to remind me of one of the characters out of a Jane Austen novel. She had a zest for life and all the new ideas that were going around at the time.'[37] It was clearly

understood that he and Betty could not marry because there
was no money but that they would have if there had been any.
It was perhaps also clearly understood that the Master would
not have liked one of his apprentices to have married outside
the fold; Don would marry once he left it, after Gill died.

Betty, however, had a different view. She wrote (to her new
lover) four years after her friendship with Don had ended:

> When I was 18* I first met Donald who was then nearly
> 30. He fell in love with me (although at the time I didn't
> know) in an ordinary grown-up way, and I hero-
> worshipped him in the innocent, nebulous way one
> does at 18, I used to sit for him when he wanted a
> model and was pleased & proud to help him & hear
> him praise me. I wanted nothing more – only to talk,
> talk to him & his friends. When he began to make love
> to me I was furious & disillusioned & in any case he
> did frighten me physically . . . I had nothing without
> him. My life at that time was dreariness itself, especially
> as I had made up my mind that I was naturally frigid
> and would never marry and have children.[38]

It is difficult to know how to read this passage. Donald, a very
reliable witness, was at first adamant that they were lovers,
although he later retracted this. Betty, still only 26 when she
wrote this, might not have wanted it to be known that she had
had a love affair before meeting her future husband John

* She was in fact 19.

Taylor, or it may have been the truth. Not long afterwards she would write that 'words like "darling" I can't say. I have used them too easily in the past';[39] it can only have been to Don. And in 1969 she would tell her friend Francis King, in response to reading his latest novel, that it had 'roused in me long-ago emotions – not memories of memories, which is what middle-aged people usually get; but the thing itself. Jealousy. I had forgotten that pain.'[40] Again, this can only have been about Don.

Yet, seventy-five years later, one cannot but feel sad for Betty. Don was charismatic, an artistic genius and, in the words of the Bryanston school magazine, imbued with 'dedication to the making of things of beauty . . . modesty, patience, encouragement, concern.'[41] 'He was the single most important influence on my life,' Terence Conran was to say.[42] Donald's opinion of Betty was that 'she had great wisdom and that she taught him a great deal – along with Baden-Powell and Eric Gill.'[43] Betty might have been very happy indeed with him and would have blossomed in different ways.*

The ending of Betty's affair with Don, in the winter of 1933–4, was why, she said, she 'went away to work to be apart from him, terribly troubled & lonely,'[44] so troubled that during these months she wrote four volumes of diaries (which she later destroyed). She gave up the kindergarten, much to her pupils' regret, and went to work at the Boots Book-Lovers' Library in Maidenhead, travelling there by bus every

---

* Don married Mary Broomfield, a nurse and later a weaver, in 1945. They had two children.

day. Then, a few weeks later, she saw that Boots were looking for someone to run the new library that was to open in High Wycombe in the summer of 1934. 'By sheer personality Elizabeth persuaded them to appoint her librarian . . . She could turn on the charm and beat the band, she went to the interview dressed to kill, with a hat reminiscent of Gold Cup Day at Ascot. Above all she was determined to get the job, and she got it':[45] 'Betty Coles is in charge of Boots Library at High Wycombe,' announced the Abbey School magazine for 1935. It was a job she would do for something under two years, from 1934 until February 1936. In some ways it was not very intellectually stimulating, but she did enjoy helping customers to choose their books and her acute ear for dialogue must have been greatly developed during that time.

But there was something else in her life. The tableaux had led on to amateur dramatics. Betty joined the High Wycombe Little Theatre Club and in November 1932, at very short notice, 'Miss Elizabeth Coles' (it was the first time she was Elizabeth; it would be on/off for the next three years, until her marriage) appeared on stage. She stepped in to take over the main part of Diana in a play by the Spanish writers Gregorio and Maria Martínez Sierra, adapted by Helen and Harley Granville-Barker, called *Take Two from One*. It is a farce about a young lawyer whose wife Diana is presumed drowned and then turns up after he has married another girl called Marcela. A year later, in March 1933, Jill in Galsworthy's *The Skin Game* was 'captivatingly played by Betty Coles, who exactly caught the hard modernism and superficial cynicism of the part.'[46]

Then, in March 1934, she was Elizabeth again, playing Lois in Somerset Maugham's 1932 play *For Services Rendered* 'in an attractive, unaffected way'.[47] The play is about the patriarch, Leonard Ardsley, complacently believing that 'if you come to think of it we none of us have anything very much to worry about . . . This old England of ours isn't done yet', while unnoticed by him his family is destroying itself. Lois unabashedly runs off with a married lover because she is bored and he is rich. Ethel has tied herself to a drunk, philandering tenant farmer. Eva is deeply unhappy because her fiancé was killed in the war and she has been forced to devote herself to Sydney, her blinded, cynical war-hero brother – at the end she goes mad, after the man who was her last chance shoots himself. And Leonard's wife is told she has a terminal illness and refuses treatment because she feels 'free. Nothing matters very much any more.' [48] If Betty had yet discovered Ivy Compton-Burnett, whom later she was to admire devotedly, she would have found the theme of the play, although not the style (it is weakly written), curiously in the manner of Ivy.*

The Naphill Village Players, a group partly founded by Betty's mother, put on its first production only three weeks later. It was, again, *Take Two from One*, with Bobby Goodchild (with whom Betty would flirt in an abstracted fashion) as the lead and 'Elizabeth Coles' not only repeating her performance of eighteen months before but producing the play, with

---

* She might have read *Pastors and Masters* (1925), *Brothers and Sisters* (1929) or *Men and Wives* (1931).

the help of her stage managers Donald Potter and Campbell Coles. 'She was by turns petulantly volcanic and intensely passionate, and took command of matters every time she appeared.'[49] Then, in April 1934, a Mr John Taylor appeared in Shaw's *Candida* at High Wycombe. He played the lead, the 'self-sufficient and lovable vicar', the Rev James Morrell, and 'once or twice might have given freer rein to his virtuous indignation.'[50] The following week there was another play, Allene Tupper Wilkes's *The Creaking Chair*. The local theatre critic did not like it: 'There had been so many bewildering near-climaxes and anti-climaxes, that one was hardly surprised when, with startling suddenness, the dark villain was revealed to be no other than . . . well, you will see.' Nevertheless, 'Miss Betty Coles acted intelligently and with admirable restraint although, perhaps, with hardly sufficient emotion in one or two instances.' [51]

Betty/Elizabeth had appeared in three plays within the space of six weeks: yet the following year, 1935, she did not appear in anything, even though John Taylor was in *The Distaff Side* by John van Druten and was, slightly offensively, remarked on for being 'well suited to the role of a young man who thought of love in terms of lucre.'[52] There was a reason why she did not do any acting in the spring of 1935. One 5 November, and it seems very likely to have been in 1934, there was an accident: a firework lodged in the collar of her coat, badly burning the right side of her neck and resulting in her lifelong dislike of exposing it unless the scar was masked by make-up. But the firework did more than burn her neck. It damaged the sight of one eye, with such long-term effects that her daughter would claim that she had lost the sight of her left eye. This is almost impossible to believe, but what is certain is that the damaged eye deteriorated over the years, causing her to give up driving in the early 1950s and be handicapped in other ways. 'You noticed it when she was drinking a cup of tea in the morning and reading letters – the tea cup would be in her right hand, her letters in her left, but she would have to curve her arm round to the right so that she could read them with her right eye, but then it would look funny with her right hand up holding the cup and a curved left hand.' The eye looked completely normal and most people did not know that it had such poor sight: 'It was not really a handicap.'[53]

But it surely *was* a handicap for Betty gradually to experience diminished vision in one eye; more than that, it must have been a vast, unknowable grief; and the scar on her neck cannot have been an ideal boost to the confidence of a 22-year-old girl. Twenty years in the future she and Ivy Compton-Burnett would discuss why her American publisher did not like her novel *The Sleeping Beauty*; Ivy would suggest it was perhaps because of Isabella being scarred from a motor accident. As Ivy said this 'she kept her eyes lowered to make sure that she did not look at me at this moment, at my own quite irrelevant scars. I kept my hands clasped tightly to avoid the habitual gesture of hiding myself from sight. The room froze with our self-control.'[54]

Betty would reveal her true self to very few people; the majority of those who were acquainted with her, even those who thought they were her friends, did not know about her eye – and did not know about very many other things as well. After the accident, in some respects Betty became more shy but in others she became more wild, almost as though the after-effects and her decision to conceal them took away some of her youth. Before she could, if necessary, 'beat the band' (as was said about her being able to persuade Boots to give her the job); afterwards she developed quieter skills.

It was not long before the accident that she had met John Taylor at the High Wycombe Theatre Club. He was 26 in 1934 and living with his parents and three sisters in an Edwardian pile called Atlast set amidst shrubberies and a tennis court, looked after by cooks, maids and gardeners. His father, also John, had been one of the leading businessmen of High Wycombe and was soon to be Mayor; he had been brought up in an orphanage from the age of 10 onwards; at 15 he was apprenticed to a sugar-boiler and in 1903 started his own very successful High Wycombe confectionery business and shop: Taylor and Webb, later JK Taylor, in Easton Street, was famous for 'Aunt Anne's Winter Mixture' to ward off coughs and colds. However, on doctor's orders he retired when he was 45 (thereby ensuring that he lasted until he was 93, outliving Betty by six months). He then turned to local politics, was Senior Councillor in 1934, and in 1935–6 was Mayor and therefore responsible for proclaiming the death of George V and the accession of Edward VIII. His world was the intensely pompous, male one of meetings and official functions.

John Taylor the younger won a scholarship to the Royal Grammar School in High Wycombe and had begun his working life as a clerk at Paddington Station; three years after his father's retirement, when he was 23, he was considered old enough to work in the family business. For Betty he represented something to which she was now – most inexplicably – beginning to aspire. Power is an acknowledged aphrodisiac and even though the Taylors were only big fish in a tiny pond, the Mayor's son offered a chance for escape from the cottage in Naphill. Just as important, and more crucial to Betty's future, in that she had very little control over her feelings, the physical attraction between the two of them was intense. 'I expect this was a sort of rebound [from Don Potter] but he gave me confidence in myself again.'[55] Then, two days after the death of George V, on 22 January 1936, the worst happened – Elsie Coles died.

CHAPTER THREE

HIGH WYCOMBE 1936–37

I think my letters, anyhow, sound to be the kind they read out in court, and the press seizes on one line and throws it out of focus.[1]

Elsie had gone into hospital at the end of December: she would not have wanted to 'bother' her doctor over Christmas and was taken ill at supper. It turned out to be appendicitis, undiagnosed because it was in the middle of a gastric flu epidemic, and although she was eventually operated on, she died one afternoon three weeks later. ('My mother used to say: "I can't think why so many people are supposed to die at 2 a.m. – I am always asleep then. *My* time will be four o'clock in the afternoon." [This was so.]'[2]) She was just 46. Betty, who had gaily gone off to enjoy herself at Christmas parties, would wonder if she could have done more: '"If I had been quicker . . . I should have been quicker. She must often have been in pain and said nothing"'[3] says the heroine of *A Game of Hide and Seek*, Harriet, who is more like her creator than any of Elizabeth's other female characters, about her own mother. 'No one who didn't know my mother could understand how this was for me. To see her die so unexpectedly and so horrible a death knocked all life out of me.'[4]

Betty was still working at Boots. 'One Saturday evening I had been allowed out to see my mother who was dying,' she would write a few years later. 'I came back just before closing-time, with an agonising picture on my mind – my mother lying there, nothing but bones and enormous eyes, saying frightful things because she was drunk, for they were trying to keep her alive on champagne.'[5] What she longed for was 'a cat to be on her bed, & there was nothing I could do about it. "Have you brought the cat?" she would ask – rather light-headed from champagne.'[6] For Betty, January became forever associated with the 'First Death of Her Life' (this would be the title of a late 1940s short story), marked by death, champagne and lilac.*

Snowflakes turned idly, drifting down over the hospital gardens. It was four o'clock in the afternoon and already the day seemed over. So few sounds came from this muffled and discoloured world. In the hospital itself there was a deep silence . . .

A small lilac-flower floated on a glass of champagne, now discarded on the table at her side.

The champagne, with which they hoped to stretch out the thread of her life minute by minute; the lilac; the room of her own, coming to her at the end of a life of drabness and denial . . .[7]

* But would there have been lilac flowers in January?

Yet Elsie's life had not been all drabness and denial. It was more that, like her daughter, she could sometimes be angry and melancholic, 'moody, over-emphatic, uncalm. Exaggerating everything.'[8] This contrast was to be described over and over again in Elizabeth's novels: the suburban calm on the surface, underneath the seething passions, the 'uncalm'. And mother and daughter argued.

> 'I wasn't good to her,' [Harriet] suddenly said.
> 'You were always good.'
> 'No. We quarrelled.'
> 'It can't be helped. One takes it out of one's nearest and dearest. It doesn't matter. It's the other side of love, part of the same thing.' [9]

But Elsie, if not exactly merry, was nevertheless someone upon whom her daughter could utterly rely, being, like Harriet's mother, 'full of wavering courage and unwavering integrity: nervous, ill-at-ease, uncompromising, loyal.'[10] She loved her daughter better and more uncritically than anyone else ever would, and Betty loved her; she had always, morbidly perhaps, feared that her mother would die, and would write, 'I loathe Sundays with all my heart & wherever I am. It used to be my day – when I was a child – for being afraid that my mother would die.'[11] And now she had.

A few days later Betty was driven 'to Golders Green (a long way) to my mother's cremation (a stupid word). I sat in a car and watched the one in front, with the coffin which was draped in violet cloth and covered with violets. Because of traffic we kept getting left behind. I had the feeling that I couldn't bear her to be going on by herself, always borne on, a little out of reach. That I had failed her in letting this happen.'[12] To someone taught to use 'spit' not 'expectorate', 'cremation' is, it is true, a stupid word compared with, say, 'burnt'; but then a funeral is always appalling, and the conventions of vocabulary cannot change this.

'The flowers, the coffin, the family waited. For what? So that Saint Paul should set himself questions and then answer them inadequately, inventing dupes to sharpen his wits upon, that contemptible trick of the argumentative.' Afterwards, 'Saint Paul having had his say',[13] Campbell, Betty and Oliver went back to Naphill. Oliver returned to work, in his Rover, and Campbell went back to his job at the local garage.* And in February Betty left her job at Boots. Yet this was not because of Elsie. Employers, after all, are used to people's mothers dying. Kneeling on the waxed hospital floor, the girl in 'First Death of Her Life' tries out different letters to 'Mr Wilson': 'I shall not be at the shop for the next four days, as my mother has passed away' or, alternatively, 'My mother has died. I shall come back to work the day after tomorrow.'[14] Betty left Boots to get married.

She had been 'going about' with John for the last year and his parents can hardly have approved: first-generation respectability – John Taylor senior had so recently gone from an orphanage to a house called 'Atlast' – is always the one that

* He was to run the garage, Coles & Blackwell, for the next forty years.

values social status the most. Yet Betty did not seem particularly to admire their bourgeois values, rather the reverse, and for a while it cannot have occurred to John's parents that they would marry. There must have been consternation when they did, and some bewilderment. And the question would be asked over and over again by Betty's friends and acquaintances – why did she marry John? It is asked, as well, by this biography: here are a few answers.

Her pupil Oliver Knox, Pigotts and Don Potter between them had shown Betty a way of life to which she by now aspired. And yet John represented something quite other. On the one hand there were houses that smelt of woodsmoke, where good paintings hung on the wall, men wore corduroy and if lunch was only bread and cheese no one minded; and on the other hand there were men earning their living in sweet factories, driving Rovers (like Oliver Coles) and reading the *Daily Telegraph* over their bacon and eggs. It was these kinds of differences, the small but vastly significant details of English middle-class life, that Elizabeth Taylor would analyse, point up, laugh at during the course of her writing life. That she rejected the corduroy trousers was, at the very least, surprising: 'I would have expected her to marry an artist, someone more bohemian,' said her schoolfriend Josephine Bales.[15] But that she chose the gin and tonic and the *Daily Telegraph* is one of the great mysteries of her life.

The reason for it (unsurprisingly, and as so many hundreds of thousands of times before and since) was not exactly thought out; Betty, who was after all only 23 in the spring of 1936, was pregnant. She had started a baby. (I used to get pregnant with the greatest of ease.) I was wildly excited by this. We decided to get married and have hordes of children . . . Then my mother died very suddenly and nothing else went right for me again . . . I lost the baby, as I had lost everything.

But there were other factors: Elsie had died and her grief was enormous and it is true, as Betty wrote about herself, she 'didn't care what happened to me';[16] she was on the rebound; she did not want to housekeep for her father and brother ('she made herself get married. She wanted to get away from home,'[17] Don Potter would comment); she did not consider herself to be that young any more – Elsie had been married at 21, Joanna Gill at 20 – in fact, in the 1930s, 23 was not so young to be married; she wanted financial security so that she could write; 'I was furiously attracted to him';[18] and she did not deplore the status that comes with marriage – having her own home, children and the time to write.

Finally, the thought of marrying the son of the Mayor of High Wycombe made more of a difference to her than she would ever like to admit. When, later on, some of Betty's schoolfriends would be surprised that she had not married someone bohemian, they were pointing up the contrast between a corduroy-trousered artist and the person she *had* married whose father symbolised respectability by being mayor. In 'Sisters', the short story about Mrs Mason being visited by the biographer, being mayor would again be contrasted with the bohemian, the raffish: 'Thank heavens,

Mrs Mason had always thought, that [Marion] *had* gone to live in Paris, and that she herself had married and been able to change her name. Still quite young, and before the war, Marion had died. It was during Mr Mason's year as mayor. They had told no one.'[19]

Seven weeks after Elsie's death – in itself this was all the excuse that was needed to have a quiet ceremony – John Taylor and Betty were married – on 11 March 1936. The wedding took place at Caxton Hall in Westminster because otherwise so many people would have had to be invited to the reception: when the newly-installed Mayor and Mayoress had given a reception in November of the previous year, four hundred people had come. John's London address was given as 47 Knightsbridge and Betty's as Flat 34, 27 Old Bond Street. How they came by them it is impossible to say.

On her marriage certificate Betty was called Dorothy Betty Coles otherwise Elizabeth Coles: her wedding marked a demarcation line between the old name and the new. Although her father went on calling her Betty, as did some of her High Wycombe friends, in future she preferred to be known as Elizabeth. For the wedding she wore 'a green corduroy suit [which she would go on wearing all during the war, with red sandals] and John was in oatmeal-coloured Harris tweed. We drove together to our wedding. None of it was what his parents had envisaged.'[20] Lunch was at the Cumberland Hotel; in the evening they went to The Crazy Gang at the London Palladium; they spent the night at 47 Knightsbridge. Then they went home – because they both had rehearsals for the play opening in a week's time.

It was *The Case of the Frightened Lady* by Edgar Wallace, put on by the High Wycombe Operatic and Dramatic Society; Elizabeth played the lead. 'For many weeks High Wycombe's amateur players have been preparing,' wrote the local paper. This was on the left-hand side of page 12. In the right-hand column there were seven paragraphs about the wedding. The bride and groom had met when they acted together; in view of the death recently of the bride's mother there were no bridesmaids; 'flouting superstition, the bride wore a neat green costume'; preparations for a honeymoon in Paris had been cancelled; Mr John Taylor had been secretary of High Wycombe Hockey Club for several years and secretary of High Wycombe Wholesale Tobacconists' and Confectioners' Association; and among the many wedding presents was a Swedish glass hors d'oeuvres dish from members of High Wycombe Hockey Club and something from Mrs Disraeli* at Hughenden.[21]

The play, which ran for three performances, was well received. 'Elizabeth Taylor revealed unsuspected histrionic ability in her simulation of terror as the "frightened lady",' wrote the local paper. 'She achieved with distinction the semblance of haunting fear in her eyes and terrified detachment in her manner . . . John Taylor, playing appropriately enough opposite his bride of a week ago, gave a natural performance.'[22] That Sunday they would have perhaps gone to lunch with the Taylor parents at Atlast and tea at

---

* the widow of Coningsby Disraeli, nephew of Benjamin Disraeli, the Earl of Beaconsfield

Burnhams with the newly-widowed Oliver. The next morning John would have left their flat and walked to the factory two minutes away in Easton Street, leaving Elizabeth – to what?

She was by now a thin, intelligent-looking girl of 23, 'not so much pretty as very beautiful' as one of her friends once said,[23] in the situation of so many millions of women before and since – alone in a small flat* (but theirs was on the top floor, two flights of stairs above a shop, with the sun pouring in), her new and equally young husband departed for work, wondering what to do with the rest of her day and the rest of her life given that all she really wanted to do was write. We can imagine it – the new bride's shopping list (wax polish, material for new curtains, a potato peeler); John coming home to lunch (as he had always done when he lived with his parents and was always to do in the future); and the two of them feeling like a cliché of a young married couple, the first meals cooked by Elizabeth, the evenings reading by the fire, the occasional trip to London to go to the theatre.

Elizabeth was happy to have her own home and not to have to worry about money, for she would never forget the atmosphere of straitened circumstances in which her family

---

* They lived at 25 Crendon Street, a turning off the High Street in the centre of High Wycombe. The building was neo-Georgian and had been built the year before when the west side of Crendon Street was demolished and rebuilt as part of the High Wycombe 'improvements'. Their flat was above Dyson & Sons, Music Stores – Pianos and Tuners, and between the Crendon Dairy and Beryl Money, Ladies' Wear.

had lived in Oxford Road. She wanted the baby she was expecting and was, we can be sure, miserable when she miscarried, probably during the early summer of 1936. (Or later perhaps: in *At Mrs Lippincote's* Julia has had a stillborn daughter.) But she was still firmly resolved to be a writer, which meant that she was not going to settle easily into being a mere wife and mother. Luckily, the Taylors' flat was just up the hill from the public library* and within walking distance from the Boots library where Elizabeth had worked. For she was now becoming extremely well-read. The writer of a PhD has listed all the literary, visual and musical 'interflects and allusions' in Elizabeth's novels.[24] The basis for these was acquired during these pre-war years when she read widely and deeply, trying to have a sense of English literary history of which, she subconsciously thought, or dreamt, she would one day be part.

It was just before the wedding that Elizabeth did something that was to be almost as momentous for her as her marriage: she joined the Communist Party. Later she would claim that she did so 'the day after' her mother died because 'I had been meaning to for months'.[25] This may have been true or the timing may have been misremembered: in the same letter she claimed that she was married two weeks after her mother died when in fact it was seven, a miscalculation which is both unimportant and important.

Whenever she actually joined, at some point in 1936

---

* The public library (by now it was thought old-fashioned to call it the 'free library') was opened in 1932.

Elizabeth became a member of the Communist Party of Great Britain, and not just a member but an active one. It is curious, of course: she had a lifelong hostility to organised religion, indeed to organised anything, and she did not seem like a 'joiner'. Yet during the previous five years, the years of her early twenties, she had become increasingly politicised, rather as if she had been an undergraduate: indeed, but for the absurd strictures about maths, Elizabeth might, by 1936, have recently come down from university, where non-political engagement was far more of an oddity than engagement.

Her brand of communism was remembered by Don Potter as being more akin to religious conviction. 'She was not religious in the conventional sense and her communism was not of the Russian brand, although at that time it had not turned into a police state with Gestapo as it did later under Stalinism, the communism was more after the teachings of Christ with the sharing of possessions and private property.'[26] The seeds had in fact been sown both at St Michael's and at Pigotts. Although Elizabeth was a confirmed atheist (once, she copied the words in her Commonplace Book, 'I could not make a close friend of a deeply religious person, because of that large area of their minds which reason has handed over to faith'[27]), nevertheless she very much approved of the concept of communal living, of sharing possessions, of working and living in harmony, and would write ten years later:

What I meant by Communism when I joined the party, was not what they have – Russia is not anything to which they appear to work towards – I thought it meant

69

all the opposite things. I did not see why economic freedom would not lead to the other more important liberties – of speech & thought & expression. I thought men & women might have an equal chance, brought up together from childhood, & a woman respected first as a person, not as a machine for reproduction . . . I thought having enough money people could turn to the important things – I did not visualise all the signboards saying 'Forbidden'.[28]

By the time Elizabeth first joined the Party it had changed fundamentally in England 'from a conspiratorial party, to one that was a part of a wider popular front fighting unemployment and fascism.'[29] During 1936 the Party was becoming much more militant than the Labour Party against the Means Test (it organised hunger marches), and against Mosley (the Battle of Cable Street in the East End). This was the time when intellectuals were joining, for example Philip Toynbee became the first Communist President of the Oxford Union, and even Virginia Woolf wrote for the *Daily Worker*. Thus, during the later 1930s, the CP operated at two levels. It was able to draw in many writers, artists, undergraduates and so on who saw it as the most active force against unemployment and fascism, and who believed that capitalism was discredited. Yet it was still controlled by a small clique which took orders and money from Moscow, and who persuaded the British public that Stalin's trials and purges, which were at their peak at this time, were the inevitable teething troubles of building socialism in the Soviet Union.

It was likely to have been Eric Gill's son-in-law René Hague who was the impetus for Elizabeth joining the CP: of him *The Times* obituary writer would observe, 'like many idealists in the 1930s he had a brief flirtation with the Communist Party, a step of which Gill could not have approved.'[30] He was seven years older than Elizabeth, Irish but brought up in England, and had thought of becoming a priest. After he met Gill he had gone to live at Pigotts, married his daughter Joanna and become a full-time printer running the printing works known as Hague & Gill. Besides being intelligent and clever he was fun-loving: 'My word, we did like having a good time: old motor-cars and parties and pubs.'[31] A friend described him as a 'classical scholar, ex-seminarian, wise, witty, drunk, holy, bawdy, very free in his vocabulary, and having a keen and loving interest in oneself, a very personal person'[32] who must have been an ideal friend for Elizabeth, indeed an ideal. Mostly Elizabeth loved listening to René talk. As a one-time Pigotts resident, Brocard Sewell, would observe, Elizabeth's novel *The Wedding Group* gives 'a very accurate reconstruction of the sort of conversations that went on at Pigotts. She captures very faithfully (under fictional names) the speech of Gill's son-in-law René Hague and of his chaplain Dr JP Flood.'[33]*

Elizabeth (René was the first friend who apparently never knew her as Betty) gravitated to him for intellectual companionship, to the extent that 'Petra [Gill] once mentioned to me' (wrote Gill's biographer, Fiona MacCarthy) 'that her

* He is Father Daughtry in the book – Flood/Drought/Droughty/ Draughty/ Daughtry.

sister Joan[na], René's wife, was jealous of her evident attractions for him, not just her beauty but her qualities of mind.'[34] Elizabeth for her part found René something of an anchor. When, in the months before the outbreak of war, she was in emotional turmoil, she went to René: 'I wouldn't have flown to him except that our relationship was trivial – and so peaceful to me. The only peace I had at that time.'[35] René, circumspectly, remarked:

> I knew Elizabeth much better in her communist days, when I used to see her at meetings at the High Wycombe Trades and Labour Club and Institute – my word, what a dreary place! The situation at the time made it easy for the communists to pick up any number of 'fellow-travellers', and Elizabeth was very busy at this. It was a time of great enthusiasm: we thought that something was really going to be done – that there'd be a real change, syndicalism, social credit, fascism, national socialism, communism, anarchism – one of these, we thought, would surely free us from the rule of money. That was the time of the 'Peace Front', into which everybody was roped from the Vicar of High Wycombe to the boy whom I remember as selling the *Daily Worker* in Wycombe High Street on market days, Friday and Saturday.'[36]

The 'boy' was Raymond Russell, the closest friend Elizabeth would ever have. Ray was a local boy born in 1913 whose father, before his early death, had worked on the railways as a mechanic checking signals, track etc; his maternal great-uncle was Ebenezer Gomme, whose furniture company would become G-Plan. Ray lived with his mother a quarter of a mile east of the centre of High Wycombe at 59 Queen's Road. Although considered extremely bright and allowed to skip two years at elementary school, he did not get into the Royal Grammar School but instead went to the Technical Institute until he was 16. Here he learnt woodwork, maths, science and English. But his contemporaries were mostly far less intelligent than him and his deep-rooted antipathy to any kind of privilege or distinction began then, in a kind of lonely sense of inferiority and anger.

At first Ray was apprenticed to William Bartlett, one of the many furniture manufacturers in and around High Wycombe, but after a while he gave this up and worked first at a paper and then at a fibreboard mill. He had been in the same year at the 'Tech' as Robin Day, who went on to the Royal College of Art and became a world-famous furniture designer; but although Ray himself designed and made some outstandingly beautiful tables and chairs (which still exist), there was something in his temperament that made him stick with the mill and reject the idea of becoming a full-time designer. Clifton Reynolds, a local High Wycombe novelist who wrote rather uninteresting but successful books, would put it well when he described Ray in a 1942 novel called *Valley of Chairs* about pre-war High Wycombe: John Blair is a young radical who goes out to Spain to fight for the Republican cause (as Ray would probably have done if it were not for his mother and for Elizabeth).

[He] was not a mixer. He was not the type who could call at a strange furniture shop and exercise enough personal charm to jolly the proprietor into giving him an order . . . The escape from manual or clerical work for anyone without capital lies either in the field of higher technical training than is required in the furniture trade, or else in the solid soul-destroying job of selling goods. [37]

Ray did not have the kind of conviviality that is necessary for a skill like furniture design, where the initial concept may be one person's but the manufacture has to be a team effort; in any case, more than anything he wanted to paint. What he did have was immense strength of character and good looks. Clifton Reynolds' description of him is acute:

A fresh-complexioned young man, with a firm mouth and steady eyes. Although not much over average height, and far from broad, his was a well-knit figure, and implied a reserve of physical strength. He had strong bushy hair which would take no parting, and made his face seem larger than it really was. He had a trick of speaking with almost closed lips and without moving them. He gave the impression of having little sense of humour, of taking life rather too seriously.[38]

Elizabeth noticed Ray before he was aware of her ('we cannot always remember our first glimpse of those who later become important to us. Feeling that the happening should have been more significant, we strain back through our memories in vain'[39]). He was 22, she was just 23, when they both started going to German evening classes at the 'Tech' in September 1935; but Elizabeth did not last very long because she disliked German as a language. The later meeting they both remembered was the following year at the Communist Party offices in the High Wycombe Trades and Labour Club and Institute, always called 'the Club'; here Elizabeth used to go and be unpaid secretary and skivvy and attend evening meetings. Ray found her there when he left the Labour Party and became an active CP member during the summer of 1936; during their first conversation he drew a cartoon and she addressed envelopes.

Over the next few months they often met again and started selling the *Daily Worker* together in the High Street on market days. By now Elizabeth was pregnant once more, but this made no difference to her joining a group of young CP members who would often go out together to political meetings in London or to other 'Clubs' in London or Reading. Later she wrote to him:

> The first time I became aware of you, after one of those drives. After Hyde Park in the rain. Came back to the flat . . . Boiled eggs in that small high-up dining-room. Hot & bright in there, I sat on the floor with my back to the window. You were sitting across the room. I made some remark about William Morris, and you suddenly flatly contradicted me. For some quite unknown reason, the other people in the room receded. We

didn't continue the argument; but to me it was as if we did – all by ourselves.[40]

Sometimes they would go out on Saturday nights, these were 'thumb-pressed on my brain. However old I live I will never forget. Bumbling along the dark countryside in that old car, outside Woolworth's at Chesham, that tea-shop, I was happy in a sort of agonised way.'[41] It is possible too that in October 1936 Elizabeth 'was actively involved in meeting the Jarrow Marchers when they stayed overnight in school halls or such. [It is likely] that she actually washed some of the men's feet.'[42]*

The Communist Party friendships and the political engagement were to be evoked in *At Mrs Lippincote's*, in descriptions of the flat in 'Vasco Street' above a shop, where people are always clattering up and down the stairs. 'It was different,' Mr Speed, the grocer in the shop, thinks, 'from his daughter-in-law's, where people only came to tea on Sundays.'[43] Then there are the evening meetings. At one the speaker goes on talking for too long, as speakers do, about the victimisation of Hindus in Bombay; his listeners cannot help thinking about the last bus or their back-ache or whether they will be able to open a tin of pilchards without a key. And

at the end of the room – and it was very much like a little white-washed Sunday School – Lenin, leaning

---

* If she did so it would have been at St Albans, the nearest place to High Wycombe on the Jarrow Marchers' route.

slightly forward, pointed upwards with one hand, giving an impression, perhaps correct, of crowds surging beneath him. Then there were others: William Morris, she felt she recognised, and either Karl Marx or Ibsen, but of course Karl Marx (she blushed), and another very historical-looking man wearing a nightcap. Her eyes, after their furtive wandering, assumed the proper look of expectancy, fixed determinedly on the platform; for surely the meeting could not last much longer?[44]

Then, in June 1937, when she was not quite 25, Elizabeth gave birth to a boy: 'There he was,' she would write in a short story, 'frilled, feather-stitched and ribboned, rushed into the uniform of civilisation, so quickly tamed, altered, made to conform. His head bobbed grotesquely, weakly, his lashless eyes turned to the light.'[45] They called him Renny not, it seems, after René Hague but partly after a character in the popular novelist Mazo de la Roche's Jalna books and partly after the hero of *The Song of Renny* (1911) by Maurice Hewlett;* the name must have caused comment at Atlast. Then there were a few weeks when Elizabeth was preoccupied with her baby to the exclusion of all else.

Just before the baby was born she and John had left the flat in Crendon Street, where they had been for a year, and

---

* 1861–1923; he was a popular writer of historical romantic fiction often set in fourteenth-century France.

moved to a newly-built house. Lower Grounds Cottage* was in Daws Hill Lane on the outskirts of High Wycombe and was virtually in the country since it backed on to a wood. Here Elizabeth had a husband, a baby, financial security, a daily help (until 1942), a gardener, even a car (although she usually pushed the pram down Marlow Hill or bicycled into High Wycombe). She had all the accoutrements of a conventional young-married life – plus her membership of the Communist Party and Ray.

It was around the time she gave birth to Renny that she realised she was in love. For a year she did nothing, in any case it was now more difficult for her to go to CP meetings or to London; instead Ray used to visit her at Daws Hill Lane. Then, in the summer of 1938, when Renny was a year old, she wrote to confess her feelings. Ray, unsurprisingly, was astonished. She had a salaried husband whose father was the Mayor, a house, a baby; whereas he, Ray, was a working-class boy living at home with his mother, working shifts in a paper mill. He thought their friendship was based on their shared devotion to the Communist Party, to his painting and her writing.

We can understand what drew Elizabeth to Ray. He was '*there*'; he replaced Elsie in being interested in every aspect of her life; he embodied within himself the romance of the working class; he was kind, reliable and devoted; he was

---

* Now called Wood's Edge, 80 Daws Hill Lane, the last but one house before the bridge over the M40 motorway.

a painter and she a writer who always considered herself a painter manqué; and he was very good-looking, in a Rupert Brooke-ish way. 'It is odd that we could have fallen in love with Rupert Brooke as much as we did,' Elizabeth would say one day. 'He was well on the wrong side of twenty. I knew most of his poems by heart and he became my measure for English manhood, which fell, of course, lamentably short of him.'[46] And, in *The Sleeping Beauty* (1953): '"I rather like fair young men," Emily said demurely. "I used to be disgruntled because, after all, one never did meet anyone looking in the least like Rupert Brooke. I expect he is the cause of a lot of disgruntlement among women of my age."'[47] But what Elizabeth loved about Ray most of all was that he treated her as an equal. 'You did not make the fact of my sex a burden to me, or tiresome. You did not shut me out from any part of your life, or expect me to do less because I was a woman.'

Ray later destroyed the letter Elizabeth wrote to him 'revealing her hopeless love for me for over a year.'[48] At first he demurred, for he had had no thought of love and treated her, as she said, 'as if I have lost my reason . . . I was prepared for anger and disdain but no I wasn't prepared for being treated as if a middle-aged actor was saying "nonsense" to an infatuated schoolgirl.'[49] But not long afterwards he revealed that he loved her. Elizabeth was equally amazed. 'You had never given me any possible reason to believe that this might be so.' Yet she often wondered why he bothered to come and see her since she thought he despised her 'for being hopelessly slack and bourgeoise and so on'.

> *Please* believe that if I had guessed the truth for a
> second I would never have been such a little fool as to
> write what I did . . . Believing my love entirely one-
> sided I felt no wrong in telling you of it, but now I
> realise how I have complicated everything for you . . . I
> suppose at the back of your mind you think of me as the
> worst type of prostitute. This is how I can't help feeling
> myself. I can only say that until about a year ago when I
> first fell in love with you, I didn't know I had the
> capacity for loving anyone as I love you.[50]

Before long their affair had begun. It was to last inter-
mittently for ten years, although for four of these Ray was in
a prisoner-of-war camp. During that time Elizabeth wrote
Ray hundreds of letters, perhaps a quarter of a million words
in total; the majority of these have survived. The letters are
unique for two reasons: they chart an extended love affair
and they reveal the development of a writer's art over the
decade that Elizabeth would call wasted because she was not
published.

What the letters are not about is contemporary events,
for example the approach of war or the course of the war once
it had started. Mostly these are letters between two people
in love who write about the thing that interests them more
than anything else except their feelings – Elizabeth's writing
and Ray's painting. It is almost certain that Elizabeth never
realised the letters had survived. She did ask Ray to destroy
those she had written until he went into the army in 1941,
partly because she did not want his mother to see them; these,

very curiously, he copied into a notebook ('Green Notebook'), deleting all dates, leaving blanks for the proper names and giving Elizabeth the name of Anne. He seems to have assumed that thereby their identities would be totally obscured. Meanwhile his early letters to her were burnt: once she had a pregnancy scare, had a boiling hot bath and took 5–6 grams of quinine, then, not unnaturally feeling faint and sick, became convinced that she was going to die and that Ray's letters would be found. 'Every single loving word you have written to me is gone. I cannot endure the thought of it. No one has ever written to me like that before, or said such wonderful things to me, & now I have nothing left. I must have been quite out of my mind.' [51]

(Reading the letter Elizabeth would write to Ray only minutes after she had parted from him seems embarrassingly if not callously intrusive. Reading the letters in an upstairs room in Hull with the elderly Ray sitting and watching me copy them out, sometimes reminiscing, sometimes producing photographs, sometimes sketching me, was exhausting and depressing: exhausting, obviously, because of the sheer physical labour involved in getting to Hull and then copying, copying, copying; depressing because one knew the sad end of the affair, yet one of the lovers was sitting there, his sadness written in every line of his body. A great love affair is all very well in literature; it's not so cosy when the reality means a period of misery for both parties and, however successfully they create a new life for themselves – as Elizabeth did and Ray did not – the misery is tangible. I tried to feel light-hearted about it, 'well, that's life' or, like an old-fashioned nanny, 'this will end in tears', or 'it's only a novel'. But it wasn't, it was real and somehow none of this worked. I only rarely glimpsed the exhilaration that a biographer is meant to feel when he or she stumbles on a cache of papers; mostly I muttered over and over, 'life is so sad'. How can one reconcile Elizabeth's writing to Ray that 'there were never two people so near to one another as we'[52] with the sadness of what would then happen to the two of them?)

It was not sad to begin with. Elizabeth now had someone to whom she could write long letters, virtually a daily diary, and who would reply. This was so for the next two years. John was at the factory and, on Saturday afternoons, played hockey (a lifelong enthusiasm, and he umpired when he was older). Ray worked shifts and was therefore quite often free for part of the day on weekdays. Elizabeth had the 'cover' of her work for the Party and, on the domestic front, her writing. John, meanwhile, seems to have been consistently good-natured about her life and the first hint in *At Mrs Lippincote's* that Julia's husband is being unfaithful comes so early on ('she had begun to rummage in the pockets of Roddy's great-coat. She did this aloofly, for husbands' pockets, since they were the subject of music-hall jokes, were always to be scorned and avoided'[53]) that we can be sure that this, the most auto-biographical of Elizabeth's novels, lightly describes the modus vivendi of her own marriage; very quickly some consensus must have been reached that they would present the appearance of a young married couple but, within the structure of their relationship, pursue their own inclinations.

We can imagine what John's parents felt about their daughter-in-law's political activities, and her friendship with Ray. High Wycombe was a small town and it would have been almost impossible for the affair to have been secret. Yet in many ways, because Elizabeth looked lovely, looked after the house, was kept occupied by her writing – in these ways she behaved perfectly unobjectionably.

CHAPTER FOUR

LOWER GROUNDS COTTAGE 1938–42

The old personal novel is done for – the subjective snivel &
whine & snigger . . . Lawrence, Huxley & Joyce. I think now
we'll have a bit of Elizabeth Taylor instead.[1]

Through all this she was trying to write, but was, unsurprisingly, deflected by Renny and by John and Ray. She found
many perfectly justifiable excuses for not working, claiming
for example that she had lost her way stylistically. Ray told
her to write exactly in the way she wanted and she replied:
'I think you are right . . . years ago Miss Sprules put me off
my stroke by trying to shove me where I would not go. Now I
don't know what my own way of writing really is.'[2]

Miss Sprules may have been hypercritical, nevertheless
Elizabeth could not quite forget her because she had never
found anyone to replace her. She was still angry that arbit-
rary rules of grammar and style had been imposed on all
Asrogs (as Abbey School leavers are called: '"What is Asboga?"
she asked dully . . . "Abbey School Brighton, Old Girls'
Association"' Miss Despenser says in *Hester Lilly*[3]); but no one
since the time of Miss Sprules had tried to influence Elizabeth
either for good or bad. If she had gone to university and
been able to publish in small magazines, or even had a job as

a secretary and made sympathetic literary friends, her writing life would have been very different. It is of course possible that someone with innate literary ability will write whether or not he or she is encouraged by a teacher, mentor or friend; but I believe that because Elizabeth had none of these she was greatly disadvantaged. She had had no family to encourage her, apart from her grandfather in Canada; no one at school; and during the '30s she had no intellectual stimulation other than from Donald Potter, her friends in the CP, René and Ray. Although loneliness can be an excellent, if unenviable, discipline (Beth in *A View of the Harbour* remarks, ' "I suppose one knows one's to be a writer from very early on. And trains oneself. Noticing things . . ." '[4]), Elizabeth knew that to be a writer demands infinitely more than being merely 'noticing'. More than most writers, she did it all on her own.

She never allowed herself to stop writing. Renny was still a baby when she told Ray, 'I am writing like bloody hell again – I mean furiouser & furiouser in a tremendous storm of energy and creativeness. You have let something loose in me, unless it is a miraculous coincidence. Oh I will wring tears out of your heart yet, with what I am able to write.' And some time later, during the last weeks of 1938, she began three novels, 'got mildly excited over each – & then suddenly got disillusioned & dropped them like hot bricks – or hot cakes – whatever.' Ray sometimes thought she was too intense about her writing. 'But I can't help myself. I have no choice whether I should write. If I had, I should choose *not*, I believe.'

Yet Elizabeth had graver difficulties than many. She had no one to talk to about her work apart from Ray, except that, once, in January 1939, she gave her novel to an (unknown) woman who 'encourages me disinterestedly. Well, I sincerely hope she is not being kind, she thinks it beautiful & full of poetry'.[5] And although she was running a house, looking after a baby, doing the things that young married women have to do, worrying – presumably – about the political situation, she did not stop her work for the Communist Party; and work she certainly did – she was more than just a paid-up member, and clearly felt that only by doing back-room office skivvying could she satisfy her conscience.

There was another reason for her active CP involvement. The justification for her life was to be a novelist but she did not identify politically with writers like Elizabeth Bowen, Rosamond Lehmann, Enid Bagnold or even Virginia Woolf – even though their names were often mentioned in reviews of her books (and the first of these would become her friend). The writers with whom she identified most were more radical, they were people like Naomi Mitchison, Winifred Holtby or Sylvia Townsend Warner, women who wrote for *Time and Tide*, the *New Statesman*, the CP monthly *Country Standard* and, most influential of all, *Left Review* (which ran from October 1934 to May 1938). When, in the summer of 1936, around the time she joined the CP, Victor Gollancz started his most famous venture, the Left Book Club, Elizabeth subscribed at once.

Since she and her CP friends were all so politically engaged she became convinced that her writing should be as well; in addition, her constant dialogue with Ray about painting and writing was distractingly theoretical. It would be a long time – more than three years – before she started to listen to her own voice and would tell Ray, 'we talk too much cock about writing & painting. We ought to think less about it, have fewer theories . . . Sod it all, I now think, I will write what I bloody will, & not worry whether or not it reflects the times.'[6] But she *was* worried during the 1930s. Sometimes in the future she would declare that she had wasted her twenties: 'The company I have got into since I was grown-up has been . . . bad for my writing. It took away what I had & gave me nothing in exchange. It wasted ten years & I have to start all over again.' Also 'it made me ashamed of the sort of talent I had, so that I stifled it, & was shy.'[7]

This was the time when, had Elizabeth been a man, and had not had a child, she might have gone to Spain: as with many of her contemporaries, the Spanish Civil War was 'the political event that had the most effect on her life' (these are the words of Dame Janet Vaughan).[8] Elizabeth would write one day, 'I think I, too, stopped at the Spanish War. After that, it was too late. I was fair wore-out, too, and cannot take such emotional interest in a war ever again. Only cold dread.'[9] Instead of going to Spain, she tried to help the Spanish cause in a tiny, domestic way: for a few months during the second half of 1938 she and John had a Spanish refugee child called Antonio to stay. Soon her personal engagement led her to raise money for, and to help at, a nearby camp* organised by the Basque Children's Relief Organisation. 'Elizabeth was

---

* It was at Booker, a village just outside High Wycombe, two miles west of Daws Hill Lane.

prominent in raising money for them and persons to work at
the camp,' wrote René, 'this as a practical demonstration of
communist infiltration, the party providing the leadership
for, and controlling, a popular movement.'[10] Normally the
Basque children did not go into private homes, but because
Antonio was a bed-wetter Elizabeth offered to have him to
stay with her, and he was cured. After the camp was disbanded
she never saw him again but often wondered what had
become of him. 'And do you remember the great Antonio?'
she would ask Ray. 'I dearly loved that child & think of him
often. I wonder what he is doing now – is he rather fat & florid
& making girls miserable? You have really got to hand it to a
child who can carry his humour & dignity & his warm-
heartedness through all of his experiences and it's a strange
land.'[11] In the 1951 short story 'Plenty Good Fiesta' 'the
doctor told me that his father, a schoolmaster, was in hiding,
his mother in prison, and his one brother, grown-up, had
been killed by the Fascists.'[12] As she said at the time she wrote
the story, 'I heard that his mother had escaped from Spain
and that they met in Belgium, and I hope that was true.'[13]

In early 1939 Elizabeth began a novel which she thought
she would force herself to finish, 'however stale & lifeless it
becomes'. She sent Ray a few pages she had copied out from
pencil scribbles on scraps of paper and backs of envelopes.
She wondered if they could give him 'any idea of where it is
all going or what it is like. I am nervous about you reading
it, because *honestly* for all I know it may be utter rubbish. I just
write it & do not know whether it is good or bad . . . As I write
I become lost & submerged.' She wanted to be published 'to

relieve myself of it, & have done something', felt she was going forward on hands and knees into darkness, but forced herself to choose the right word, balance the sentence, to convey the essence of what she wanted to describe. 'Perhaps it is not worth while to do this, since I am hypersensitive to words & other people may not notice.' Her readers would notice.

The approach of war preoccupied everyone. When, in the early spring of 1939, she had written a quarter of her novel in three months and estimated it would take another year, she remarked: 'In a year's time who knows where we shall be. I shall probably be digging a deep hole in the earth to bury such stuff as this I have written, for fear of my life.' Not only was she in danger because she was a CP member; since we know, from a letter to Ray, that Joe, the central character in her novel, is killed, perhaps in Spain, we can deduce that this lost novel was more politically engaged than any of her subsequent books. It was also about a love affair: in a letter to Ray she claimed to be willing to face 'any consequent publicity' if the novel was published because 'I see it objectively that there is no danger for either of us, that no one will guess, that we can keep our secret.'

A month or so later she thanked Ray for reading the chapters and taking trouble over them. 'It helps me enormously to feel you are with me on the way.' But she felt despondent, that the novel was going from bad to worse, and anticipated that, as so often before, the fire would get it in the end (as it did). 'I *must* do well. And you *must* stand by me while I do it. I am lost & alone without you. I can never go on.

I can never tell you how important it was to me – what you thought about this. I scarcely dared to open that letter, it meant so much to me.' But after a few days she fears that the novel will 'die' on her, which did not mean that 'I don't know where I am going, but that I lose heart & feel that it is not worth doing at all. I lose faith in myself. If for once I could do something well, I feel I should overcome it.'

By the spring of 1939 she had nearly got to the end. 'Just for the moment, I think it the most beautiful, heart-searching thing ever written. I hope this feeling will tide me over till I am through with it.' The heroine was real and complete to her, even though she could not imagine where she came from. 'Perhaps she is like what I would like to be (& that is why she is far removed). I shall be lost without her, for she has obsessed me lately.' There were two more chapters to go and one Tuesday evening she finished. 'Allons. We'll begin our offensive against Messrs Gollancz, Woolf, Wishart etc. I can dare anything with such a united front.'

It is the last reference to this lost novel, for the united front was to be less united for more than two years. Elizabeth discovered she was pregnant. 'No luck at all. There is nothing more that can be done, so I shall go up to London & fix things next week, & then the worst will be over. As soon as [the doctor] agrees, I shall be quite happy & not mind anything that comes after. So don't worry. Because I'm not. I feel all right.'[14] She had an abortion at a London maternity home, in May. Afterwards, unsurprisingly, they were both depressed. Elizabeth felt wretched, physically and mentally. Renny was being difficult. John was often out. There were 'sickening rows', once in the street after Ray was jealous because Elizabeth had gone to tea with someone else (probably René Hague). In September 1939 Ray volunteered and the following May he went off for training in the Tank Corps with the 4th Battalion Queen's Own Hussars, first at Wool in Dorset and then at a camp west of Edinburgh. That month Elizabeth conceived her and John's second child. By now she and Ray were no longer writing to each other. 'There was bitterness & constraint between us. We were quite strangers. We dealt one another fearful hurts because of the turmoil we were in.'[15]

Then, in the autumn, he came back to High Wycombe on leave. He had not told Elizabeth he was coming and they met only by chance at the Club. 'I wish that that leave was to be had over again. I looked so bloody ugly & was shy unto death & everything was left unsaid & unexplained.'[16] She wished 'we could have said goodbye with kindness.'[17] Instead of which she walked away down the hill as if Ray was only going away for the weekend, went into Boots and stood in the queue at the library counter, and felt despairing and wretched. After this she again began to write letters to Ray. However, these letters never reached him and when they were returned to Daws Hill Lane she threw them in the fire. This is why we know so little about Elizabeth's life for the two years between the summer of 1939 and the late spring of 1941, which was when Ray was reported missing. As soon as this happened she started to write to him again, he received the letters – and kept them.

He went abroad in January 1941, embarking at Glasgow and travelling across the Atlantic to the south of Iceland, down the East Coast of America and hence across the south Atlantic via Freetown to Cape Town and Alexandria. Here Churchill had assembled 50,000 troops, including the British 1st Armoured Brigade, the New Zealand Division, and the 6th Australian division, in order to assist the Greek army to defend Greece against a potential German invasion. Ray was trained as a tank gunner and a reserve tank driver (although he had had no previous experience in driving a tank). In March they were suddenly ordered to Greece, and by the time of his birthday, on the 25th, Ray was in Athens, and managed to send Elizabeth a postcard, which reached her six months later, from the Parthenon. On 6 April the Germans (500,000 of them) invaded both Yugoslavia and Greece and by the 24th Greece had surrendered. A huge evacuation was implemented over the next five nights: '80% of Empire Troops Out of Greece; Remarkable Feat Against The Odds' was the *Times* headline. But it was a calamity, one of the low points of the war.

Ray was on the southern Peloponnese coast at Kalamata, part of the 'Empire Forces' Heroic Stand in Greece; Special Despatch; Anzacs Resist To The End In Hopeless Fight; "The Few Against the Many."'[18] In reality 'Way down south in Calamity Bay, Sat Ten Thousand men waiting to get away.'[19] Almost all of them were captured on the 29th and Ray spent a grim month in a POW camp in Corinth, before being taken by train to Athens and then on foot to Salonika. A fellow prisoner kept a diary: they left Athens on 8 June and marched 'over famous Thermopylae Pass [where Churchill had hoped the Allied armies might make a stand], 32 miles of dust and hell. 100s fall out, 5 die on the way. Proud to say I made it, but only just. Dead beat, sore, stiff and hungry . . . Greeks are great – throw food to us at risk of being shot.'[20] After two terrible weeks at Salonika the POWs, who were addressed by Himmler, were sent by cattle truck to southern Austria, to Stalag XVIIIA at Wolfsberg. After days of hunger, thirst and lack of sleep, Ray arrived there on 10 July.

He had been reported missing while he was in Corinth in May. After his mother heard, she asked their mutual Communist Party friend Martha to ring Elizabeth up and tell her (she presumably thought they were all three 'comrades'). Elizabeth sobbed broken-heartedly.

> For weeks I had been waiting for this. I was in the middle of my lunch when she phoned. I had a little chat about I don't know what. Then walked out of the room & upstairs, my head and hands icy cold. I felt simply stunned, though I expected it for so long.

She was convinced Ray was alive and wrote to him imme-diately. 'Perhaps you have never had any of my other letters. There must be dozens. I wrote 2 or 3 times a week. And I shall go on writing & keep them here until I know where you are. I have written to the Red X. If you are still alive I will find out somehow.'[21] She did find out: on 1 August she came home to find a scribbled message by the phone – Ray's mother had rung again – saying that he was in Austria. 'It is as if for a long time I have been breathing in a shallow superficial way & now at last I can take a good breath from the belly. . . .' From now on she wrote two or three times a week; the letters generally reached him and were preserved.

Elizabeth had given birth to a daughter on the first day of February 1941. 'If you never had my letters you will not know about Joanna,'* she told him. 'She is 6 months old & heavenly . . . I was alone most of the time. John rushed out to get the nurse . . . no pain . . . only sensation . . . she is my dear little girl and a great comfort to me.'[22] For the next few months she was too busy looking after a baby and a four-year-old to write anything except letters. However 'the autumn starts me off again' – it was always her best time – and in October she wrote a (lost) short story about a little boy at school, 'one of my best I think. I haven't written much for a very long time. I thought I never would again.'[23]

In the same month her life became more difficult and more solitary. John had wanted to go into the Navy, but was too old (he was 33), and was also too old to join the RAF as a pilot; instead he was drafted as an officer into the RAF

* She was given the same name as Eric Gill's 31-year-old daughter Joanna (Joan), the wife of René Hague, whose birthday was also on 1 February. This may have been because of the coincidence of their birthdays; or Elizabeth was used to hearing the two names together and thought Renny and Joanna had a pleasant, familiar ring; or it was because her closest friends at school were called Joanna and Josephine; or of course it may simply have been that she and John liked the name. The shortened version, Jo, would have reminded Elizabeth of her (destroyed) Spanish Civil War novel written in the early years of the war, in which the central character was called Joe.

Voluntary Reserve Administrative Commission and at the end of November 1941 went away to Uxbridge for a month to be taught how to train Air Crew cadets in drill, RAF law and aircraft recognition. Elizabeth was now completely alone, unable to think of working part-time in a factory or canteen, unable even to go out to the evening meetings of the Women's Institute (she had long since given up CP meetings because of the logistical difficulties), unable to write because of the children; in any case, 'how can I have anything to write about when nothing ever happens to me?' [24] The best she could manage was that very occasionally she left the children with Oliver and his second wife (he had remarried in 1939) or with John's parents and went up to London for the day; it was what she saw here, walking about or sitting in the Café Royal, that made her such an admirer of Elizabeth Bowen's work. She was, she felt, the only person who wrote convincingly about London in wartime.

But Elizabeth did manage to finish a short story 'which is on the funny side'[25] and in January of 1942 'a story about a murder – quite funny, if immoral.'[26]* In May she wrote 'the most heavenly long short story & I am trembling with it & quite done in . . . I've written nothing for so long. I was down in one of those troughs when you feel you never will try again. Then something started me off. This green lush fertile world at the end of May. I began to smoulder . . . I Have Started Again.'[27] Five days later she wrote 'a very fine short

---

* In fact she never read detective stories because she found them too upsetting.

story called "The Woman Who Died in the Snow"' and another called 'Beer' about a woman who wishes to confess a sin but has not the courage to do so until a glass of beer 'softens and weakens her, but not enough, for she confesses o.k. but not to the right sin.' None of these stories have survived. She told Ray,

> One day I will write well. I have not done so up till now. I have written very badly & sentimentally, with only here & there the seeds of reality scattered among the falsity of the whole. I wrote before because I wanted to get things straight. Well, that's understandable. It may be necessary as a means of finding one's way. Now I am grown up. I took a long time doing it. My childhood went on too long. But now I begin to understand.[28]

This kind of outpouring would have sounded egoistic beyond words to other people; but Ray understood her.

Soon she was writing 'quite furiously. All short stories. They are called this – "Thank God You Laughed", "I'm Not Flattering Myself" and one about Renny called "God Is In Your Heart." '[29] The latter was based on Renny coming home from staying with his grandparents and saying:

> 'Who comes in & makes your home lovely when you're away? God, I suppose.' I could understand with what rush of love & recognition he saw his familiar things – his name written on the wall (also 'WOT ROT'), the feeling that all that expanse of wall was his own to

draw upon, the cupboard full of his own books & down the lane the voices of his own friends. 'This is my corner of the world.' People don't need to take up much room but they do need a focal point, somewhere private to come back. Children, perhaps, especially.[30]

During the summer of 1942, from mid-July until mid-September, Elizabeth and the children went to stay in Scarborough. John had been posted there at the beginning of the year, to the 17th Initial Training Wing. He was Flight Commander in charge of sixty cadets at a time on two-month courses – his role was not unlike that of a housemaster in a boarding school. The Taylors decided to live in a guest house so that Elizabeth, who had been misdiagnosed with a tubercular condition (she suffered from intermittent pains which must in fact have been endometriosis), could have a rest from housework. But Renny, aged five, did not like being taken away from Daws Hill Lane, where he played with other local children and even went down the hill to High Wycombe on his own, to 'a boarding house full of silence & old people, over which his exuberance breaks like thunder. How many times today have I said "Not so much noise"? . . . There are two-and-a-half hours to go till tea time . . . Just thought of a grand new game – eating raisins with his gas-mask on. Should last at least five minutes.'[31]

Despite the two years of 'bitterness and constraint', as well as not having seen each other for so long, and with Ray only being allowed to write to Elizabeth once a month (his other fortnightly letter went to his mother), the two were once more very close. She needed someone to write to, while for him she was the only link to his old life before the war – and he adored her. But when an old CP comrade asked Elizabeth how Ray was and said that when he came back he ought to get some nice girl and settle down, 'this put me into a dreadful misery, for I felt that I had been standing between you & the happiness of a normal, settled life.'[32] She never pretended that after the war they could be more to each other than dearest friends: 'Nothing can be different in the future from how it was when you went away. I can never give you anything but my friendship & the sort of love which is unacceptable to you. I have never written otherwise however consumed with loneliness & longing for your companionship & understanding.'[33]

She knew, and occasionally admitted, that she was behaving deplorably; but because she was so lonely she could not bring herself to give him up and, naturally, told herself that by continuing to write to him she was making his life as a prisoner of war more bearable. It *was* more bearable and her letters were the only thing he lived for. At the time he was proud of her letters, but disconcerted in retrospect: 'What she did wasn't fair, or wasn't fair to the other prisoners. I got two or three letters a week and they got almost none. Sometimes I read them out, but they were so different from everyone else's. She wasn't really writing to *me*.'[34]

Ray, by this stage, was having 'a cushy war' (his words, years later), living in a work camp, adequately fed, spending his days chopping timber and the evenings lying on his bunk reading books sent by his mother and by Elizabeth. He was never in danger, except when he escaped, twice, and twice was recaptured,* and did not have to work long hours or break stones with three-kilo hammers or endure the horrors suffered by many other POWs; but naturally enough he was bored and unhappy. It was also bad luck that most of his fellow POWs were from Australia and New Zealand; they were friendly and civilised but Ray had little in common with them in terms of shared experience. Nor was life going to be easy after the war. Unless he was to stop loving Elizabeth, find someone else and begin a career rather than a convenient job, his future would be bleak.

For her part she had never, and would never, contemplate running off with him, because of the children and because the comfortable way of life she had created allowed her to write. The furthest she would go was to say, in various different ways, 'one day in the future we will paint & write & work together'[35] and, as an alternative refrain, 'I am sure I was a desperately bad person for you to meet, & I know you should have loved someone cheerful and normal and got married. And I want you to do that one day. A good sock on the jaw for me, which I deserve.' And yet she knew, and Ray knew, that 'we are both awkward & difficult sods & understand one another as other people never have understood us. We see unguessed things in one another . . . I love you so dearly . . . I can't help loving you because you are part of myself, as if I were split in two & half in Germany.'[36]

* in November 1941 and August 1942, resulting in three weeks' solitary confinement both times

Elizabeth sent Ray totally original, beautifully written, detailed letters which (for example in the summer of 1942) are a mixture of apologies for moaning about her pain, descriptions of domestic life, and paragraphs about books she has read (*Black Narcissus*) and films she has seen (*Citizen Kane*). She mentioned writing 'the shortest short story' called 'The Seaside in Wartime'. 'I don't know if it's good. I suppose not. Since nothing that I ever write is.' And she described to Ray a discussion she had had with Clifton Reynolds about the art of the short story. He thought they should be 'plotty' but she was already a modernist:

> I don't like ones that are compressed novels (or rattling good yarns). It's a new & exciting form of literature. It is something done quickly, all in one atmosphere & mood like a Van Gogh painting. And is very much akin to poetry (well, lyric poetry) for that reason. And is an expression of urgent inspiration.[37]

In the autumn Elizabeth and the children returned to Daws Hill Lane and a 'wonderful welcome' – the gardener had put flowers in the rooms and heated the water; he had even put the best sheets on her bed, where she lay looking out at the beech trees and listening to the owls. When she woke next morning to sunshine pouring in ('after weeks of dark & heavy rooms the house looked strange indeed'), the sound of Renny playing football with his friend John and the sight of sixteen bunches of grapes ripening on the vine, she was perfectly happy – apart from being alone. 'I have just arranged a nice little wicker basket full of brown pears &

apples & nuts, lying on vine leaves. And then I thought, "what a bloody waste of time". No one to look at it. I had stuffed vine leaves & coffee for my supper.'[38]

As the winter of 1942–3 set in, Elizabeth was only too conscious that, far off in the future, when events like the Battle of Stalingrad were mentioned, all she would be able to say was 'oh, yes – I was at home minding the children'.[39] But she tried to tell herself that keeping them well and happy was something worthwhile, and in any event she had no desire to return to Scarborough, especially in the winter and especially with John being away every other night. Officially this was because of his work. But, Elizabeth told Ray, when she visited John for the weekend, 'it is an odd sensation coming up here & meeting one's husband's girl-friends.'[40] It seems to have been accepted by the two of them that John was unfaithful: when Julia in *At Mrs Lippincote's* looks in her husband's pockets 'aloofly' (see p 84) the word cleverly reveals that she is doing something both squalid and necessary, something she despises herself for doing but has to. And the novel ends because the intelligent and kindly Commanding Officer returns a handkerchief belonging to 'Muriel Parsons', thereby betraying Roddy as a philanderer; posting him home is the only way the Wing Commander can think of to save his marriage.

Elizabeth was still thinking endlessly about creativity as a concept. 'I am in a bad way,' she told Ray, and

so hag ridden with this bloody need to write. Some dreadful strength rushes through me. What is it? Do all human creatures experience this? If I knew, I would direct it to some other channel – though I don't quite

see how. Always I have the feeling that *not* to write is
evil. I shall never get over it now. And I despise those
who write *about*, instead of write.[41]

She wrote about seeing scenes in pictures, about the artistic
process generally, about the stylistic inspiration of the parable
of the Good Samaritan: after reading it 'then I go back &
strip my own writing a bit cleaner of adjectives & adverbs.
That's the best bit of prose I know – & the simple way the story
is told is bloody moving. The nearest approach to this kind
of writing now is Hemingway at his best.'[42] It was almost as
though, by thinking so much about the abstract aspect of
writing a novel, she was preparing herself, taking a deep
breath, a breath which she would hold until she felt ready to
start another. She did so finally at the beginning of October
1942, more than three years after she finished the 1939
novel, and used as a basis one of the stories which 'seemed
such a skeleton & I thought it would make a good frame-
work,'[43] almost certainly 'The Seaside in Wartime' written
in Scarborough in August. In the middle of the month she
went there for the weekend, not just to see John but because
'I want to be there & feel it in the autumn.'

Soon 'my novel goeth forward. I begin to write creatively
– I mean, without myself being in the way.' She was not sure
that it was very inspired but, despite this, and the lack of
encouragement from Ray in person, 'I am fairly happy with
it. I think it is good workmanship.'[44] After a month a few
chapters were finished. John read them when he was home on
leave and 'said it was too staccato & I feel he's right & have no

power to put it right. Also I am still walking round the outside of the heart of it & cannot strike the centre.'[45] By December she was a quarter of the way through.

Never and Always is set in a seaside town at the beginning of the war. Perhaps because of the legacy of all the years when she believed a novelist had to be politically engaged, Elizabeth tells the reader that London was 'unscarred yet except by sand-bags'[46] and

> at that stage of the war there was a great deal of talk about despondency and alarm, which was later replaced by ideas about the dangers of complacency. To be truly patriotic one must be forever condemning one's neighbour of one or the other. To say: 'We shall have to wake up a bit before we'll win this war' was wrong at one stage but laudable three years later. [47]

The central character is a young woman called Emily Hemingway who, no longer hoping to have her own children (she is perhaps in her early thirties), marries Hugh Meredith, a widower who has two – Prudence who is 20 and Stevie who is a baby; when, in the first chapter, Hugh tells his daughter, 'I am going to marry again', the statement is both Forsterian and callous in its abruptness. But his new wife falls in love with a painter who lives in the town; Prudence marries Emily's father Bertram, an eccentric and characterful retired naval officer who is 'rather Rabelaisian yet romantic & I love him so much & wish I knew him. He keeps me company & is real to me. (I have suddenly realised that to *look at* he resembles Sir

Henry Wood. The pet. I love him so)';[48] and Emily renounces her lover, whose name is John Innes* and who is apparently impotent because of war wounds.

The most memorable figure is Prudence, considered by her father to be 'entirely self-centred, pursuing her own pleasure single-mindedly . . . He could not abide his daughter,' he tells himself with unabashed frankness. Prudence's thoughts 'had usually a certain dirty elegance' and she expresses herself in 'an archaically literary way' ('my novel goeth forward'); she was permanently cold and 'nothing ever warmed her but her glasses of port'; and she dislikes feminine women with hand-bags – she once snoops inside one with 'greasy grey leather, and a clasp which would not' – and prefers her muff with its 'familiar animal smell'.[49] Yet she is extremely percipient and senses immediately when her stepmother is pregnant, even though this revolts her.

Emily at first appears rather vapid – quiet and God-loving was how Elizabeth described her to Ray – but is brought to life by her lover; she is an early version of Emily in the 1953 *The Sleeping Beauty*. The affair is described with such delicacy and conviction that it is hard to imagine what High Wycombe would have made of it if the novel had been published. In the final scene Emily renounces John Innes and tells her

---

* A young painter at the Slade, Rhoda Glass, exhibited a painting called 'Portrait of a youth wearing a brown waistcoat (John Innes)' in 1938, which Elizabeth might have seen. It has recently been used on the front of the Persephone Books Classics edition of *Little Boy Lost* by Marghanita Laski.

unsuspecting husband that she would try to be different in future; this naturally anticipates *Brief Encounter* in 1945, although Elizabeth might well have seen *Still Life*, the 1932 Noel Coward play upon which the film was based; or in her mind she might have rehearsed possible future scenes with John if she gave Ray up.

Never and Always, which is 60,000 words long, is in some ways similar to the longer novel Elizabeth would write in 1946 and publish in 1947, *A View of the Harbour* – and she in fact changed the title of *Never and Always* to *A View of the Harbour* when she finished it, and then re-used it three years later. Both books are set in a seaside town, but in the later work Bertram Hemingway is the painter and the other important female character is a successful novelist called Beth: she is married to Dr Cazabon (sic) and they have twenty-year-old Prudence and Stevie, who is by now five. Tory, a widow with a son who is Beth's closest friend, falls in love with Beth's husband; again their love is unconsummated and she agrees, expediently, to marry Bertram and move away from the town.

In most respects the two novels are not at all similar, which makes it all the more curious that Elizabeth recycled so many of the names and characters; again, as with her letters, she cannot have realised that the earlier book would survive. Yet it should have been published, because apart from the re-use of names and types, the two novels are very different. The greatest difference is the thematic focus: in the later, 1946 book Elizabeth mocks the creative process and the pretensions of the painter (Bertram) and the novelist (Beth).

It was to be the theme of her thirty years of writing life, that she always professed not to take herself too seriously, and can be summed up in her realisation, while she was writing *Never and Always,* that she was pleased with what she had written – 'until I ask myself, "what good does it do?"'[50]

It is hard to know whether she asked herself this because she was writing during wartime; whether writing books about human relationships during the siege of Stalingrad made her feel guilty; whether she had a genuinely existentialist feeling of futility; or whether she was simply shoring up the ironic carapace that would always surround her and her work, leaving even her most devoted friends and readers uncertain what she herself thought. Alas, the early intensity with which she approached her work would have stood her in better stead with critics; her future stance as the housewife and mother who put her writing second and did it rather to keep herself busy than for any other reason may have been a pretence, but it was a pretence that was divined by very few; and it would have an important effect on the way her work was received.

Never and Always was finished in June 1943. Elizabeth told Ray, 'I am writing terrifically these days, & think this last year has taught me something immensely important, & perhaps I am on the right track at last.'[51] Very quickly one evening, in the midst of packing up to go to Scarborough for, as she thought, a year, she wrote the wonderfully funny 'Ever So Banal'. It was based on a pipe having burst two weeks before, when her neighbour rushed round with her lodger – 'a pale graceful sissy in tennis-shoes. We sat on the lavatory together

& tried to stop the pipe up.'[52] In the story the sissy is called Veronica and she sits very happily with Bernard, both of their hands clasped over the burst downpipe, while his wife frantically tries to find the stopcock. At the end she absent-mindedly gives the plumber all the whisky; Bernard reaches for the bottle but '"There's none left" Grace said happily. "We finished it while you and Veronica were up in the lavatory." Said like that it sounded frightful . . . '[53] Yet this excellent story was turned down because none of the literary editors wanted to publish a story set in a lavatory! And when it was eventually published three years later by a small Reading magazine, the accompanying illustration showed Veronica and Bernard decorously standing up to clasp their hands round the pipe.

Just after her thirty-first birthday Elizabeth took the children up to Scarborough to be with John, to a house where she thought she would be until the end of the war. Here in 'Mrs Lippincote's House' (the original title) she found the setting for the first novel of hers that would be published. Her life as a published writer was now not so far off.

CHAPTER FIVE

SCARBOROUGH 1943–44

She realised that now, having no life of her own, all she could hope for would be a bit of Roddy's, what he might have left over and could spare.[1]

The house the Taylors moved into in Scarborough in July 1943 was called Strathmore in Sea Cliff Road and they appeared to have bought it outright since 'Elizabeth Taylor' stayed on the Scarborough voting register until 1948 (buying would have been shrewd because the house was cheap). News reached them that in High Wycombe gossip was claiming that Elizabeth's CP sympathies meant that at Lower Grounds Cottage 'I would not have any furniture in the house but only packing-cases brought up from the shop. The simple life. Of course that would enrage people in a furniture town. But how do such stories start?'[2] Now she was the owner of a second house stuffed with roomfuls of furniture.

Its previous owner was a Mrs Turton, an uncommon name which would remind a Forsterian of 'the Turtons and the Burtons', the English ruling class whom Forster describes with such damning precision in *A Passage to India*. A month after Elizabeth went to live at Strathmore she sent Ray two Forster novels, telling him that 'I respect this man more than any other writer now living'.[3] And since she was steeling herself to begin another novel, she may well have spent a week or two immersed in her favourite living novelist (as he was then; he would soon be supplanted by Ivy Compton-Burnett). Mrs Turton might also have made her think about Mrs Beeton:

> Here we live like impoverished gentry. This house is enormous, but all we can get. The owner, long ago defeated by lack of staff, packed up & retired to a private hotel, there to await the return of her broken world. This is like Mrs Beeton's – one imagines servants with long ribbons to their caps & there is a soup-tureen the size of a church font. The four of us spread ourselves meagrely round an enormous oval mahogany table, & the knives are like Bluebeard's scimitars . . . The place is full of china, but there are two saucepans, a burnt frying-pan & a very dirty gas-stove, which makes me feel sick. [4]

It was Mrs Turton's maids she sided with, the young women who once sweated at Strathmore and were now far more happily in factories, on the land, in the forces. 'It is incredible,' she told Ray indignantly, 'that women could ask so much of their fellow-creatures – the cavernous gas-stove, the sink, in its black corner, the high-up shelves, the uneven stone floors. Ah, it's unbelievable.'[5]

While she was living in the house, shopping, cooking, taking the children to the beach or to school, it was almost impossible to write. But within six months, by the January of the following year – Elizabeth often began, or tried to begin, a new novel in January – the words she wrote to Ray would have simmered and synthesised and would reappear in her book: 'And now it's all finished . . . They had that lovely day and the soup tureen and meat dishes, servants with frills and streamers, children . . . and now the widow, the bride, perhaps at this moment unfolding her napkin alone at a table in a small private hotel down the road.'[6] Her powers of observation were becoming a uniquely honed turn of phrase, the ordinary, almost homely description of tureen and streamers and napkins had come to symbolise something much more than the sum of their parts, a whole 'broken world'. This is why her friend and fellow writer Barbara Pym would write this passage, from 'And now it's all finished' down to 'down the road', into her diary two weeks after Elizabeth's death in 1975; she was using it as a representative image of the first book Elizabeth ever published and as a tribute to a prose style quite unlike anyone else's.[7]

Strathmore (now demolished) was rather like some of the grander houses Elizabeth used to bicycle past in Reading, but unlike them had been left to rot by its servantless owner. 'A little light came through some blood-red glass at the front door. Through an archway hung with plush, [Julia] came to the kitchen. It was like the baser side of someone's nature.'[8] However, Elizabeth did not regret coming to Scarborough: she knew that 'one must take risks sometimes & I was in an awful rut at home.'[9] Even though the 'rut' had left her some time to herself and a house like Strathmore allowed her none as (in the words of a contemporary *New Yorker* writer Mollie Panter-Downes) it demanded, ruthlessly, 'Clean me, polish me, save me from the spider and the butterfly,'[10] even so Elizabeth was in good spirits. The reason for this was Reginald Moore.

He was the editor of *Modern Reading*, a writer himself, a kind and sensitive young man of 28 who had founded his magazine two years before and would soon manage to get its circulation up to what is nowadays a staggering figure. '*Modern Reading* ran for twenty-three issues, from 1941–52, and at its peak its circulation of 150,000 rivalled those of *Horizon* and *Penguin New Writing*.' Moore spread his editorial wings wider than Cyril Connolly or John Lehmann, not being afraid to publish unfashionable writers such as John Cowper Powys and James Hanley. 'He understood that if young writers are to maintain any degree of self-confidence they need to see themselves in print, preferably in good company.'[11]

Elizabeth had been sending out both her short stories and novels for a long time, since she had been at school in fact, and the rejection of the former must in some ways have been almost the more frustrating because a 'little magazine' would not have had a great deal to lose by fitting one in, whereas of course the acceptance of a novel has much greater financial implications. The previous February she had told Ray that the editor of *Horizon*, Cyril Connolly, had turned down a story but had written to her again to ask if she had anything else to show him. 'As they turned down the best I have ever written, it isn't much use.'[12] In a few months' time, in early

1944, Cyril Connolly would set out a manifesto about what he was looking for as an editor. He wanted 'well-written, adult, thoughtful war-pictures' and asked that anyone who had been over Berlin or taken part in landings should please send in an account of their feelings. Poets were told that mere thinking aloud on a typewriter does not constitute poetry (what he especially deplored was 'an impression of resentment, bewilderment, or self-pity'); and he said he was particularly interested in cultural developments in other countries and in the sciences that 'impinge on art, in psychology, biology, anthropology, philosophy or physics.' Above all, Connolly was more impressed by the quality of an author's mind than the correctness of his opinions. Finally, writers of short stories stood more chance if there was something unusual in them:

> *Horizon* will always publish stories of pure realism, but we take the line that experiences connected with the blitz, the shopping queues, the home front, deserted wives, deceived husbands, broken homes, dull jobs, bad schools, group squabbles, are so much a picture of our ordinary lives that unless the workman-ship is outstanding we are prejudiced against them.[13]

(Three years before, Connolly had published an article on 'War Books' by Tom Harrisson in which he said dismissively: 'Many of our lady novelists have reflected the paper war' (in that they wrote books about it). He then named a few writers – Helen Ashton, Daphne du Maurier, Vera Brittain, EM Delafield. And that was that for the ladies.[14])

Since Elizabeth's surviving work from 1943 onwards (she destroyed everything written before then) is exclusively about the home front and about ordinary lives, and since Connolly failed to see that her workmanship was outstanding, his prejudice remained intact. Yet she went on trying to get her stories published; one reason she did so was that there were so many places to which she could send her pieces: the number of literary magazines that kept going during the war, and indeed started up, is unimaginable to the modern reader. She could have sent her work to *Penguin Parade*, the *Evening News, English Story, Kingdom Come, Life and Letters*, the *Spectator, Horizon, Modern Reading, Truth, Argosy*, the *Manchester Guardian, Lilliput, Housewife, John O'London's Weekly, Tribune, Rangefinder, Time and Tide, Windmill* and several others.

At first it was only Reginald Moore who gave her any encouragement; while refusing to print her stories, he told her that she could certainly write and that 'you have a fine caustic touch'.[15] And he may have sensed he was not enthusiastic enough (he too was just beginning his career) for he wrote again in August 1943 in response to Elizabeth's sending him two more stories. 'Dear man,' she told Ray, 'because they are not the kind he can publish himself, though he, personally, likes them, he has gone from door to door with them, with no better success. I can't tell you what this means to me. For someone to take an interest. It's pathetic, that it should, but it does. I could never forget his kindness & patience.'

One of the stories (apparently written before the war) was rejected for being 'strong meat, this; but one day you'll find someone who can take it';[16] it is about a bored schoolteacher with continual stomach pains who accuses her doctor of molesting her. But how could Moore not realise that he was reading a unique new voice, a voice that not only needed encouragement but deserved it? Here, for example, are the first two paragraphs of this story, 'For Thine is the Power':

> Coming down the hill in the bus. The tyres lick the hot road. Four o'clock is dazzling. Down the new roads of the estate, the houses ranked shoulder to shoulder; thin trees let down into the asphalt; double daisies, dirty pink, dirty white, with dirt scraped up round them, in new gardens, descending the hill.
>
> Eva mooned, fringing her mauve ticket, her case lying squarely on her lap. When you opened it, out flew the smell of cardboard and egg sandwiches and rubber soles. [17]

And here are the first sentences of an incomparable story called 'Mothers', the only story Elizabeth wrote in Scarborough in the 1943 summer, about a young mother visiting her son in hospital, in which the atmosphere of the hospital and the strong and touching relationship between mother and son are perfectly evoked in a thousand words: 'Outside the hospital entrance the gravel was bright and unrelenting. She stood with the other mothers and waited for the doors to open. Each had a basket; the clean clothes and picture books, barley-sugar, the bunch of pansies from the garden.'

This has never been reprinted, either in one of Elizabeth's four collections or since,* although her future genius is encapsulated within it. She would have assumed it was too 'ordinary'. And she may have regretted the word 'dirty' and been persuaded that the maturity of the child's language is implausible (it is not):

> 'One of the nurses said I'd wet my bed. "Oh, you dirty little boy,"she said to me. And I hadn't done any such thing.'
> 'Oh, darling. So what did you say?'
> 'I said, "Go on! You! Liar! Rat!" To myself.'
> She bit her lip.[18]

This, we can be sure, was Renny aged seven; a short piece of dialogue tells the reader everything about the mother and son. But would a male editor recognise this and admire it? What female editors were there? Had they existed, which of them would have valued the domestic and the maternal? And where was the editor who could see the brilliance in the words 'she bit her lip'?

(Renny's wartime stay in hospital would reappear in *At Mrs Lippincote's*. On the way home Oliver tells Julia that he was afraid of what the nurses would do to him but he got out before they could do the worst thing of all. ' "What would

---

* except in the free magazine sent to readers of Persephone Books, the *Persephone Quarterly*, in the autumn of 2001.

the worst thing be?" "I kept hearing them say I would have to have my bowels opened."'[19] Later Elizabeth remarked, 'It was a true thing that had been said to *me*, and made me realise the abyss of terror into which children are thrown by careless and misunderstood words. They brood and feel, super-stitiously, that to ask for an explanation will make the horror real at once.'[20] It is the *extra* understanding and insight of this last sentence that confirms Elizabeth as one of the great writers about childhood.)

Moore was perceptive, yet it would seem to most people that anyone with any feeling for language would at once recognise that this as-yet unpublished writer's way with words was extraordinary, that publishing her would have been a *coup*. But he simply did not seem to realise that he was confronted by a spectacular new voice. This may have been because Elizabeth was a woman and, like Cyril Connolly, Moore believed that the pram in the hall was inimical to the creative process. And, because 'the vocabulary of modernity is a vocabulary of anti-home,'[21] Moore failed to see that nevertheless *in her way*, in a domestic context, Elizabeth was a modernist in the tradition of Chekhov and Katherine Mansfield, choosing to dispense with conventional narrative form ('and then and then') and preferring to write in scenes, in 'moments of being'. It was to be a running theme over the next thirty years: because she was a woman, and because she wrote about 'women's subjects', very few critics, or readers, would see her as a modernist; they would see her as a woman's writer, a mere lending library writer. Virginia Woolf was a modernist but because she eschewed the domestic she could be labelled as such; Elizabeth, because she wrote about women and children and housework and dailiness, could not be.

In September, Elizabeth sent Ray a long description of a short story (now lost) which ends with the woman making up a personal disaster because 'the point I wished to arrive at was that if . . . that *type* of woman . . . dare not confess one thing, she will make up something different. But she will *confess* – & shatter & demolish & lay waste (or hope to) the emotions of the other.' (She was, it seems, returning to the theme of a woman confessing a sin but not the right one: in the lost May 1942 story called 'Beer' the same thing happened.*) Alas, Moore wanted the story to be simplistically rounded off so that the man, Vinny (another name that would recur, in *The Sleeping Beauty*) 'gets his chance of her after all those years. Then we are tied up neatly.' Elizabeth could see what Moore meant but thought, with some justification, that then it would have been an entirely different story, and a rather boring one. She realised that Moore liked her style but not the 'little shapes'[22] her writing made.

Before there was time for Elizabeth to decide whether she would even try and start a new novel in Mrs Turton's house, the news came that John was to be posted first to Group Headquarters at Sunningdale and then to Bomber Command at Shinfield Park near Reading, seventeen miles from High Wycombe. One reason may have been his 'girl-friends'. In *At Mrs Lippincote's* the Wing Commander is outraged by Roddy's philandering: 'I didn't know the sort of man you were

* see p 98

– that you would use your wife to preserve the *status quo*, so that you might conduct your amours with a new safety and immunity because of her presence, that you would use her, in fact, to save yourself from your mistress.'[23] Perhaps the real-life Wing Commander did indeed hope that John would be more uxorious if he was posted nearer home, and that Elizabeth would be better off writing in her own armchair.

Whatever the reason for leaving, in early September 1943, after only two months in Scarborough, they packed everything up, John went off to Sunningdale and Elizabeth went to stay with a friend who was living in a bungalow near Totteridge, a village outside High Wycombe. And it was here that she had a reply from AM Heath, the agent to whom, from Scarborough, she had sent the typed manuscript of *Never and Always* (Heath's were Clifton Reynolds' agent). They wrote a 'very nice letter' and said they would send her novel to Constable and put it in for the Best Modern Novel prize. 'Personally, I don't think it at all the sort of novel to go winning prizes, but I shall let them try . . . I feel a bit set-up by this letter . . . Small crumbs feed me completely after all these years of going without.'[24] As she instinctively knew, she never would write the kind of novel that wins prizes. She also knew she would be a writer, and an exceptional one. How else to explain the calm acceptance – as opposed to the joy and amazement – with which she heard the news that Heath's wanted to take her on as a client?

She was in Totteridge for a month, and we know what it was like from a September 1943 story called 'A Nice Little Actress':

On bad mornings, as she washed up by the kitchen window, she could see the sides and backs of other bungalows and their doors would be shut fast beyond the sheets of rain which fell and fell over the slate roofs and into the rows of cabbages. But on bright mornings, the doors would fly open like the doors of those little weather-houses, and women in coloured overalls would pop out and shake mats, go from one fence to another for a chat, clean shoes on the back door-step, hang out washing and go down the garden with a basket for runner-beans. And from all their wirelesses would come the sounds of the cinema organ.

'Oh, God!' Iris would cry, wringing out the dish-cloth and hanging it at the edge of the sink . . .[25]

In October, when the tenants in Lower Grounds Cottage had left, Elizabeth was able to move back home. It was autumn, her favourite time of year, she had a potential agent, an editor who took an interest in her, she was no longer so painfully thin (she had gained twenty pounds and weighed eight stone now) and she was back in her house with its white walls and modern pale-beech furniture and the garden where the children could play in safety. Unusually,

there is such peace in me, coming back here now . . . this exquisite month, when I feel full of energy & strength. After other people's houses, to get back to this room with my books and your pictures, on the window-sills bowls of grapes ripening & on the table a flat basket of green & yellow tomatoes . . . and on the other sill two fat yellow-ochre marrows with lemon stripes. In the garden those preposterous sun flowers turning their faces at ours.[26]

As winter set in, she took another deep breath, this time a much calmer, more measured one. It was as if she knew, although she did not say so to Ray, that the twenty years of solitary writing were nearly over. She wrote 'Better Not', 'a little story about a conservatory'.[27] It describes a woman called Helen at home in the country with two children; her husband has gone away and their closest friend Lecky, who is on embarkation leave, is on the verge of declaring himself in the conservatory but just avoids it.[28] Inevitably Moore returned it. But then John Middleton Murry, to whom Moore had presumably passed it on, said he would publish it in *The Adelphi* in October of the following year. It was Elizabeth's first story to have been accepted. If she is to be believed, and there is no reason to doubt her word, she had been sending out her novels and short stories for ten years. Here at last was recognition. Nor could it have been more appropriate that the person who first recognised her talent was Murry, who had discovered Katherine Mansfield thirty years before.

Indefatigably, in early December 1943, Elizabeth now typed off and sent to Moore an essay called 'EM Forster as a Poor Liar', her own tribute to her favourite modern novelist. It is about Forster's plausibility – do we or do we not accept that Leonard and Helen in *Howards End* conceived a child together when 'we do not know what we are expected to believe. How much is *actual*, and how much the *meaning*, or symbol?' We have no idea, Elizabeth concludes, but 'we must tighten ourselves against the shock'; unlike Jane Austen who, 'if there was ever any poet in her, she knew how to subdue it . . . he does not.'[29] Moore thought the essay too sketchy and it never appeared anywhere; but Elizabeth always kept it among her papers.

The Forster essay also clarified her thoughts, or made her confront again some of the questions which she often touched on in her letters to Ray, those she could write to him about but to which she could not hope to have a response for three months. Should we believe in Art for Art's sake or should it have a political dimension? Should novelists draw on their imagination or write about what they know? Did novels have to have action and drama? Should they explore 'important' issues or were human relationships important enough as a topic? It was as though, that winter of 1943–4, she was putting herself through a miniature English literature degree, the theoretical element in particular, and had by now made up her mind what she thought.

First of all, she had rejected the political angle that had obsessed her for so long and was finding the courage to be true to her own voice: she was at one with Jane Austen when the latter wrote, '"I must keep to my own style & go on in my own way & though I may never succeed again in that, I know I should totally fail in any other." Or words to that effect. We are rather bored by now,' continued Elizabeth, 'of being told how she ignored the Napoleonic Wars. She ignored a great deal more than that.'[30] As she said to Ray:

And you write because you must, not because it would be a useful thing to do, & this effort to direct it into useful channels has been death to my writing in the last seven years[31] [since she joined the CP] . . . I am simply hustling back into the ivory-tower & moan for the wasted years & the delusions I had. What utter cock it all was. And so unnecessary, for we had only to look around us to see what literature *is*. What it does *not* do is reflect contemporary history. All the great novels shriek this to the housetops . . . Only private life there, how this & that person lived.[32]

She had also become quite content to accept that 'I've no imagination and can only write of what I know',[33] that she had to fall back on her own personal experience. Obviously she would always refute this when questioned about her sources. But over and over again in her letters to Ray she would describe going up to London to sit in the Café Royal or in a pub simply to watch people, or outline a story which is based almost in its entirety on a real incident. Her best novels – *At Mrs Lippincote's* and *A Game of Hide and Seek* – would stand out because their heroines, Julia and Harriet, are her (*Madame Bovary, c'est moi*).

Lastly, Elizabeth knew, and accepted, that she was uninterested in drama as opposed to 'the drama of the undramatic'. She had copied into her Commonplace Book a quotation (allegedly from Maurice Hewlett, but the tone of voice is her own): 'I have often wished that I could write a novel in which, as mostly in life, thank goodness, nothing happens . . . What we look for so wistfully in each other is the raw material of poetry.'[34] And she once told Ray: 'I always feel disappointed when I get letters from people describing what they've been *doing*, & much prefer the kind which might just as well have been written in Epsom. Just as my very dearest books are those in which people *do* hardly anything at all.'[35]

Elizabeth's letters to Ray give a very good idea of her literary influences. These were definitely not her mother's favourites (Hardy, *Adam Bede*, Gissing) and Elizabeth has grown out of Dostoevsky, dislikes Dickens, finds Lawrence a 'bloody crosspatch' and thinks Katherine Mansfield moaned too much. 'It is easy to see who is behind me: Jane Austen & Chekhov & EM Forster & Virginia Woolf. I know it, acknowledge it. And I know that there are always the unhappy ones, who struggle without being noticed, but they are ones who are before their time. Jane Austen, for instance. But she had something to do, which had never been done before. (Nor has been since.) A new sentence to built up, for one thing.' From Austen, Elizabeth claimed to have derived the importance of precise craftsmanship in constructing the novel in which no word is redundant (unlike the stream of consciousness school, or the subjective writers like Lawrence). Even more important was Jane Austen's ability to move the story forward by the characters interacting with each other rather than through an omniscient narrator.

From Chekhov she took the ability to capture a moment of emotional epiphany or development or revelation rather than plod through a long story. 'I break in at a certain stage of people's emotional developments, not the beginning, and leave them with the end merely indicated . . . All this makes difficulties of which the narrative novelist can have no conception.' As to EM Forster, she admired his directness and the Chekhovian way events and characters relate to each other; his abruptness; and the significance of Only Connect – which was that most human beings were such an incoherent jumble of thoughts and emotions that they were hard put to pursue their own life, let alone interact usefully with others. And for Virginia Woolf, it was her radicalism of form and her unmatched ability to explore feelings and perception. Other important writers for her were Sterne (for his relationship to the reader), Richardson and Fielding.

Above all she revered Jane Austen and Turgenev. 'He is one of the dear ones, like Chekhov. A writer's writer. So that one feels personal affection for him. When you read Jane Austen, with every reading there is something fresh, a sly hint one has not taken before – Turgenev too. [But] when you read Tolstoy a second time, it is the same as the first, but not so exciting. When you read Dickens and Defoe it's the same.'[36] And, finally, she loved *Madame Bovary*, which influenced her both for its technique and its theme. Since it is about the romantic longing for a happiness which the everyday world can never provide, she was perhaps partly persuaded by the fate of Emma Bovary not to run off with Ray but to stay soberly with her own Charles Bovary. '"I must say, darling,"' says Harriet's friend Kitty in *A Game of Hide and Seek* when she is trying to persuade her not to run off with Vesey,

'do be clear; don't drift. Think of consequences. Remember Madame Bovary. No, I'm sorry, I don't

Dear Ray. How many times have I read your last letter. You say you stretch out your hands to me. They don't reach me. I need you so. If only to restore my self-respect. But not only for that. When I think about the war I am in great agony of spirit. There is nothing I can do, and I never imagined it being like this. I am quite useless. Worse. A liability rather. When I get back I have got to make an effort somehow. The thought of being there alone all the winter, never able to leave it or make contact with other people, except contact with you through letters like this — all that seems a bit insipid when everybody else is so busy & hard-working. You always have given me self-respect. From the very first. You treated me with equality. No one else has done. You did not make the fact of my Sex a burden to me, or tiresome. You did not shut me out from any part of your life, or expect me to do less because I was a woman. I always recognised your tact and delicacy. It wasn't inborn, for in our generation it wasn't so, but was something you knew to be right. You never embarrassed me and I was happy with you & knew that from all our discussions we should start with the same basis. No prejudices between us. Even in the early days I saw that you were thus & no one else I had met had been so. The early days when occasionally you came in to see me at the flat. I can't remember much about those days and I should like to. I sometimes try to and nothing much comes. All is quietly dark. I remember once when you had all been to London and got wet,

mean to be offensive, only – well, Charles snapping and
snarling, everything uncomfortable, storms in the air;
glasses crashing to the ground; blood flowing . . .
because someone's face, or voice, obsesses you. When
really everybody is the same.'[37]

After Elizabeth had been back in High Wycombe for a
couple of months, had had a story returned by Moore, coped
with a second flood ('I think of my mother's equivocal
statement: "Once funny, twice a bore." . . . Christ, how I
loathe plumbing'[38]), she wrote another short story and sent
it off to Moore without much hope – 'the ones I love always
have been scorned & rejected.'[39] It is based on a real incident
in the middle of the night when a gypsy woman living in
the wood behind the house screamed and screamed because
her husband was beating her up. The police said they could
do nothing: 'If a man chooses to beat his wife and children
they cannot interfere.'[40] The story, 'Husbands and Wives',
describes a woman, who is childless, staying alone in a house
like Lower Grounds Cottage while her husband is in the army.
She encounters a gypsy woman living in the woods whose
husband, as she hears in the night, beats her. With great
courage she goes out and confronts him, then returns to her
prim little sitting-room. Her own husband comes home on
leave.

There was the log-fire, the home-made cakes, the little
sandwiches, the book he had brought for her, his
approval, his kindness, their quiet intellectual understanding. They had a serene pleasant evening, talking,

listening to the gramophone, supper by the fire, with chops and a little omelette laced with rum. Everything went peacefully, as of old, until he said: 'Our minds are like brother and sister, close, sympathetic. Nothing could ever part us' and she burst into tears.[41]

Moore did indeed reject the story and it was eventually published in a small Reading magazine called *Here Today* in the spring of 1945.

'This war has put years on me. The silence, the isolation, the quiet at the heart's centre . . . In the end, one is alone.' Throughout the war it was a constant refrain: 'I am very lonely indeed here now . . . If only I had someone to speak to. I wouldn't get so filled with self pity if I were not so much on my own . . . I am a prisoner, too, you see. And I do not even have fellow prisoners. Very rarely I see anyone . . .'[42] It was the evenings that were the worst because she knew she ought to work but was usually too tired.

The children's bedtime [Helen thinks in 'Better Not']. After that, began the worst part of the day. You would pour yourself a drink, perhaps. 'Ah, this is gay,' you would think, kicking the coals on the fire, watching the sparks fly. The gin rolls on the tongue, a little oily. You go to the window to have a last look at the day and stand there, wringing your hands like a woman in a play. And at night you lie down calmly and quietly in the big double bed. Another day gone. A sense of achievement in this. Going cheerfully towards the grave.[43]

Women's loneliness in wartime has never been better described. But it was a writer's loneliness, the kind that would be defined by Charles Morgan in a lecture called 'Creative Imagination'. In it he quoted George Moore: 'An artist's life is like an acrobat's, he must exercise his craft daily, when inspiration is by him and when it is afar . . . [He] must dine in and alone very often.'[44] And it was because Elizabeth *was* alone that, at the beginning of 1944, she could begin another novel. This was first of all called Mrs Lippincote's House (the name may have come from Charles Morgan's history of the publishing company Macmillan,* which mentions the firm of JB Lippincott) and it was inspired by Mrs Turton's house. (The name also has an echo of Mrs Dalloway.)

At Mrs Lippincote's, as it was eventually called, is about one of the most memorable heroines in fiction, Julia Davenant. She is a young woman of perhaps 32, like Elizabeth, and she has come with her seven-year-old son Oliver to live in a rented house in the town to which her husband Roddy has been posted. (His name echoes Ronny's in *A Passage to India* and he is not unlike him.) With Julia comes Roddy's cousin Eleanor. 'She was forty and unmarried, she had a little money in Imperial Tobacco, a royal-blue evening dress, and was in love with her cousin, for whom, as they say, she would have laid down her life with every satisfaction.' Her contribution to the war effort is sending letters to a POW: 'She wrote her

---

* Five years later Vesey in *A Game of Hide and Seek* would be called Vesey Macmillan; Renny by then had two schoolfriends who were called Macmillan.

letter, signed it "Your E", wrote on the envelope that monstrous word "*Kriegsgefangenenpost*", and put it proudly on the
mantelpiece.' [45]

Julia is sardonic, highly intelligent, difficult, sharp but
good-hearted; above all she is original (as Elizabeth herself
would put it, 'her family found it tiring and annoying because
she came to everything freshly and without preconceived
opinions and wasted time and came to odd conclusions all
because nothing was taken for granted'[46]). Roddy is stolid,
dull, accepting, well-organised, and 'a leader of men'; when
the two of them are unpacking Julia dives 'like a mole' for a
handkerchief, he consults a list: '"Handkerchiefs, stockings,
small blue suitcase," he read out . . . But she had already, in
desperation, blown her nose upon a piece of tissue-paper
from her hat-box' (and partly needs to blow her nose to cover
up the hint of tears caused by what she had found in Roddy's
pocket); thus, with tiny domestic details, Elizabeth dissects the
faltering relationship between the two of them.

The focus of the book is the Davenants' marriage. But
the war is the background to everyone's life: an ex-waiter is
escaping the Blitz; Roddy's cousin alleges she has suffered
a nervous breakdown because a 'dear friend' was reported
missing and now is a POW; the Wing Commander's daughter
has learnt to recognise different kinds of aeroplanes; Julia is
confronted by Nazi atrocities in the paper. How, Elizabeth
is asking, should people lead their lives while the war was
on? Should they try and live 'normally'? Should they think
constantly and with compassion about those on whom the
atrocities are being perpetrated? Should they be miserable

because all around them others were sacrificing their lives? And how appropriate was it to nurture romantic fantasies? At the end Julia asks herself: 'But why any longer desire the remembrance of having been cherished – however meagrely – by other men than Roddy? I never wanted to be a Madame Bovary. That way for ever – literature teaches us as much, if life doesn't – lies disillusion and destruction. I would rather be a good mother, a fairly good wife and at peace.'[47]

Yet this last comment, about Julia renouncing romantic longings and contenting herself with being a fairly good wife and mother, was presented in an entirely different context in the original draft of the manuscript; in this Julia is not thinking about another man but about her own success or failure as a writer. Just before she leaves Mrs Lippincote's house she destroys a manuscript:

> She . . . glanced at the top page of a pile of typescript – *Fugue For Marionettes* – a novel by Julia Davenant. A letter with a publisher's printed heading was pinned to the title-page – 'You may yet write a good novel. This is not it.' She flicked through the pages, without emotion of any kind. Once, she had felt emotion for it, once the letter she now crumpled into a ball and threw towards the grate, had frozen her, the words biting into her brain like acid. It was no longer part of her life. By abandoning that, she had covered her vulnerability. Once it had meant life itself, and more, to her, so that death became a menace foremost to her uncompleted work, only a breath later, dying would mean also a

threat to Roddy and Oliver and tears might come to her eyes because of it, and it was the finest thought which had caught her breath with its urgency. It was odd, now, to remember how much it had once meant. 'Why did I not go on?' she wondered, and faced the uncomforting truth that she had allowed her talent to disintegrate. 'I am a person of little character. I am deflected easily from my path, I am diffused, I fritter away my time and my enthusiasm in listening to gossip, being inquisitive and meddling in other people's affairs. I desire to be shaken out of myself, but how I can never picture. Neither love nor fame attract. I never wanted to be a Madame Bovary . . . '

After starting to tear up her manuscript for scrap, she tells the Wing Commander, who has come to say goodbye to her and says mournfully, '"I should have liked to read it myself"':

'I am beginning afresh. I am rather one of those people who can only start being good at the New Year. I shall be rid of Mrs Lippincote's domination, free of the slavery of this house – oh, I know I managed ill about that, but the very thought of work to be done is stifling. *This* sort of work . . . ' She looked round the room. 'Yes, I'll begin again.'

In the published version of the novel Julia resolves not to start writing another book but to be more patient with her family. The Wing Commander leaves and she feels depressed; then the thought of London lifts her spirits and she thinks about the waiter, Mr Taylor. But in the draft Elizabeth makes it explicit that Julia plans to write about him: 'and with that, the thought of writing, of beginning another book.' Ruthlessly she would use him for her own purposes, as novelists do. Julia thinks, in the draft, 'by the time I have finished, I shan't have him at all, with all my building-up, destroying, suppressing this and embroidering that. But I'll be rid of myself. I am rid of myself now and ready to begin.'[48]

Would it have been Elizabeth's publisher who asked her not to make Julia so recognisably a would-be novelist and to turn her into someone a little more maternal, more dutiful, more *complaisante*? Or was it Elizabeth who at the last moment decided that she did not want to be accused of being too overtly autobiographical, or give away so many intimacies about her working methods – Julia caring about her work more than her family, being interested in Mr Taylor only in order to put him in a novel? The second is more likely. Elizabeth, in everything she would write, would use an aspect of herself, a real incident, a real person, as the canvas; then she would stitch away upon it. But without the canvas she could not begin. And it seems very likely that she did not want to proclaim her dependence upon it right at the start of her career, to announce to the world that 'I've no imagination and can only write of what I know' (see p 126). She would spend her entire working life denying that the characters, incidents, settings for her novels were 'real', although they invariably were. But why admit it from the outset?

At the end of January 1944, as she was finishing the first chapter of *At Mrs Lippincote's*, Elizabeth heard that the story about Iris, 'A Nice Little Actress' written in Totteridge, would be published in *Writing Today* edited by Denys Val Baker (in the end he was to publish it in something else he edited, *Modern Short Stories*).[49] Then in March she 'had a letter from that dreadful George Orwell, saying he's keeping one of my stories & wants to print it some weeks hence in the – yes – *Tribune*. Moore sent it to him. I wrote it before the war & it's one of my worst.' *Tribune*, of which Orwell had been literary editor for four months, had, she thought, become 'a mild, literary review now. Very insipid & timorous',[50] and this dulled her joy that the 'strong meat', 'For Thine is the Power', the story about the woman who accuses her doctor of molesting her (see p 118), would at last be in print; yet her curious lack of exultation about finally finding publishers for three of her stories is a measure of her innate belief in herself – she knew it would happen eventually.

Although Orwell's biographer has described him at this stage of his a life as being 'a known character, hard-hitting and good-humoured, a quirky socialist but with a love of traditional liberties and pastimes,'[51] he was renowned for being vigorously anti-Communist, unlike many contemporary intellectuals, which is why Elizabeth disliked him and why she was not more positive about a left-wing writer who turned out to be the first person to publish one of her stories. (A book of Orwell's *Tribune* writings has recently been published; it points out that although Orwell managed to write *Animal Farm* while being a literary editor, he 'was less successful at coming clean when struggling writers sent him their work; stuffing his desk with unpublishably awful short stories that he could not bear to return with an honest appraisal.'[52] At least he recognised the excellence of Elizabeth's.)

She told Ray about her triumphs but was tactful, being only too conscious of him saving her letters to read alone on his bunk, his days stretching ahead in a fog of watery soup, pine trees and boredom. And the change in her fortunes was not yet dramatic. In February she wrote two short stories: one – 'Violet Hour at The Fleece', about a couple in a pub who were lovers before the war but four years later find conversation uneasy – was turned down by Moore and never found a publisher;[53] the other, 'It Makes a Change', is about a man leaving the office who is reluctant to go home to 'the smell of parsnips from dinner. Up in the steamy bathroom taps rushing, cistern refilling, child being slapped; through the steam the voice. The Voice. "What did I tell you . . . Always the same . . . When *I* say a thing . . . Now here's your father . . ."' and so on. His profound unhappiness is evoked in a few paragraphs; and when he goes into a church and meets a prostitute the reader can only feel joy for him. This story went first to *Horizon* and then to Moore, and neither of them took it; eventually Murry published it in *The Adelphi* in the autumn of 1945.[54]

Elizabeth was now beginning to think less highly of Moore, and no wonder. Even though she told him that 'I can never explain what I think of your kindness and the trouble you've taken,'[55] she never accepted his suggestions and in particular would not dream of writing the 'social documents'[56] he apparently wanted, or of altering the end of a story. 'The end is in the beginning – even I, with my lack of structural stuff, see that – and if the end is wrong then the beginning is too.' There was a pattern: Elizabeth would not take advice. And yet we must respect it. Did Miss Sprules know what she was talking about? Did Moore, with his longing for neatly-tied ends and social commentary? As Elizabeth said to Ray, 'I have never been given any good advice, except once by a tramp at Reading going in to the workhouse, & he said: "Never describe what a character looks like." I was 18, & I think it was early to learn that lesson. I salute him.'[57] In the end Moore only accepted one of her stories, 'Aunt', later retitled 'A Sad Garden', written in September 1944. It is about Kathy, her small daughter Audrey and her sister-in-law Sybil who is 'always queer, always moody and lazy and rude.' Kathy is kind-hearted and tries to 'explain, excuse'; [58] until Sybil pushes Audrey's swing with murderous intent. This was published as the second of 'Two Studies' (the other was by a writer called Maureen Boyle) in *Modern Reading* in March 1945.

But Heath's, who had by now officially become her agent and were to remain so for the rest of her life, had Elizabeth's unreserved approval. She could not get over that they, in the person of Patience Ross, continued to champion her writing even when *Never and Always* was turned down by Constable, Hamish Hamilton and the Cresset Press (run by Marghanita Laski's husband, who was one person who should have recognised its outstanding prose). 'There is a strength there which will – I hope – move mountains. For none of this do they get one penny, unless they are successful. They take risks gallantly. I feel moved at their faith in me. That they do it.'[59]

Moore, too, she credited for having saved her from despair. But it is after all not surprising that, despite his hunch as to her excellence, he could not like her work. Among his papers in the British Library there is a page of notes for a proposed survey of contemporary English fiction. The three writers he admired most were Graham Greene, Aldous Huxley and Henry Williamson. After that he put Somerset Maugham, George Orwell, HE Bates, James Hilton etc. 'Then there are the writers of repute whom I nevertheless cannot read.'[60] These included Elizabeth Bowen, Rosamond Lehmann and Rebecca West – in which case it was surely unlikely that he would ever admire Elizabeth's work, despite his kindness and wish to help.

In *Tribune*, at the end of March of that year, 1944, George Orwell published 'For Thine is the Power'. It was the first piece Elizabeth had had in print since she wrote about a visiting hockey player at the Abbey fifteen years before, and although, twenty years hence, she would assert that 'as far as published writing is concerned [I] was a late starter',[61] in fact she was 31, not so very old. Now other people would read her work and could, and would, criticise it. First there was Renny (he was now nearly seven):

Renny, who reads nearly everything that comes into the house, rushed to me when I was bathing Jo. 'A lady with the same name as you is in this book.' 'It is me,' I said humbly & ungrammatically. So I had the pleasure of hearing him chant out all the unsuitable things I had written in his special 'reading' voice. The fact of 'print' goes to his head. That is the right idea.

What was disconcerting was that, by being published, other people apart from Ray and a few literary editors would be able to say what they thought. 'People think I am madder & horribler than ever. The more sensitive one is, the tougher one must be, then one is so tough that people feel they can say anything.'[62]

As predicted, most of High Wycombe did find the story strong meat. However, Lilian and Julius Freed, local Communist intellectuals whom Elizabeth had known since her earliest days in the CP, said they thought it was excellent and wrung her hand up and down in delight; she cringed, but had to start accepting that her writing could no longer be a private pursuit. Although she claimed, to Ray, that she disliked the idea of people she knew reading what she had written, the thought of being published was in fact a spur. A month later she told him that she was excited about her new novel and could face disaster about the other. 'I am swung deliriously up in this. My heart races when I think about it. Oh, please God I have got it this time. It is plaited. Three themes wound in & out* – I think it's o.k.' Because

---

* The three themes were the angry young wife, Julia; army life in wartime; and the comrades with whom Julia's cousin Eleanor becomes friendly.

she had her new book she felt safe. 'Either a baby, or a book. Then I know I can come to no harm, because I have staked everything on the future.'[63]

Three months later, in June 1944, one of the very few poems she ever wrote* was published in a poetry magazine called *The Decachord*; or rather the editor chopped the poem in two and ran one half in the May/June issue and the other in the July/August one. Elizabeth had submitted a poem in a despairing attempt to have something, anything, printed. But the editor's chop annoyed her and in any case her short stories began to be published just as the poem appeared – so she seems rarely to have dabbled in poetry again.[64] That same month 'A Nice Little Actress' was published in *Modern Short Stories,* and in October 'Better Not' appeared in *The Adelphi* and 'Mothers' in *Here Today.*

Now that four stories had been published, High Wycombe did indeed start to give its opinion. 'Joan T', a friend, or perhaps soon to be erstwhile friend, whom she had known through the CP, wrote telling Elizabeth that her stories were 'examples of the moral depravity of the age. She thinks JB Priestley a good sort of chap. I had given him as an example of the awful thing that happens to a writer who seeks to please the public. She thinks he is streets ahead of

---

* She had written a poem when she was twelve and sent it to *Life and Letters* (see p 27) and continued to write poetry from time to time; all that survives in manuscript is a poem for Don Potter, another for Ray Russell, and one called 'Aeroplanes'.

Chekhov.'[65] Three weeks after her grandfather Harry died in Vancouver, but just a few days after she had heard about it, at the beginning of October 1944, Elizabeth finished writing *At Mrs Lippincote's*. A month later, Patience Ross wrote to tell her that she thought it a considerable advance on *Never and Always* and she was extremely confident of placing it. Elizabeth allowed herself to feel some joy.

CHAPTER SIX

LOWER GROUNDS COTTAGE 1945–46

Writing is the one thing one never gets paid justly for. I was thinking of Jane Austen's £10 for Sense and Sensibility against Thackeray's £4000 for the bloody Newcomes. Being a woman is a lot to do with it. Written under the cover of a creaking door. What effect did that have on her nerves? To throw down her pen and cover her ms at any minute, so that she could lace up her nephew's boots or answer questions. Apologetic. A man would have roared, 'I am evolving a new sentence, changing the face of literature. I must not be disturbed.' And shut the door. 'Hush, children, Papa's busy.' It is always that way round. One day it won't be.[1]

Just before Christmas 1944 Elizabeth read Rosamund Harding's *The Anatomy of Inspiration*, which explores the way artists, writers and musicians set to work. The autumn was universally their favourite season; the morning was their best time of day; everyone seemed to like sipping something as they worked. All were true for her. 'Those are the happiest times – sitting at the table in a warm room . . . some warm, weak gin & water & the words spilling from my pen. There is no happiness like it, I am ashamed to say.'[2]

Rosamund Harding had been at Cambridge, at Newnham, and her book arose out of her PhD; that Elizabeth read it is in itself interesting. At this time, the war years, when she writes to Ray she only mentions reading her favourite writers – Chekhov, Virginia Woolf, Turgenev, the Brontës, Forster – but never once mentions reading any new fiction apart from novels by Elizabeth Bowen and Ivy Compton-Burnett. Whereas most people might have spent the lonely evenings during the war curled up with books by Ann Bridge or Dorothy Whipple or Nevil Shute (the kind of novels that Elizabeth could easily have borrowed from Boots) she did not apparently do so. She saw writing as her job and her life, and apart from looking after the children thought about nothing else and read few books that were not relevant to her work.

And it is odd that, apart from Jane Austen, she never seems to have read any nineteenth-century writers such as Mrs Gaskell or George Eliot, or contemporary women novelists such as Rosamond Lehmann, Susan Glaspell, Phyllis Bentley or Joanna Cannan, even though the last three were part of Victor Gollancz's prized stable of women writers to which she might plausibly have aspired. Was this because she considered herself in a different league or because she was uninterested in them? And although she had written a short essay about Forster, she apparently never wanted to be a reviewer and therefore did not know a great deal about contemporary literature. Was this because she believed herself to be, if not the inheritor of Jane Austen's mantle, then in her great tradition? Or was it simply that her almost blinkered devotion to the novels of Ivy Compton-Burnett and

Elizabeth Bowen stopped her being interested in other 'lesser' writers?

These two novelists, both of whom would become her friends, were the two other modern writers apart from Virginia Woolf and EM Forster for whom her admiration was unstinted. 'I am reading some books by Miss Compton-Burnett (I like the "Miss". Some of us are ladies),' Elizabeth had told Ray in early 1944:

> Not in the least up your street. The curiosities of literature. A dark madness pervades. Beyond the atmosphere of insanity, nothing happens. A bunch of rococo & unpleasant people stand talking in a room; first in one house, then in another, then back again at the first. Who shall sit down 13th at a table they discuss for a whole chapter. They all speak the same, even the children. They are all nasty. No one does any work – not even the governess.[3]

Despite all this, Ivy, mysteriously to some, was at this time widely regarded as one of England's greatest living novelists. She had emerged in the 1920s and '30s as a subversive new voice whose brittle dramas of domestic tyranny and family secrets developed through sharp, often perverse and aphoristic dialogue, Greek tragedies in the style of Jane Austen. And her 'persistent habit of setting her novels in an isolated country-house milieu, somewhat like Agatha Christie transposed back to the late years of Queen Victoria, did not, however, make her an anachronism to her younger contemporaries';[4] on the contrary, many of them admired her unreservedly.

Elizabeth was among them, although her admiration was not uncritical. She told Ray that when she read Ivy's novels she had a sensation like eating medlars – '"Do I or don't I?" A strange flavour & sudden exciting thoughts that it is heaven – followed by reactions from the cloying taste. Easy to have a surfeit of, but in some subtle way, strange & delightful.'[5] When *Manservants and Maidservants* came out in the spring of 1947 she would write to Ivy – who replied that she was 'so glad you think I am a compassionate writer'[6] – and be invited to lunch; thus a friendship would begin which lasted until Ivy's death and which would be documented in Elizabeth's letters to her friend Robert Liddell.

The words quoted above, about Elizabeth's 'happiest times – sitting at the table in a warm room', are, rather fittingly, almost the last surviving words she wrote to Ray during the war: her letters from January 1945 until the late summer of that year are missing. It is not clear whether Ray chose to keep them hidden, or whether, in the chaos of the end of the war and his return to England, they vanished; but since all the other letters Elizabeth wrote, from June 1941 to December 1944, were so carefully preserved by Ray (in his washbag), it is hard to believe that he allowed six months-worth of letters to vanish. Until or unless they are found, we have little idea about Elizabeth's life during the last few months of the war.

The most significant events for her personally were that Patience Ross at AM Heath found her a publisher for *At Mrs Lippincote's*; she began another novel, which was to be

Palladian; John was at home much more because, although he had not yet been released from his job at Shinfield Park, he was allowed the petrol to enable him to go back and forth from High Wycombe to Reading almost every day; and, in May, Ray came home, arriving at a small airfield near High Wycombe and from there setting out to walk into town. As he trudged along (it is unimaginable to think what was going through his mind after four years away) a car drove past and stopped to give him a lift. Unbelievably, it was John, on his way back to Daws Hill Lane. He took Ray straight to his mother's house in Queen's Road; and then went to Lower Grounds Cottage to tell Elizabeth the news.

Because we do not have the letters, we have no idea what happened when Ray and Elizabeth first met again, nor do we know anything about the nature of their relationship over the next few months. All we can be sure of is that they became lovers once more and when the letters restart in late July 1945 Elizabeth fears she is pregnant. It is not clear whether she went to London and had an abortion as she did in 1939, or whether she had a spontaneous miscarriage. But there are several letters about doctors and pills and bleeding and late periods. Eventually, at the end of August: 'I shall always remember as the symbol of emptiness a sunny afternoon, the drowsiness, and the whirring of the binder – the corn being cut.'[7]

She told John about her pregnancy, and even though (as she said to Ray) she managed to convince him they had only been lovers after his return from Austria, John was firm: their relationship had to end. 'He has asked me to write

& tell you he knows all about everything & he wants to feel done with it & to try to forget,' Elizabeth wrote to Ray in late July 1945 (he was visiting Haworth, *Wuthering Heights* having always been a special book for them). And she asked him to write to John:

It will be better than seeing him. Say that I have written & told you he knows. Tell him if you like that you love me, but that none of this will ever happen again. Put his mind at rest. He is willing for us to meet sometimes as long as he is not tormented by suspicion. He must never think it was more than a momentary lapse & sudden madness . . . John has not deserved to suffer as he has done & I cannot ever let him suffer again like it in the future. We must be absolutely certain that we can manage without making love, or running into danger of torturing ourselves. The world would not seem quite so empty if I thought I should sometimes talk to you. I deserve neither your love nor John's. I am completely unworthy and fail you both . . . John is very kind to me and he has forgiven me . . . I have promised not to see you – or rather not to arrange to see you or have you come here or be alone with you. If I don't keep this promise I am done for. If you like, I will sometimes write to you, but not if you feel it will be keeping open your wounds or hurting you in any extra way . . . Always know I think of you and shall never stop, and that I have only done what I have had to.[8]

So they were never lovers again: Elizabeth had decided she did not want to be Madame Bovary. She continued to write long letters to Ray, and presumably he replied, but they do not seem to have been sexually involved and there were no afternoons in the little sitting-room at Daws Hill Lane. Yet he was sometimes at the house, because in a letter Elizabeth mentions Joanna talking about him; and he and Elizabeth would still meet outside Woolworth's in High Wycombe (where they used to meet to sell the *Daily Worker*) early every Thursday morning, whether for a walk or a decorous cup of coffee it is impossible to know. Elizabeth did her utmost to continue the friendship; self-interestedly, she still desperately needed someone to whom she could talk about her work.

One therefore has mixed feelings reading the letters for the second half of 1945. Elizabeth sends Ray every detail of her triumphs, her struggles to write another novel, her daily life. He, presumably, responded; and must have been in torment. Yet, how should she have behaved? It was a tragedy for him, but he might have forged a new life for himself and relegated Elizabeth to his past and to his Christmas-card list. That he never managed to do so might have been to do with the psychological effects of his imprisonment; or with his own personality. Elizabeth felt partly responsible for his future, but Ray's bewilderment and depression were not entirely her fault.

Knowledge of his misery, and acceptance of her guilt, would, however, never leave her. And her relationship with John would be changed. She admired him because he 'could not have behaved more wisely or kindly.'[9] But her spirit of independence was eroded still further and she settled down more into the role of wife, albeit a wife who wrote novels; having made the decision to stay with her husband and home and financial security she seems to have pushed away any thoughts of emotional engagement in the future. The fact that her affair with Ray ended the same summer that her first book was published was for her a hugely lucky coincidence. But she remained admirably loyal, writing to him every other day, urging him to paint. She still believed that 'in our writing & painting we are together & nothing can separate us.' Nevertheless, she said to Ray, 'we were damned from the beginning.'[10] It was a way of reminding him that she had never held out any hope for their joint futures. But it is unbearable to think of him, writing her plaintive, intolerably depressed letters, trying to find a job (he eventually became a graphic designer for a company in London), struggling to go on with his painting, while Elizabeth was beginning to have such a success.

In the summer of 1945 when the surviving letters restart, Elizabeth is correcting the proofs of *At Mrs Lippincote's* and is trying to write another novel. Ray and John are both still away much of the time because neither was demobbed for another few months. Renny is now eight and Joanna four; he is thin, quick-witted, sensitive, she is chubby, delightful, self-contained. Elizabeth has a daily help and all the rituals of a middle-class life in the country that she was so often to write about. But what has changed is her attitude to the children. It was as if the disaster of becoming pregnant a second time by Ray, the decision to stay with John, and the impending public recognition – or criticism – of her work made her decide that in future the children would be her lifeline, her stability. 'I shall never finish my book now,' she told Ray fatalistically as she was struggling to finish the novel. 'It matters terribly to me that I shan't. But the children matter most. Writers shouldn't be mothers, for they cannot be ruthless . . .'[11] And again, 'I feel instinctively that women who have children can't write. A certain single-mindedness is denied to them. In the end, children and writing suffer. Guilt is bound up with this. Women writers do not have children – Sappho, Jane Austen, George Eliot, Miss Mitford, Fanny Burney, the Brontës, Virginia Woolf, Gertrude Stein.'[12]

And how did the fact of having children change Elizabeth's attitude to her work? On the one hand being a mother had precluded her from doing war work (in a factory for example) but allowed her to stay at home and write; on the other it had stopped her from going to London and ever meeting other writers – she was often prevented from even going into High Wycombe; her canvas was now narrower than ever. Having a family also dictated the time of day at which she could write: she would have preferred to write in the mornings, but that was impossible and she had to accept that the only time she could have to herself was when the children were in bed.

Jesus, I never can get over this – it is as bitter as gall – that I have got to choose. I *know* it is wrong that I have to. No man could ever know what it has been like, writing this novel, how much it has taken from me . . . .

I don't think anything enrages me as much as seeing in famous men's autobiographies photographs of their studies, libraries, quiet places where they work. Then I think of Harriet Beecher Stowe with the yelling baby in one arm & a pen in the other hand. What happened to that baby? How did it fare? People who've done anything in literature have practically all had a good or fair education & *some* leisure. Working-class women never do anything enduring. Naturally. There is no education & *no* leisure. Oh, now I'm doing a huge Room of One's Own, I will stop.[13]

At Mrs Lippincote's was published in September 1945 and its impact was tremendous, even though the reviews, as reviews do, varied. The *Spectator* said that 'Julia is a real person . . . She is a triumph',[14] but the *New Statesman* thought that 'Roddy and Julia do not appear vividly enough.'[15] LP Hartley wrote that Julia was 'extraordinarily intelligent and aware' and that '*At Mrs Lippincote's* is a book for the epicure, who will delight in its deftness, its compression',[16] but George Orwell (who had been the first to publish one of Elizabeth's stories eighteen months before) considered it 'a waste of talent . . . Probably this book means something, but the meaning fails to get through.'[17] James Agate in the *Daily Express* said, 'Now this is my cup of tea. I chortled from the first page to the last', whereas Graham Greene in the *Evening Standard* was lukewarm – although he did call it 'a novel of great promise'. The *Yorkshire Post* remarked that 'it is a rare & fine thing to read a book which makes the reader aware continually and excitedly of the beauty of truth';[18] but the reviewer in *The Queen* could not finish it.[19] And while the *Spectator* said that 'sometimes she over-writes'[20], LP Hartley thought Elizabeth's technique 'almost terrifyingly efficient, so rigorously does she exclude any irrelevant or adipose word. She strips the art of fiction to the bone.'[21]

In the end there were two reviews that mattered to her more than any of the others: Richard Church in *John O'London's Weekly* praised Julia by saying that she reminded him of Mrs Dalloway.

> Nothing much happens. It is all in the telling, the nuances, the odd moments. And how sensitively and with a balanced sophistication Mrs Taylor collects those moments and displays them on the little velvet pad of her humour. A philistine will wonder what it is all about . . .[22]

And Elizabeth Bowen praised Julia as well, for being 'erratic, melancholy, elegant and dishevelled – a charmer' and said that Elizabeth was a writer to watch: 'distinction, sensibility and originality glow on every page she has written here.'[23] Since Elizabeth had once allowed herself to daydream that Forster might review her (he never did), this, from the author of one of her most beloved novels, *The Death of the Heart* (1938), was the next best thing.

What most of the reviewers failed to realise is what a funny novel *At Mrs Lippincote's* is. Some did. But it was not until 1950 that it was compared to *Tristram Shandy*. An

American academic quoted the passage when Julia is swatting flies and says to the curate, "'I never hit them when they're copulating. It would be simply the limit." Then: "Would *you* like that?" she asked with a show of innocence.'[24] Readers of *Modern Language Notes* were told rather ponderously that this is 'a drolly expressed Shandean mock-sentiment – any doubt of the author's acquaintance with *Tristram Shandy* and with the currents of humour it instigated is not readily conceivable.'[25]

The negative reviews were disconcerting but the general response was extraordinarily positive for a first novel. We do not know how Elizabeth genuinely felt about the reviews because she did not – now – disclose her deepest feelings to Ray. We have to guess that she was pleased and upset in equal measure. The letters to him are chatty, interesting, quite a lot about her writing and local life (John, for example, re-joined a High Wycombe amateur dramatic society) but generally unrevealing. Sometimes she was quite harsh to Ray: once he sent her a sheet of proof-reading signs but she said she didn't have much use for them. Above all, she did not seem to be very interested in the book jackets which Ray was now doing.

Peter Davies had begun to commission these in the summer of 1945 and we know that Ray did the jackets for both *At Mrs Lippincote's* and *Palladian* and for several books by other authors since, at one point, he refers to a 'spate' of commissions from Peter. But Elizabeth did not seem to take Ray's work seriously and she was more critical than, one imagines, his battered ego could cope with: there was muted praise and some extended criticism of the proposed jacket for *Palladian* because it was not how she had imagined or hoped it would be. Yet these two jackets are among the few things by Ray ever to have been published and could have led to a career in the art department of a publishing house. (Instead he chose to work as a graphic designer in a large commercial firm.)

Elizabeth's British publisher for *At Mrs Lippincote's* and indeed for her first few novels was Peter Davies, who ran the firm of the same name under the Heinemann umbrella. It is not clear whether Patience Ross sent him the manuscript of *At Mrs Lippincote's* while he was still in the army or whether someone else in the firm accepted it; but as soon as he came home Elizabeth became 'his' author. Peter was a highly intelligent, sensitive man whose life had not been made easier by being the Llewelyn Davies boy who inspired Barrie to write *Peter Pan*, or by fighting in, and surviving, the First World War (when he won the Military Cross). He had been a publisher since 1926 and was to be consistently good to Elizabeth and generous about her work: their relationship was a very happy one during the publication of her next six books. It would go on being so until his death in 1960.

Peter's first communication with Elizabeth was in September 1945, a few days after his return to work, when he wrote to tell her that she had written 'a beautiful book and it will get some very appreciative notices'.[26] He was right, and he wrote again a week later about reviews in *The Sunday Times* and the *Times Literary Supplement*. The latter he liked because of the reviewer's admiration 'being so very reluctant but entirely compelling'. 'It is unusual,' Peter told Elizabeth, 'to say the least of it, for a first novel to have such a reception,'[27] and suggested lunch at the Café Royal where, during the war, Elizabeth sometimes used to sit and watch people. After their first meeting Peter Davies wrote a thoughtful letter saying something of great perception:

> that whereas it is damnably often the case that talent of the highest order is doomed to appeal to comparatively few readers, I have an extraordinarily strong presentiment that you are one of the exceptions, and that you are going to have both kinds of success, the critical and the popular.[28]

He then went on to ask Elizabeth not to tear anything up without giving him the chance to read it first. (What we do not know is if he read *Never and Always*.)

So she was now a published writer. She had received on the whole excellent reviews, was at work on another novel and was doing her best to comply after John 'asked her to try hard for the sake of the children to be happy with him'.[29] Two months after the publication of *At Mrs Lippincote's*, in November 1945, she finished *Palladian*. The title refers to the architectural style of the house in which the novel is set; it warns the reader that the background is the English literary tradition, and that the book is a romantic satire both on the classical tradition and on the Gothic novel – in fact a deliberate period piece. And because the Palladian façade has been built onto a medieval house nothing, of course, is what it

Chapter Fifteen.

They went for their walk into the country. Going out that afternoon was like laying a hand upon damp wool. None but lovers could have borne it. And all the country they could find for a long time was of the kind where every bend in the road reveals a sheet of orange tin, or royal blue, announcing the names of blends of tea or tobacco, mostly tea. These were often outside shacks where lorry-drivers played darts and tunes out of machines and drank Oxo.

"Oh, it's frightful!" he cried suddenly, for they had both until this moment been shy of the failure the walk had turned out to be. They had walked steadily along the gravelly roads on which rain had lately fallen. Neither would have minded for themselves, but were nervous for one another. Also, there were obviously things which must be said before they could be at ease, but so far Emily would not cease her bright anecdotes, which she brought out desperately, one after another, as if she could not help herself. All the time, the gravel sucked at their rubber soles. When he said that 'Oh, it's frightful', she acquiesced at once in some relief, and relaxed.

"We will strike down the first cart-track we

seems. The title also warns the reader that the author has no pretensions to political engagement: her sympathies are not with gritty social realism but with the kind of decorative, ironic, period drawings and paintings done by Rex Whistler. (When he was killed in Normandy, six months before she started writing *Palladian*, *The Times* 'received a larger mailbag about the artist than for any other person killed in the war' and 'comparisons were drawn with the death of Rupert Brooke.'[30]) Although Elizabeth was now forcing herself to remain true to herself and her own style, to write in exactly the way she wanted, she still thought she would be censured for sidestepping the post-war world: 'At no other time would writers have fretted because they did not belong to their age. It is something which the Marxists have bred in us. There is no censorship so terrible.'[31]

Instead there are references to Jane Austen (whose sister was Cassandra, like the heroine), *Wuthering Heights* ('She turned me into a sort of glowering Heathcliff'), *Jane Eyre* (the house in which the action is set is Cropthorne, an allusion to Thornfield) and Forster (the 'rows of sashed windows and not quite central pediment' evokes the house in *The Longest Journey*). The most overt homage is to Ivy Compton-Burnett. Cassandra has just arrived at Cropthorne and is having 'cauliflower cheese from a silver dish' with the family. 'The cheese had seethed and bubbled and was a curdled mass.'

'Forgive my mentioning my own private affairs,' said Margaret casually, 'but I find, mother, that I am expecting a child.'

The old woman started, her fork jagged across her plate. 'Why, Margaret, what a way to say such a thing! What a way to tell your mother such a thing! In the middle of a meal.'

'It was the way I preferred,' Margaret said cruelly.[32]

This was an ironic squint at Ivy Compton-Burnett's style rather than literary hero-worship, since Elizabeth's kind of readers would have understood the half-mocking, half-curtseying allusions. Barbara Pym, for example, wrote to a friend the summer that *Palladian* was published, assuming a common currency: 'I have so much news that I had better just fling it at you in Compton-Burnett style. Hilary and her husband have separated and my father has married again and given us a very nice stepmother of suitable age . . . '[33]

Palladian is about Cassandra Dashwood (the surname too comes from Jane Austen, as well as being the name of the local High Wycombe aristocracy) who has just been orphaned and left school, and goes to live in a crumbling country mansion to be a governess. 'She was setting out with nothing to commend her to such a profession, beyond the fact of her school lessons being fresh still in her mind and, along with that, a very proper willingness to fall in love, the more despairingly the better, with her employer.' The household consists of eleven-year-old Sophy Vanbrugh, whose mother had died when she was born, her father Marion, his aunt Tinty, his cousins Margaret and Tom, and Sophy's nanny.

The glance at romantic fiction is satirical. Thus, when Cassandra meets Marion she replies to him 'in a little governessy voice. She knew that Jane Eyre had answered up better than that to her Mr Rochester.' About ten minutes later: '"He will do to fall in love with," Cassandra thought with some relief.' No one mentions earning their living and even Nanny 'had taken her standards from lives of idleness and plenty and despised those who worked for their living'. Marion has retreated into a Palladian world and spends his days reading the Greek classics in the original, while his cousin Tom spends his drinking. Sophy ('myself at eleven') writes essays about 'The Death of Chatterton' and 'Shelley's Funeral Pyre'. In the end she is killed, in a scene which is reminiscent of the one at the end of *Howards End* when Leonard Bast is killed by falling books; reminiscent as well as of all the other sudden deaths in Forster's novels (because after all, Elizabeth is saying, this *is* only a novel). Marion proposes to Cassandra, as we knew he would from the beginning, and she accepts him, as Tom knows she will: '"What if she refuses [him]?" "She won't. It is never done."'

This 'it is never done' is the key to *Palladian*: through and through it is a satire, of past literature, of future literature, of what the novelist herself was trying to write. Elizabeth informs her readers that she knows they read for pleasure but along the way she will make some ironic comments on literature and on the way we live our lives. And, as in *At Mrs Lippincote's*, the key element is her style. It is evident that Elizabeth had now found her voice: in sentences like Cassandra's deliberately clichéd realisation that after she marries Marion the only obstacle between them will be his first wife, 'his memories of her perfection, in the light of which I shall always fail'; or the final sentences of the book when Marion and Cassandra return to Cropthorne and 'the hen pecked between the cracks of the terrace paving stones and wandered into the hall. But as the dark shadows of indoors fell coldly across it like a knife, it turned and tottered back into the sunshine';[34] in sentences like these the subtlety and humour and ironic observation are by now so characteristic of Elizabeth's style that one could not imagine them being written by anyone else. The other characteristic (the dark shadows, the knife) is bleakness. It was to be her typical style: the sadness and pathos mixed with a unique feel for language – and humour.

Before *Palladian* came out in England Elizabeth had to try and pretend she did not mind about the mixed reception of *At Mrs Lippincote's* in America. This had been accepted by Knopf in October 1945, just after its publication in England, and the two readers' reports were unanimous. One thought the book had 'humor, a sort of gentle irony, a light, elusive dream-like quality in presenting Julia's soul, and a dryness somewhat reminiscent of EM Forster.' The book was too quiet, 'in a sense too slight', to be one for the millions; but another Knopf reader should take a look at it. Herbert Weinstock did so, agreeing with everything the first reader, Jane Lawson, said, even though Elizabeth would be compared

> without sufficient reason to Elizabeth Bowen or Virginia Woolf, all the while that she is less complex, less really good, and less difficult to understand. But she writes well and sparely, tells a tale that holds

the attention, and creates a credible and interesting (though often depressing) atmosphere.

He concluded, 'I'm for At Mrs Lippincote's'.[35]

Six months later, in the spring of 1946, the American papers began to do their worst. Elizabeth quoted some of the reviews to Ray, with the *New York Times* being the most upsetting:

> The reader is continually shocked by inept dialogue, emotional non-sequiturs and irrelevant literary references . . . Mrs Taylor is much concerned with the embarrassing things people often say under pressure. Reading her book is like sympathising with the harassed inventiveness of a raconteur who has forgotten his joke midway.[36]

However, *The New Yorker* got the point:

> Here is one more proof that the English can do a certain kind of novel – intelligent, ironic, and just this side of penetrating – better than anybody else. Even if it does not seem to some people as worthwhile as chronicling the growing pains of American youth or life among the homicidal inhabitants of the Georgia gullies, it is at least vastly more entertaining. [37]

Elizabeth did not tell Ray that she was wounded by the bad reviews, although she must have been. Instead she wrote him several very long letters about the art of fiction, most interestingly for us about the difficulties of writing novels that do not have defined narrative. 'Either I have got to go on failing & being irked & finding it all perilous & difficult, or I have got to change, & start writing novels containing sentences like: "When Veronica was 25 she . . . " "A few months later . . . " "In the spring of the following year" "Meanwhile at Lyme Regis our heroine . . . " No, it is not worth doing.'[38] That she did not do it was to be one of the characteristics of her writing.

Elizabeth was now working on *A View of the Harbour*, which she had begun in the New Year of 1946. It must have been difficult returning to an old setting and old characters (see p 109), for although some things – such as the harbour front where all the characters live, and 20-year-old Prudence – are exactly the same as in *Never and Always*, yet there are major differences between the two novels. Firstly, the persona of the creative artist is much more mockingly described: Emily in the earlier book takes her lover's painting very seriously, and so do we, the reader, whereas in the later novel Beth is portrayed as being far too self-important about her writing. Secondly, the later novel focuses on the ultimate isolation of one human being from another whereas in *Never and Always* this theme is covered in a more diluted form; there is, it is true, a certain amount of solitude, in that Emily returns to a husband who does not understand her, but the two of them are, and will be, we are meant to think, good companions. That, Elizabeth is saying, is as much as any of us can hope for.

Also, the later book is much bleaker in mood – Beth is an egoist who thinks only of her writing, Robert Cazabon and Tory would clearly have been well suited but are forced to part, Bertram is an old bore rather than a delightful Rabelaisian figure, and Prudence seems condemned to remain at home doing the cooking. (This is partly because her life is blighted by a bronchial cough, rather as Emily's, in the 1953 *The Sleeping Beauty,* is blighted by scars from a car accident.) In the earlier book, however, Emily no longer hopes for children, Prudence escapes into an unlikely but very happy marriage, Hugh has his academic work and the calm presence of his second wife, and John Innes has his painting which (the words are Emily's) 'has blocked her vision with greatness'.[39]

The Cazabons in *A View of the Harbour* (which is set in a fairly recognisable Scarborough, but in fact it is possible to get up to London for the day) live next door to Beth's school-friend, Tory Foyle, whose husband abandoned her during the war for 'one of those woman officers'; her son has just gone to boarding-school and she is lonely. The relationship between Beth and Tory is the most interesting aspect of the novel because the two women are so much at ease with one another. '"But nothing with men is so good as our friend-ship,"' says Tory. '"If women love one another there is peace and delight, fun without effort. None of that wondering if the better side of one's face is turned to the light."' The unspoken question throughout the book is why on earth society is so organised that women live with men and accept their sub-servient role. And why is Beth able to find fulfilment by being a novelist while Tory has nothing to do and no one to talk to? Elizabeth does not explain this inequality; but she implies that if Tory were less beautiful, and had more self-confidence, she would stop simply mouldering at home waiting to be noticed by another man. Nor does she have any explanation for men's dominance, for the way 'they implant in us, foster in us, instincts which it is to their advantage for us to have, and which, in the end, we feel shame at not possessing.' The two questions remain an unexplained but ruefully accepted leitmotif throughout the novel; in this respect it was Elizabeth's most feminist, written a quarter of a century before the feminism movement put an end to some of the things she was writing about.

Beth is luckier than Tory because she has an occupation, writing novels having long been a perfectly acceptable thing for women to do. As the book opens she sits at breakfast 'among her press-cuttings. "Her perception," she read, "her broad humanity." She held the strips of paper high, sipping her coffee, rather pleased with the picture of herself which was suggested.' Then she has a happy morning.

> Ink filled the nails of her right hand. She sat with her back to the window and thus, the words pouring out of her own darkness, she had taken her characters for a nice country walk and brought them back successfully, drawn them together at meal-times and let them talk (but not eat) and now, her eyes burning hotly, was hoping to have an only child dead before luncheon.

Yet her relationships with real people are timid. 'Only on paper did she employ sharp words or risk a conflict. She had a sluggish nature and was lazy physically, but her head was full of clamour, her imagination restless.' [40] In some ways, but not all, Beth resembles her creator, although Elizabeth was defensive about this from the start. When she had written the first few chapters she showed them to Ray and he apparently expressed misgivings about Bertram. Elizabeth asked him:

Why do you hate Bertram? Because he is a hypocrite? Or more than that. How can you so early on tell that he is a harmful old man? Something ghoulish. I am no more Beth than any of my characters. I am Tory, too, & Prudence, certainly Beth, & I am those two day-dreamers Mrs Bracey & her daughter Ivy, and the brisk, tart Maisie. I have never written about any character who had not part of me in it – Julia and Eleanor, Cassandra and Margaret, Tom and Mrs Veal and Marion. Does this make them all the same? I know my self so well, I find *funds* of material there. Beth's eyes & her writing don't make her like me. I have not her vagueness, lack of perception, unworldliness, contentment, frigidity. And I am not literal nor even very truthful, although I love the truth. [41]

Beth is egocentric, yet knows that she is not a great writer because whatever she writes someone has always done it before: 'And, even if I were one of the great ones, who, in the long run, cares?' And, she knows, men have cleverly organ-ised society in such a way that 'I (who, if only I could have been ruthless and single-minded about my work as men are, could have been a good writer) feel slightly guilty at not being back at the kitchen-sink.' Because she has a pram in the hall her work has to be stitched together, it cannot flow uninterruptedly. When she looks at her books she knows that: 'Here I nursed Prudence with bronchitis; here Stevie was ill for a month; here I put down my pen to bottle fruit (which fermented); there Mrs Flitcroft forsook me.'[42]

When Elizabeth said, as she often did, that she wrote in scenes not narrative, perhaps she was suggesting that women *have* to write in scenes because narrative needs leisure and an uninterrupted run of time to write it. And when she imagined *A View of the Harbour* as a film, 'as if a camera, by the fact of resting on a person, object or scene, gave it significance, I wanted the author to be able to move about freely in and out of people's houses, without boring transitional passages',[43] perhaps she was implying that women didn't have time for the boring transitional passages, they had to seize the moment to write the next scene. Or perhaps her modernism – the way she looked at life in fragments, at the single moment – was nothing to do with being a woman but simply because 'I myself hate reading about arrangements & how people get from one place to another and always skip stories which so conscientiously enlarge on everything.'[44] In some ways her technique was cinematic. This was why she loved films like Marcel Carné's 1938 *Le Quai des brumes* (she told Ray it was worth seeing half a dozen times). Set in a damp, gloomy Le Havre, it conveys a world-weary romanticism, an atmosphere of melancholy and a sense that nothing in life is more important than passion. Above all, it revels in its economy of expression – we certainly have no idea how the characters get from one place to another. But that is not the point of it: what is the point is to convey emotion and atmosphere and the moment, and this the film does to superb effect.

So too did a short story called 'Simone', written at this time. It is about a bed-ridden woman, a variation on the bed-ridden Mrs Bracey in *A View of the Harbour*, who is given a Siamese cat but dislikes her because the cat is the more domineering of the two of them; in the end 'her strength suddenly cracked'.[45]

The last chapters of *A View of the Harbour* were being written, in the autumn of 1946, at just about the time *Palladian* was published; Rosamond Lehmann's was the first review to appear, in *The Listener* in October. It called Elizabeth

> sophisticated, sensitive, and brilliantly amusing, with a kind of stripped, piercing feminine wit not unlike that of Elizabeth Bowen, and a similar power of creating and maintaining a fine nervous tension . . . The idiom of this novel is highly intellectual and contemporary, its matter is innocent of social realism or of any hint of bracing moral tone.[46]*

LP Hartley started his piece by saying, 'What a pleasure it is to salute a new artist, and an artist of the quality of Miss Elizabeth Taylor!' He thought the book as good if not better

---

* The first few words of this would be, and still are, used by Virago in its promotional material for all of Elizabeth's novels.

than *At Mrs Lippincote's* and especially admired the way Elizabeth's 'watchful sense of humour never seems out of place; it darts hither and thither like a will-o'-the-wisp in a graveyard. And what feats of compression she achieves, what marvels of foreshortening.'[47] Elizabeth Bowen was more measured than before; although she still thought Elizabeth was a writer to watch, she hoped that she would not continue to go off at too marked a tangent from everyday life. *Palladian*'s power lay in its strangeness but 'its weakness lies in the strangeness being carried to excess . . . Genius inspires some of the incidents, and the often unnerving veracity of the talk. Between those lightning flashes there are domestic touches which Mrs Angela Thirkell could hardly better'[48] (whether this was an insult or a compliment is hard to work out).

It was the end of 1946. Elizabeth had published two novels and finished a third. She was being reviewed by writers of the stature of Elizabeth Bowen and LP Hartley. The word 'genius' had been used. She was a coming novelist.

CHAPTER SEVEN

PENN COTTAGE 1947

It embarrasses [Roddy] when I try to overhear conversations in restaurants, or sit and stare with my mouth open in trains, and what good does it do, since other people's lives remain an illusion?[1]

Elizabeth's sadness at having to stop seeing, indeed stop loving, Ray was slow to leave her; for more than ten years she had thought of him as her closest friend and companion and she did not yet have anyone with whom to replace him. Yet she was no longer quite so lonely for John was back in his old rhythm (the factory, coming home to lunch every day, hockey); the children, now five and nine, were turning into friends to whom she could talk and were to a small extent beginning to replace Ray as companions; she had a daily help and would soon have living-in help, which gave her more time to write; among her new friends one in particular, Robert Liddell in Greece, would slide into Ray's role of recipient of, and responder to, her letters; and, as well, she would soon be thirty-five, the age at which most people have to accept that they are grown-up. When, on Boxing Day 1946, the Taylors left High Wycombe and moved to a small Buckinghamshire village, the transformation into the successful, middle-class, happily-married woman novelist living in the country was complete.

Moving away meant that they left the town, and the place, where for the last ten years Elizabeth's thoughts had been to such a large extent about the lover whom she had just given up. John, perhaps, insisted that they go somewhere to which Ray (who would not have believed in anything as bourgeois as a car) could not walk or bicycle. And it is true; although Elizabeth and Ray continued to write to each other for a few years and sometimes, once Ray was working in London, met for tea on a Friday if he could leave work early, it would be impossible for them to go on meeting outside the High Wycombe Woolworth's or Town Hall, whether by arrangement or by chance. In fact Elizabeth rarely went to Wycombe again – she almost always went to Beaconsfield.

Ostensibly the Taylors moved because High Wycombe Borough Council had announced in the last months of the war that 'there are to be forty houses on our wheat-field. At night I lie in bed & listen to the wind washing gently through it – the whole field sways & clashes. I cannot bear about the houses, or the little footpath turning into a road.'[2] Another factor was that there were squatters living at the American Air Force base opposite them in Daws Hill Lane. These were not the only reasons: it was the changes in High Wycombe that made the Taylors want to leave.

When Elizabeth and her family had first come to Naphill, its identity, as a community, was that it was one of the many villages surrounding High Wycombe where wood turners and 'bodgers' made chair parts out of wood from the surrounding beechwoods and sold them to the Wycombe factories that produced, famously, Windsor chairs as well as numerous other designs. But in the 1920s High Wycombe had begun to expand from being simply a 'chair town' to the second largest furniture-making town in the country and in the '30s it was very prosperous, benefiting from the house-building boom in south-east England and the Midlands; scores of companies, large and small, produced between them every grade of furniture – handmade and mass-produced, reproduction and modern, church and cinema. Unfortunately, a brutal 'slum clearance' scheme began in High Wycombe in 1932 (John and Elizabeth's first flat in Crendon Street was newly built as a result of the scheme) and continued after the war; despite some local protest, it would be a long time before the people, or at least the councillors, of High Wycombe (who in the 1930s had included Elizabeth's father-in-law) realised what they had done. When, many years hence, a far-sighted conservationist (far-sighted because he *was* a conservationist) told a Parliamentary Committee that 'the lovely town we once knew has gone' he was thought an eccentric; it was not until the late 1970s that the people of High Wycombe accepted that they had allowed their beautiful eighteenth-century 'chair town' to be destroyed. Then the planners were blamed – but in truth it was the fault of both the 1930s councillors and the later ones who condoned the pre-war clearance and the post-war 'Blitz of the 1960s that tore the heart out of the town'.[3]

At the same time as many of High Wycombe's historic streets were being cleared, the planners were allowing huge sprawling suburbs to be built, to house the people whose homes they were tearing down and the new arrivals attracted by High Wycombe's industrial prosperity. Even by the mid-1930s the town had become virtually surrounded by a two-mile belt of suburban housing (fifteen hundred council houses were built in the inter-war period); after the war, Lower Grounds Wood, at the back of the Taylors' cottage, was meant to become part of this, part of the process that HJ Massingham wrote about in his influential 1940 polemic *Chiltern Country*. In this he despaired that High Wycombe, which used to be a fine Georgian market-town, could now be seen in 'the scoop of the valley used as a gigantic rubbish-dump. It is a vast dustbin of houses'; it was now surrounded by Suburbia, which 'is non-productive in character, art and principle of life':

> In the average Suburbia, a Dorothy Perkins prettiness is its only aesthetic ideal; its pleasures are imitation-urban, its work largely parasitic. The places where it settles become neither town nor country because itself remains urban-minded within a rural environment.[4]

The growth of the town led to people's increasing nostalgia for village life but also to suburban sprawl. Yet, as EM Forster said on the radio in the spring of 1946, bemoaning the destruction of the countryside round Stevenage, '"Well," says the voice of planning and progress, "why this sentimentality? People must have houses."' They must, Forster agreed, but 'I cannot free myself from the conviction that something irreplaceable has been destroyed, and that a little piece of England has died as surely as if a bomb had hit it. I wonder what compensation there is in the world of the spirit, for the destruction of the life here, the life of tradition.'[5]

John and Elizabeth wanted to prop up the life of tradition as best they could, to live in a real village from which John could drive to the factory but have a life in the country at weekends. Elizabeth, conscious of Jane Austen's own 'recipe for a nice novel – two or three families living near to one another in the country',[6] knew that a novelist's best inspiration is, after all, her neighbours and that these are more easily acquired in a village. Imagination was not her forte; what she excelled at was observation of her immediate milieu – but she needed a milieu to observe. At the same time she wanted some privacy, and life in a village would provide that without loneliness – there would always be neighbours whom she could see if she wanted to. (This is what she thought. It is possible to argue that village life gives the observer an impoverished – a restricted – milieu and that Elizabeth might have been an even greater novelist if she had lived in a town . . .)

Village life did, however, have its own rules. In the 1968 short story 'In and Out the Houses' it is the local villagers that Kitty Miller indefatigably visits.

'Then Mrs de Vries pulled her socks up, and made a big apple tart,' Kitty told her mother. 'I have warned you before, Kitty. What you see going on in people's houses, you keep to yourself. Or you stay out of them. Is that finally and completely understood?'

She does not understand, or chooses not to, persisting in her comments and indiscretions. As her mother says, '"You are becoming a little menace to everyone with your visiting, and we have got to live in this village."' [7] Like so much of Elizabeth's work, this story is more profound than its gentle and opaque style makes it appear. The real subjects are the way neighbour gets on with neighbour, or fails to; the conventions by which information is disseminated; and how trivial gossip can become destructive of good relations. 'In and Out the Houses' makes plain that in a community people need to be informed about their neighbours' business, but there are accepted ways in which they are given that information. For thirty years Elizabeth would stay at home and send Robert Liddell local news. Yet face-to-face with her neighbours she understood the rules and obeyed them; her indiscretions were the reason she persuaded Robert to destroy her letters after her death.

Elizabeth thought that village life would be good for her writing. Robert Liddell was to write in his 1953 book *Some Principles of Fiction*: 'The organic community, which still exists as a permanent background to the novels of Jane Austen or Hardy, is no longer a living thing – and every modern novelist feels or exhibits its loss.' This is because his or her characters can no longer be grouped in a village – no one stays anywhere for very long, they are always going away or, worse, commuting, and have to meet in a hotel or a country house-party or on a ship. But, Liddell points out, 'there is much more to be learnt from living in a constricted neighbourhood, and from seeing the same people again and again, year after year . . .

For the novel is a form of story-telling, and has a close affinity with a very humble intellectual activity, Gossip.'

However, you can only gossip effectively about people whom you know well or know a great deal about. 'And gossip, and leisurely, gossipy letter-writing is the best breeding-ground for the novelist . . . It is not great travellers who have been the best letter-writers – it is people who have stayed at home, and have talked about their neighbours.'[8] After she moved in 1947 Elizabeth would spend the next thirty years staying at home. She made a conscious decision that a quiet life closely observing what was going on around her would be better for her art. Neither she nor John wanted to live in isolation in the country; a village would be a good compromise between being alone and being in a larger, more bustling community. As Elizabeth would put it one day when the car had broken down and a neighbour came out to tow it home: 'It is a good thing to live in a village where people help one another.'[9] On the other hand, for social and managerial reasons John would not have wanted to run into his employees in High Wycombe; like his father-in-law before him he would drive to and from work in his Rover.

Another reason for leaving Daws Hill Lane was that the Taylors wanted to live in something old rather than in a house that had been recently built. So Elizabeth spent the autumn of 1946 house-hunting. She knew that Elsie had wanted to leave the Oxford Road because she had seen a ghost on the stairs; and claimed herself to have seen a ghost at Montacute ('a young girl in an eighteenth-century dress in an attitude of utter despair . . . But . . . there was nothing there. This frightened me very much. Either I am going off my head as my mother more or less did or there are vast territories against which I stiffen my hands in horror'[10]). So she rejected the kind of house 'which I know was loaded with poltergeists, bricked-in with nuns & the screams of the damned.'[11] What she found was Penn Cottage, an originally sixteenth-century house in the village of Penn just outside Beaconsfield, a few miles east of High Wycombe. It was on the main road through the village, although partly screened from passing traffic.

Penn suited the Taylors in several ways. In the background of their lives for the last ten years had been the chair-making industry. Penn, surrounded as it is by beechwoods, is one of the many places where the wood came from and where the chairs used to be made. 'But the chair-makers by no means confined themselves to the beech, the seats were mainly of elm or cherry and the small market-towns were centres for the harvests of the cherry orchards.'[12] This resulted in an extremely balanced local economy in which everyone was involved (mattresses were stuffed with beech leaves; cherries were made into pies; timber was made into chairs or carved into something elaborate). By moving out of High Wycombe back to a small village nearby, Elizabeth felt, even if sub-consciously, that she was perpetuating tradition rather than colluding in its destruction. Nor was she isolating herself: 'Buckinghamshire contains all of England – suburbia, indus-trial squalor, great estates, even valleys remote and rural where most of the families have the same name.'[13]

The village of Penn had an illustrious history and there were many rather grand houses as well as some lovely old

cottages. In the early eighteenth century the then Princess
Anne, later Queen, lived at The Knoll, from which she could
see Windsor Castle and the vast panorama below (Penn is
six hundred feet above sea-level). The fourteenth-century
church, with its flint-walled graveyard and, outside, a War
Memorial on the site of what was the village stocks, has
monuments to the Penn family and to the Curzons; Viscount
Curzon, the son of Earl Howe, was living at The Knoll by
1950. ('In the Penn country one can tell who is anyone,'
Elizabeth would remark. 'It depends on whether a woman
kisses Lady Curzon or not.'[14]*) Sir George Grove lived at
Watercroft House, and Arthur Sullivan stayed with him and
there composed 'The Lost Chord', the music for 'Onward
Christian Soldiers' and *The Mikado*.

As well, Penn is in itself beautiful. As Alison Uttley wrote,
'the air at Penn seems to be coloured, for the land falls sharply
away from the ridge, with cornfields in the foreground,
with woods in the distance, and a violet-blue mist hangs
over those far trees and hills. The atmosphere is charged
with sweetness, and sun and light, with the open spaces
there.'[15] There are indeed amazing views from the ridge
north across the beechwoods and south to the Thames Valley.
In her 1961 novel *In a Summer Season* Elizabeth would write
about the family being drawn 'evening after evening, year
after year' to The View, 'wooded hillsides and orchards, roof-
tops, in the distance the gas-holder at Staines, the grand-
stand at Ascot and, with the setting sun striking the tops

* In *A Game of Hide and Seek* Mrs Curzon is the daily help.

181

of towers and ramparts, the Castle itself, set high against the horizon.'[16]

Finally, by moving to Penn the Taylors would lead a much more prosperous lifestyle in 'the Chelsea of the Chilterns'. This is what John Betjeman allegedly called it, not because it is modern (on the contrary) but because of the people who lived there: as the 1972 author of *Portrait of Buckinghamshire* was to put it, Penn 'numbered among its residents some famous actors, an eminent surgeon, a brilliant fashion designer and artist, and others distinguished in rather less obvious ways'[17] (such as novelists). With the success of *At Mrs Lippincote's*, and the reviewers seeing a future for her as a writer, Elizabeth and John wanted to move to a house where they could have a live-in maid and from where the children could go to boarding school and bring their friends home in the holidays; and where they might make congenial friends. In fact Elizabeth's closest friend in Penn would be her neighbour Gerry, whose husband Barry Ercolani was the son of the founder of Ercol,* which was about to launch the first machine-made Windsor chair.**

The cottage the Taylors bought, Penn Cottage, made another kind of statement because it *was* only a cottage, and it

---

* He had worked for Frederick Parker at Parker-Knoll, and Ebenezer Gomme at what was later G-Plan, and founded Ercol in 1920.
** However, once Windsor chairs became machine-made they became less desirable: when the Taylors moved to a new house in the 1950s they commissioned hand-made Windsor chairs from the Goodchild family at Naphill.

was pressed right up against the road. Elizabeth would write: 'It is the typically English set-up of cramped cottage in large garden. The garden, of first importance, edges us into the lane, so that our noses are close to the "traffic" and all behind is space.'[18] And as she would say in a short story, 'the village had a preponderance of middle-sized houses. They lay at the end of short but curving drives, embowered in flowering trees. [She] was unusually placed in being able to see the road. Only rather low beech-hedges separated her.'[19] Being next to the road was in contrast to many of the families Elizabeth was to get to know, who tended to live in large detached houses, 'six-bedroomed villas, built twenty or thirty years ago in what she called Underwriters Georgian. They had gardens full of flowering trees, bright gravel drives and tennis courts.'[20] Penn Cottage was more modest than this, more of a compromise between the little terraced house in the Oxford Road and the kind of villa which John and Elizabeth could by now have afforded but deliberately rejected (and in any case she would not have wanted to have anything to do with the values of Atlast). Finally, their cottage was definitely not 'jerry-built' and like a miniature Pigotts it represented Elizabeth's dislike of anything to do with 'materialism, and devitalised food' (see p 41). [21]

The winter they moved, 1946-7, was the coldest it had been for many years.

So cut off from normal life have I been, by snow, floods, children's illnesses and the death of Siamese cats and several other acts of God, that there had been nothing to do all winter but pursue the Life of the Spirit, until I am at breaking point and take a lot of little sips out of the cupboard. (I read in an American magazine that the first sign of dipsomania is requiring a drink in the morning.)[22]

The sense of being cut off, and the way a drink can fill in for happiness, was evoked in a story written at this time. In 'Shadows of the World' Ida, who is bored and impossible, is entertaining a friend: '"I have nothing," she said moodily and dramatically. He looked surprised and alarmed. "The empty days," she continued, to his great relief, "the long, empty days."' But at the back of the house in the maid's sitting-room 'life was gayer'; and in the shed her son watches over his cat who is having kittens. '"Whatever will you do with them?" George asked. "Four kittens." "Do? What do you imagine? Need we go into details?"'[23] asks the appalling Ida.

Nevertheless, it was during this terrible winter that something wonderful happened to Elizabeth – she met Maude Eaton, the woman who would be the closest female friend she would ever have. Maude had been asked to give twelve weekly WEA lectures at High Wycombe on Literature and Psychology; these took place between October and December 1946. 'One evening she was horrified to observe Elizabeth Taylor sitting in the audience. She already knew her work and therefore knew what she looked like and was amazed at her own temerity in lecturing to Elizabeth on literature.'[24]

At first Elizabeth was rather critical ('that awful flat voice!'[25]), and she resented Maude saying that Virginia Woolf was schizophrenic. But after the lectures finished in December, Maude wrote and accused her 'in a sweet & kindly way of perhaps trying to force human-nature into the Marxian strait-jacket.' She had been unable to say anything while the classes were going on because 'argument involves her emotionally & she hates it & feels flayed alive'; in any case, she told Elizabeth, she had not liked lecturing to people in whom she 'felt an instinctive antagonism to & contempt for art and artists.' And 'she must have divined my odd horror of reading aloud' because she asked every single other person to do so: 'Perhaps she is a witch. She looked rather like my idea of Joan of Arc.'[26]

There are very few letters for that winter, and for two months during the early part of 1947 Elizabeth was marooned at home with the children because they had ringworm ('the cats are the chief suspect . . . If they must be destroyed I'll die'[27]). By the spring Maude was staying at Penn and had evidently become one of Elizabeth's two closest friends apart from Ray (the other was 'an unhappy little priest' called Ronald about whom we know nothing): the two women grew close so rapidly that it was like a platonic falling in love or the discovery of the female best friend neither of them had ever had. Soon Elizabeth complained to Ray, only half-jokingly, that now she does not know how to finish her letter – 'I was going to put "your loving Liz" as I would to my children, or to Maud [she had now dropped the 'e'] but I am afraid to be thought flippant.'[28]

The two women were solitary, intelligent, and deeply interested in literature and the arts; indeed, Maud seems to have nurtured hopes that she would one day write herself – in Elizabeth's posthumous novel *Blaming* Martha is the author of 'sad *contes* about broken love affairs, of depressed and depressing women.'[29] Above all, Maud and Elizabeth were similar in temperament, being sensitive but hidden in their shells, compassionate but realistic, highly observant but introverted; when a relation of Maud's said that she was 'not quite of this world . . . she never actually opened up – you felt very protective towards her – you felt she might step off the kerb and be run over'[30], the same might be said of Elizabeth. The difference was that the circumstances of her life had made her better at fending for herself – 'being a writer has taught me in a hard school, and I have found I have immense reserves & great courage about everything unconnected with my children. I am ambitious and tough and all the soft parts of my heart were gnawed away by vultures long ago'.[31] Maud, for better or worse, and in the end it would be worse, still had the soft parts of her heart.

She was 25 in the winter of 1946, nine years younger than Elizabeth, and had been born and brought up in Christchurch, New Zealand. A contemporary described her as 'shy, thin and slight in build and to men not immediately attractive. But she had a thoughtful and rather beautiful moulded face and golden long hair',[32] and a cousin remembered 'an elfin creature, who watched and listened and did not impose herself on others.'[33] Maud went to a girls' school not unlike the Abbey, shone at Canterbury College, Christchurch and completed her undergraduate degree when she was 19. She had studied under the philosopher Karl

Popper and in his classes 'spoke with slight hesitation, in a quiet voice which showed firmness of convictions, but was never assertive and certainly never aggressive in argument . . . Her gentleness and firmness were most clearly expressed not just by her voice but by the way she would bend forward when she spoke, and tilt her head to one side, as if she was questioning rather than affirming. . .'[34] She also edited the university newspaper and contributed several incisive articles with titles such as 'A Better World', 'Nationalism or Commonsense' and 'Education in Nazi Germany'.

After completing her MA in industrial psychology, Maud spent three years doing the research for a paper on 'The Forewoman and her position in Industry' (1946) and for the topic that would be published in 1947 as *Girl Workers in New Zealand Factories*: 'an attempt to understand factory girls and their problems with a view to improving their conditions';[35] despite her elfin physique she herself worked part-time as one of the 35,000 women employed in New Zealand factories from 1942–5. Then, when the war ended, she went to England, enrolled at the London School of Economics, and started research for a PhD (which she never completed) on the working conditions of domestic staff in London hospitals; she lodged in Turner Close, Hampstead Garden Suburb, in the house lived in by the political economist Friedrich Hayek. He was a friend of Popper's and had brought him over from New Zealand to the LSE philosophy department, where Maud worked part-time as his assistant. Hayek was by then rarely at Turner Close because he had all but deserted his wife; in *Blaming* she is a widow called 'Mrs

Francis' (German refugees called Friedrich, Frederick or Fritz often called themselves Francis in England).

Martha in the novel is almost absurdly without vanity, for example she brushes her hair without looking in a mirror, 'cut her own pale, streaky hair' and wears 'the old raincoat, the denim trousers';[36] Maud 'always dressed badly, hair just scraped across her face, totally indifferent to how she looked or how you assessed her'[37] although others described her as looking like Dora Carrington.[38] Both women, the fictional and the real-life, had an ambivalent attitude to men: 'Maud often told me,' a university friend remembered, 'that men-women relationships were bound to be difficult because "women, in the end, are always disappointed by men."'[39] Yet there was a young man to whom she was close, William ('Bill') Geddes, who had also arrived at LSE, to finish a PhD in anthropology.

Maud had first met Bill in Christchurch in 1945. In London they became lovers, perhaps out of loneliness and perhaps, like Martha's 'Simon' (who is 27, as was Bill in 1945), he 'wasn't all that good at it, but neither am I'. They remained lovers in a semi-detached way, and when Elizabeth visited Turner Close she must have sympathised ruefully with Mrs Hayek: '[Mrs Francis] did not like Martha having sex under her roof. After all, she did not have it herself. She would clatter about in the kitchen, next to Martha's room . . . knowing perfectly well what was going on on the other side of the wall, and thinking it bad manners.' We know from the tone of *Blaming* and from the surviving letters that although she was indisputably 'my dear Maud' the relationship was not pure joy for Elizabeth: Maud's shabby clothes and neurotic fiddling

– she had a tendency to strike matches and blow them out, as does Martha, and to have rather primitive table manners – could be annoying.

Sometimes Maud came to Penn Cottage and looked after Joanna while Elizabeth went to London (Renny had just gone to boarding school); or, because the Taylors had a live-in housekeeper for a short while at the end of the 1940s, Elizabeth was able to leave Joanna and walk with Maud in Highgate Cemetery or go to her room in Hampstead Garden Suburb, 'at the back of a semi-detached house with french windows giving onto a small lawn with trellis-work concealing dustbins, and pegs hanging on a clothes' line . . . Martha lit the gas-fire and a gas-ring for the kettle, and Amy sat down in a wicker chair padded with peacock-blue cushions.' Quite often they met in central London and went for long walks. Sometimes they went to galleries; in the autumn of 1948 Maud bought Elizabeth an etching by Vanessa Bell (*Child with Flowers*) and the following year a tiny Whistler drawing. These presents would be remembered in *Blaming* when Martha, before leaving England, manages to track down and give to Amy a painting ('much influenced by Vuillard'[40]) by her late husband; it becomes a symbol of Martha's generosity of spirit and Amy's thoughtlessness.

During this period, Maud's work for Popper and her research into domestic workers seems to have dwindled away, leaving her with the ambition to write or to make films and a great enthusiasm for taking photographs (those that survive are indeed superb). But 1947 was the year that Elizabeth was becoming not just a respected novelist but a well-known one;

she was hard at work on a new novel; and she had her family to preoccupy her. It was perhaps in some vague, misguided attempt to create a life of her own that Maud agreed to marry Bill. 'I am rather excited & happy,' Elizabeth told Ray, 'because my dear Maud is getting married. She is marrying an anthropologist who is going to Borneo. If she goes too, I shall be lost.'[41] (She did go, and part of Elizabeth was lost.) In early 1948 Bill and Maud were married at St Alban's (St Barnabas's in *Blaming*), the nearest Catholic church to Turner Close, with the cartoonist David Low, Maud's relation from New Zealand, as one of the witnesses.

The previous spring, 1947, the American reviews of *Palladian* had started to appear. They varied as much as the Knopf readers' opinions of it the year before, when Jane Lawson had praised Elizabeth's 'delicate sure touch, the fine phrase, the loving detail, the creation of *breath* in the air. It is a special book. It is not the modern novel on a larger scale I had hoped for to follow ET's first book. It is a book for a special taste'; Herbert Weinstock had thought it 'a modern Gothic romance, a kind of more sophisticated *Rebecca* written by a woman of real talent . . . It is not a great book, but is miles above most of the swill we see (and that others publish)'; but the third reader disliked the book very much and thought 'its only resemblance to *Rebecca* is such that most people would consider it a poor imitation.'[42]

'A good book, written with care and distinction, a Victorian period-piece which at times steps tantalisingly beyond the aura of the period' wrote the *New York Times*.[43] But then *The New Yorker* said that 'everybody is elaborately unreal . . . why

Mrs Taylor did it . . . and whether it was worth doing are a couple of other questions.'[44] Meanwhile, Elizabeth's relationship with Knopf was becoming less smooth than that with Peter Davies. It was the most prestigious publisher she could have had, but, annoyingly, her editors there were far more concerned than Peter Davies with potential sales figures and made complaining noises about Elizabeth being so English that they were unlikely ever to do more than break even. It is true that, like all publishers, their quest for excellence had to be reconciled with the accountants' quest for profits. But they were tactless about their suggestions for improvements.

In particular, they did not like Elizabeth's titles. *At Mrs Lippincote's* was acceptable, presumably because the usual American spelling was Lippincott and therefore the title was distinctive but not libellous; but they pressed hard for 'Cassandra's House' for *Palladian*. Elizabeth angrily assumed that they had not read the book, that they had to have a woman's name in the title, and that they had to change the title 'on the principle of what is good enough for Great Britain is not good enough for them'. It was a narrow-minded anti-Americanism that would, alas, never leave her. She told Ray that Knopf seemed to be 'distressed beyond words at my "attitude" about titles . . . [Peter Davies] thinks for my own good I should "keep them sweet". Because he thinks them the best publishers over there and just right for me & so on.'[45]

Even though Knopf wanted the best for her, and even though they sent kind letters and ham, butter and books (a common thing for American companies to do then when there were so many shortages in Britain), Elizabeth could not quite forget their small criticisms. Her fragile ego needed unequivocal approval and although she did not exactly bear a grudge, she did not forget. She could not know that one of Knopf's readers thought *Palladian* a much inferior version of *Rebecca*, but she sensed a lack of enthusiasm and this was a strain on her, especially since she began a new novel for four years running (the New Year of 1944, 1945, 1946 and 1947). In addition to writing as well as she could, on her own, without anyone to show her work to day by day, she also had to think about Knopf's commercial demands (thankfully, Peter Davies made it plain he would publish whatever she wrote). Thus in March 1947 she thanked Blanche Knopf* for sending some reviews of *Palladian* but said sadly, 'I hope it will do a little better than the other one, but I'm afraid it is rather unlikely that it will appeal to many people. Perhaps *A View of the Harbour* [which had just been sent over] will be more the right sort of thing, and I hope you will like it.'[46]

An author's relationship with her publisher is a subject all on its own. How, for example, would Virginia Woolf have reacted if she had been asked to change a title or had felt she

---

* Born in 1893, Blanche Wolf became engaged to Alfred Knopf in 1915, the year he began publishing. Their only son was born in 1918. By then Blanche was working full-time in the Knopf New York office as manuscript reader, editor, secretary and delivery boy; she became Vice-President in 1921. 'Her life was books and the men and women who wrote and published them. She was a petite dynamo' (*The Library Chronicle* University of Texas Volume 26 no. 1 1995 p 34).

needed to apologise for low sales or, as would Elizabeth in the near future, had had the awkward and upsetting experience of having to resist calls for rewriting? And yet did Blanche Knopf have a point? Would Elizabeth have been an even better novelist, even a great one, if she had followed Knopf's advice?

They were, however, unreservedly enthusiastic about *A View of the Harbour* and when Blanche Knopf visited England in the summer of 1947 Elizabeth felt confident enough to try and persuade her to take on Ivy Compton-Burnett in America. She decided she would, and Elizabeth told her: 'I am delighted . . . It will be like being on the same list as Jane Austen and gives me peculiar and boastful feelings . . . What can I say about her, and would she like me to say *anything*? I should like to make a signed statement that she is the greatest/only writer now living, but perhaps this will not do.'[47]

A View of the Harbour came out in England in the early autumn of 1947. Although the heading for its review was 'The Feminine Genius', *Punch* was a bit grudging ('the bigger subject seems too much, at present, for Mrs Taylor's art') but conceded that she was 'a novelist born'; the reviewer praised especially her acute relish for the appearance of things, quoting 'the greyish meat sliding off the bone, the rings of onion, the pearl barley, the golden sequins of fat glinting on the surface.'[48] PH Newby in *The Listener* said that Elizabeth had 'no doubt grown tired of being praised for her great understanding of the art of novel writing' ('Could one ever?' she might have retorted), praised everything about the book and praised Elizabeth herself for being 'wise, witty and good'. He concluded that the novel 'could have been very tedious indeed, but thanks to Mrs Taylor's keen intelligence, her repeated but unembarrassed change of viewpoint . . . it is all delight.'[49] (His one criticism was the same as Ray's – he did not like the bearded sailor.) And LP Hartley also admired the book but, saying that 'work of this quality can only be judged by exacting standards', he criticised the use of the names Edward, Teddy, Eddie and Ned. To him it was more than absent-mindedness, 'her characters are like sums of which we know all the figures, but which are not added up . . . Christian names are notoriously difficult to choose but it is as though the total personality eluded her.'[50]

Elizabeth had begun writing her next novel, *A Wreath of Roses*, in the January of that year, not long after she met Maud. It is about two young women who had been friends at school, one newly married with a baby who is called Liz and one unmarried who, for the first twenty-four pages of Elizabeth's second, handwritten draft, was called Camilla. Maud/Camilla meets a man on a train and, naïve and lonely as she is, allows herself to be attracted by him. At the end, after he has told her that he has killed someone ('making love exasperated me. Every depravity angered me . . . Some women like to be treated cruelly . . . ') Camilla thinks:

'I ought to have feared him more than I did . . . *He* is the sort of person . . . ' The other world, the world of violence, of people in newspapers, crept round about her, a world she had scarcely believed in. Parting the leaves to look for treasure, love, adventure, she inadvertently disclosed evil . . . '

In *A Wreath of Roses* Elizabeth is exploring the nature of exploitation and trust; she is not interested in the mentality of the murderer but in that of his victim.

Richard Elton ('the sort of name people don't have'[51]*) in the novel was based on the then notorious case of Neville Heath. He was born in 1917 and was, in the words of the *Oxford Dictionary of National Biography*, a 'bright, personable young man with charm and ability. Tall, broad, spruce, and fresh complexioned, with blue eyes and fair, wavy hair, he attracted many women.' But he was a 'liar, braggart, cheat, and impostor'[52] who posed as a war hero but was actually court-martialled three times. In June 1946 he sexually assaulted and murdered one woman in a hotel in Notting Hill Gate and another two days later in a hotel in Bournemouth where he had registered under the name Group Captain Rupert Brooke. For a few days before his arrest in early July he could have assaulted someone else: *A Wreath of Roses* partly tries to understand how a woman who might have encountered him at that time could have allowed herself to trust him; originally the novel was to focus on Heath/Elton but when Elizabeth realised, during the trial, that he had always been a sadist she realised it 'wouldn't be interesting to watch the growth of a tiny sadist into a

---

* But then one could say that of many of Elizabeth's characters, for example Emily Hemingway.

full-grown one. It would only be a matter of size, not a slow transformation from one thing into another.'[53]

Camilla is one side of Elizabeth's nature and Liz is the other. (It is odd that she did not choose *any* other name – but part of a pattern.) Camilla, an unmarried secretary in a girls' school, is a little like Emily in *Never and Always*. As she does every year, she travels down from London to spend the summer with Frances, who was once Liz's governess. The three of them talk uninhibitedly about anything that comes into their head, and about literature – they plan literary tea parties with Jane, Ivy, Virginia and George Eliot. Camilla tries to believe herself in love with Richard Elton; Liz tries to adjust to being married and having a child; Frances thinks about her painting:

> For was I not guilty of making ugliness charming? An English sadness like a veil over all I painted, until it became ladylike and nostalgic, governessy, utterly lacking in ferocity, brutality, violence. Whereas in the centre of the earth, in the heart of life, in the core of even everyday things is there not violence, with flames wheeling, turmoil, pain, chaos?

She faces a future, because of old age, when she will not be able to paint, the only thing she has ever wanted to do, but is visited by someone who admires her painting and who, it is hinted, might marry Camilla. At the end Camilla's admirer kills himself, and thus *A Wreath of Roses*, which has also started with a suicide when someone jumps off a railway bridge, ends with another suicide. After Maud, to whom the novel is dedicated, took her own life a few years later Elizabeth must have thought of this with agony.

The beginning of the novel is a miracle of compression and subtle scene-setting. Camilla and a young man are waiting for the train. 'Then, with a collapsing sound, the signal dropped.' As the train pulls in, a man on the footbridge jumps in front of it, 'an ill-devised death, since he fell wide of the express train.' This chapter is full of literary references, for example 'afternoons seem unending on branch-line stations' ('Adlestrop') and 'confusion and panic' and 'an ill-devised death' (Forster). And there are later allusions to Katherine Mansfield ('With a little arranging, the morning promised very well') and to Mrs Moore in *A Passage to India* ('Nothing stays. Nothing is completed') and so on. Elizabeth was writing in a way that was all her own and resented it when reviewers said she was a cross between so-and-so and so-and-so or, worse, accused her of simply imitating Virginia Woolf or Elizabeth Bowen not very well. These literary references are *hommages*, they place her in a literary tradition; otherwise she is herself.

Certain aspects of Camilla are exactly like Maud:

In her youth, discipline, over-niceness had isolated her. Shyness, perhaps, or pride, had started her off in life with a false step, on the wrong foot. The first little mistake initiated all the others. So life gathered momentum and bore her away; she became colder, prouder, more deeply committed; and, because she had once refused, no more was offered. Her habit now was negative. A great effort would be needed to break out of this isolation, which was her punishment from life for having been too exclusive.

Then, more trivially, there was her untidy hair and, as Barbara Pym pointed out, her habit of giving 'a quick little glance down from the corner of her eyes, not at him, but in his direction. This look – Liz knew it well – was a sign that she was deeply moved, but embarrassed.'[54] 'Anyone who knew Maud would recognise this,' Barbara Pym would write.[55] And Frances tells Camilla: '"You are the one I worry for . . . Because you never cry. Because you are so heavily armoured that if you get thrown, you'll never rise to your feet again without assistance."'

But what Maud must mostly have contributed to the book is an air of melancholy, even pessimism, evident from the title page onwards where Elizabeth quotes from *The Waves*: 'So terrible was life that I held up shade after shade'. Although there are many flashes of what reviewers call 'exquisite humour' ('"Welcome" said the door-mat, but to those going out'), this is not a book to laugh over, it seems instead to be a book written as a result of many afternoons walking in Highgate Cemetery. It is significant that the wreath of roses of the title is dead. Frances picks it up and thinks '"I shan't paint again . . . It is time to finish"'; significant too that we are reminded of Maupassant: the Griffin's 'shuttered façade seemed to suggest faded chambermaids sitting lost at the end of dark corridors, commercial-travellers sleeping off their midday drink on brass bedsteads, utter silence along all the passages, on all the little flights of stairs.'

Perhaps the most interesting aspect of *A Wreath of Roses* is the reflections on creativity and art, for, by implication, Elizabeth was writing about the dichotomy between modernism and the woman's novel. She writes about the art of painting, through the character of Frances, but she is talking too about the art of writing (in her long written discussions with Ray about all aspects of writing and painting the abstract thinking was about both genres).

At the start of the book Frances, who has been a governess all her life and has therefore not been able to concentrate on her painting as much as she would have liked to, or should, have done, is having a crisis about her work. She has done Vanessa Bell-like still lifes and landscapes but now she wonders whether 'she had become abstract, incoherent, lost'.[56] She rejects the prettiness and Englishness of her earlier work and attempts to express her new vision in paintings that have dark tormented skies and inhospitable scenery. Her admirer Morland Beddoes tries to get her to paint as she used to but Frances refuses, her last painting incomplete – a real wreath of faded roses, but whether it is bridal or funereal is unclear.

Morland, comments the critic Niamh Baker, 'has done what many male critics have done to women artists: tried to restrict them to their femininity'. Through the character of Frances, Elizabeth explores 'her own problems as a woman writer . . . she too struggled to find ways of expressing her horror at cruelty and violence . . . without losing her individual voice',[57] and suggests that the woman artist is wrong to allow her gender to banish her to the private sphere and exclude her from public events. Quoting a passage when Morland thinks about Frances's painting, another critic, Clare Hanson, suggests that what Elizabeth is doing 'is to articulate a painful distinction between her own art and that of the canonical texts of high modernism';[58] she alludes to Virginia Woolf ('life itself shifts round a little') but she herself is the recorder of the everyday, the mundane and, occasionally, the grotesque ('a dwarf, and a woman with dyed hair'). It was a dichotomy of which Elizabeth was nervously aware. She wrote to Ray in October 1947, when she was halfway through writing *A Wreath of Roses*,

> I am worried about my book. I have turned my back on all that people liked in my other novels – the light thrown on little daily situations (for thus they write to me) and there is nothing funny, no wit, no warmth, no children, no irony, no *perceptiveness*. It is *deadly serious*. Horribly sad. Cold. Everyone will hate it. It is also about people's bodies. They will feel insulted. The people in it are not pleasant consistently. The unpleasant are often *right*. I have come out of my range – a great mistake – and have swept in violence, brutality, passion, religion, all the things that had been better left out.[59]

CHAPTER EIGHT

PENN COTTAGE 1948–49

I used to lean out of my bedroom window when I was a girl,
watching trams banging by, & would dream of heaven being
sitting in a room with Virginia or Elizabeth Bowen talking
about books. Here it was, heaven on earth. All done by the
books themselves. [1]

Elizabeth's short stories were now beginning to sell in
America. In July 1947 *Harper's Bazaar* picked out extracts
from *A View of the Harbour* and published them as 'The School
Concert'; at the end of the year *Harper's* magazine brought
out 'The Light of Day', a miniature variation of Enid
Bagnold's novel *The Squire* (1938) about a baby being born
and the reactions of his family ('"God, I'm so tired," the
mother thought, bored'), which had first come out in *Time
and Tide* in the previous January; and *Harper's* also published
'A Sad Garden' (see p 140). [2]

Then in September 1948 *Harper's Bazaar* ran 'I Live in a
World of Make-Believe'. This is about 'Mrs Miller', eaten up
both with self-pity ('she would remain discontented for ever,'
thinks her husband) and envy, especially of 'Lady Luna' in the
big house across the road; meanwhile Lady Luna thinks
distractedly but without rancour of the days 'when nobody had

ever heard of the Labour Government and servants were grateful for their jobs.'[3] It was the most brilliant and most sophisticated story Elizabeth had yet written, and *The New Yorker* must have wished it had been offered to them. Yet neither Patience Ross nor Elizabeth's American agent appears to have thought of doing so, instead, her editor would tell her ten years hence, it was one of the *New Yorker* editors, Mr Lobrano, who 'discovered you and told me about you; he had been reading book after book during some illness.'[4] Thus began a relationship which was to mean so much to Elizabeth, and was to cause her almost the greatest grief she had ever known when it came to an end.

The first story *The New Yorker* published was 'A Red Letter Day' in November 1948.[5] This is an apparently rejected chapter from *A View of the Harbour*, 'which for some inexplicable reason you decided to omit'[6] (Peter Davies) about the appalling but unspoken misery endured by both mother and son when Tory goes to Edward's school to take him out to lunch. It is very funny; and a heart-rending indictment of the horrors of visiting a child at boarding school (something Elizabeth now knew all about because she had just sent Renny to boarding school when he was 10). Harold Ross, the *New Yorker*'s editor, was delighted with the chapter and Katharine White, the story editor, said to Elizabeth that she was most anxious that their editorial suggestions were not annoying 'because we so much hope that this will be the *first of many* of your stories that we will publish.'[7] It was to be the first of thirty-four stories written over a period of twenty years: moreover, in the fifteen years from 1950 to 1965 *The New*

Yorker published every story Elizabeth wrote apart from *Hester Lilly* (p 271), 'Poor Girl' (p 38), a ghost story written for an English anthology, 'A Trouble State of Mind' (p 316) and 'The Little Girl' (p 330). She could not have hoped for more.

Her editor at *The New Yorker* was Katharine White. A small, energetic, highly intelligent upper middle-class Bostonian with great taste and style, she had been given a job at the newly-founded magazine when she was 32 and the mother of two children. She at once became indispensable and *The New Yorker* became her life: 'She was intensely, *intensely* interested in her work,' her son Roger Angell would write. 'It was the main event of her life. It wasn't a matter of power. It was about what was on the page or what could be on the page if something worked out.' As another *New Yorker* writer, Gardner Botsford, remarked, 'She was someone whose standards and capabilities were so much higher than your own that you just sat down and shut up.'[8] As well as being rigorous editorially, she was broad-minded, and willing to reach out to writers who might not be thought characteristic of the magazine (which Elizabeth certainly was not). Above all, once they were 'her' writers she worried about them and was interested in them to an admirable extent.

Through all Elizabeth's growing success, seeing what was happening to the dream that had nourished him throughout his years in Austria, Ray was made increasingly unhappy. Elizabeth accused him of being harsh, of trying to punish her, of being insensitive, of stripping little bits away from her confidence, of criticising her appearance, of being tired of her writing; he was probably guilty of all these things. He accused her of having a foot in each camp. 'Yes, you are perhaps right. But the wrong foot in each case. In common with most people, I am uneasy in either.'[9] Ray said that she had the wrong friends, that they had 'influenced' her. He had just read the typescript of Elizabeth's latest book and it was now that he fully realised to what extent he and she were living in different 'camps'.

Something Ray would never forgive Elizabeth for was that in 1948 she left the Communist Party. At first she had not minded being a curiosity. In June 1946 she described going to a party at the Conservative Party chairman's house in High Wycombe and him teasing her.

> It is funny, I feel I do more good to the party now than I ever did selling Daily Workers and going to meetings . . . They do not often meet people who [don't] seem like themselves. When they do, they like to listen and argue. It is because of these people, who always think of me as being a communist, that I hesitate to leave the party. I feel it would shake them for ever, if I were to say, 'As a matter of fact, I've stopped believing in all that' . . . For all those people at the Cricket Club, for instance, people in pubs, John's friends and our neighbours, I am really the only communist they have ever talked to, the only one who ever puts the other point of view.[10]

But she also told Ray that 'only a cowardly feeling of hating people to say "I told you so" prevents me from leaving the party (which I have really left anyway – virtually as journalists say). Of course, what goes wrong in Russia does not damn Marxism, I know, but it makes me afraid that the machine Marxism inevitably leads to this autocracy. I do not care to help in taking such a risk.'[11] However, by 1948 'I feel that what led me into the CP at last led me out of it . . . I am lonelier than you, because now there is darkness and dis-agreement lying on either side of me. You have it only on one side. There's peace of mind in that. I am only dust blown about on the winds of other people's beliefs. I cannot find refuge in any set of rules.'[12]

Meanwhile Ray, aged 35, was settled into the man he would be for the rest of his life: earning enough to support himself as a draughtsman in London but without any wish to do much more; painting, but without much success (because success so often means sociability and contacts, neither of which he approved of); he did not even contemplate giving up his membership of the CP (and continued, inplacably, only to read the *Daily Worker* and, later, the *Morning Star* and, as a concession, the *Observer* on Sundays). He would despise the bourgeois world Elizabeth now inhabited of dinner parties, comfortable sofas, holidays in Brittany, children at boarding school, the Home Service and *Mrs Dale's Diary*; and, tragically (because to see it is tragic for the onlooker, even if it did not appear that way to him) he remained embittered for the rest of his life.

From the late 1940s onwards Elizabeth, living in this world, arranged her life in the pattern that was to continue until her death. She went into Beaconsfield, a couple of miles from Penn, to go shopping and, on Fridays, to have her hair done; she waited for John to arrive home at ten past one to eat the lunch she had cooked for him; she saw friends in Penn; occasionally she went up to London or went on holiday; she wrote thank-you letters and sent Christmas cards. She ensured that her life became full of ritual because she preferred it that way. 'I dislike much travel or change of environment,' she would tell the *New York Herald Tribune* in 1953, her tongue only slightly in her cheek, 'and prefer the days (each with its own domestic flavour) to come round almost the same week after week. Only in such circumstances can I find time or peace in which to write.'[13] Above all, she stayed at home writing. She had no room of her own but worked in an armchair writing a first draft and then a second draft in longhand in a school exercise book which rested on the arm of her chair; she would not have dreamed of doing, say, a dozen drafts. She did not talk about her work, to anyone, certainly not to her family, although probably a little bit to Robert Liddell.

In fact she was now doing very much the same things as Kate would do in *In a Summer Season* (1961). She lives 'in commuting country – an hour from London' and also has a daughter at boarding school and a son working in the family firm (as Renny would do), a live-in housekeeper, convivial evenings with neighbours that began with gin and tonic at six. This was another ritual that Elizabeth began after she moved to Penn: nearly every day at six o'clock she walked to The Crown, a variation on Mrs Mason's routine in the 1969 'Sisters': 'They were almost able to set their clocks by her, her neighbours said, seeing her leaving the house in the mornings, for shopping and coffee at the Oak Beams Tea Room.'[14]

Having finished the day's writing Elizabeth went to The Crown for the kind of conversation that she often writes up in her books, based on the friendships that happen in pubs (and, for a woman, could only happen in country pubs in 1950s Britain – although, even in the country, it was still unusual for a woman to go to a pub on her own). So, even if superficially her life was like that of the women in large houses who had their hair done and gossiped, in fact her writing was the most important thing in her life. Like Kate in *In a Summer Season* she may sometimes have thought wearily, 'we're all of us just passing time';[15] she may have believed this existentially; but as far as the everyday rhythm of her life went it was quite untrue. Time, life, what she did every day, for Elizabeth *was* her work.

In the spring of 1948, only two and a half years after *At Mrs Lippincote's* had appeared, there was an entry under 'Elizabeth Taylor' in the American *Current Biography*: Who's News and Why. Elizabeth told Ray that at school she used to look at

the History of English Literature and imagine my name going in between Coleridge and Collins. I always felt part of it, felt it streaming through me and I adding to it . . . but when I did see my own name in that very History of English Literature (though not in the Cs) I felt most peculiar. People think my writing is a sudden flowering, but I waited a long time.[16]

She was 35 and had written a novel a year for four years: it was as if, after what turned out to be twenty years of apprenticeship, she felt that once she had been given her chance to be a published novelist she must not stop; now that she had 'confirmed her right to a high place among the after-war generation of novelists'[17] she must not lose it.

Although well and healthy, and free of her wartime stomach pains, Elizabeth was often exhausted and often frenzied. These were interior emotions. Her family remember her as consistently 'there' for them, good fun, ready to put down her writing the moment she heard anyone at the door (did the door squeak? Did she think of Jane Austen covering her work when someone came in at the door?). It was a refusal to be pompous about her writing that was almost humility. She never wanted her own room, never went away to write, never boasted about her literary life. Her belief, after all, was that 'authors should be as ordinary as they can be – and not be special or removed or bohemian.'[18] Yet when her daughter would say that she never realised her mother was a writer; or when Elizabeth insisted that she cook lunch and John insisted that he come home for it: the question should be asked (and dismissed, for being unanswerable) whether she would have been the great writer, a First Eleven writer along with Forster, Greene, Orwell, Woolf, if she had not *appeared* to be almost neurotically modest about her work. (And if she had not been a wife and mother and cook and cleaner . . .)

Elizabeth *was* tired in the spring of 1948 and was in irrational despair about *A Wreath of Roses*. Ray suggested she burn it, but 'I would destroy myself first'; Maud came up with a new title (we do not know what the previous one was) and told her nothing mattered but her happiness, 'as if I have any happiness that is not bound up in my work'; Ronald (the priest) said she needed a holiday, 'as if writers are ever able to take a holiday'; and other people 'say all the wrong things to cheer me'.[19] Nevertheless, she very nearly did destroy the manuscript and told Peter Davies that she could not have the book published. When she finally and very reluctantly sent him the manuscript he suggested she might be suffering from 'nervous exhaustion arising from the abominable effort of writing, plus the very nearly inevitable anxiety which must afflict anyone like yourself who has been praised in the press.'[20] He argued her out of destruction over lunch.

The reason it had taken her fifteen months to write rather than the ten months she had spent on each of the previous three novels, and caused her so much despair, was not just because she had moved house at the time she started the new novel. It was because this book was 'my personal statement about life, that all beauty is pathetic, that writing is like Ophelia handing out flowers, that horror lies under every leaf.'[21] The quotation from *The Waves* on the title page presents the reader with an image of a dead wreath tossing on the waves; it also makes the book something of a homage to *The Waves;* and Elizabeth may have hoped it would have the same importance in her oeuvre as *The Waves* had in Virginia Woolf 's.

Two suicides, an attempted murder, an undertone of bleakness about human relationships, and a great deal of abstraction about the art of painting, all this does indeed add up to a 'statement', yet such a bleak one, and so casually done, that it did not seem likely it would appeal to reviewers. As Elizabeth said to Blanche Knopf, 'I hope you will like it when you read it, but it isn't the same as the others and I feel quite prepared for people to find it not very gay, to say the least.'[22] In the event Knopf were very happy with it, loved the title, and predicted large sales for it. And Elizabeth's chief fan there, Herbert Weinstock, said that although comparisons with Elizabeth Bowen were inevitable, and although Elizabeth Taylor would probably never equal her particular intensity, 'Mrs Taylor is every bit the older woman's equal in artistry, human under-standing, and ability to tell a compelling story.' He thought *A Wreath of Roses* her best book to date and that it ought to be treated '(sales differentials being, of course, kept in mind) as we treat Camus, Mann, Bowen, and Cather.' And he concluded that although Elizabeth would never produce commercial fiction – 'this is a novel of velleities, subtleties, nuances' – he thought Knopf had on the whole been too modest in their claims for her and should now start placing her 'in the company of the most accomplished, readable, and intelligent novelists of our time.'[23]

Despite the gratifyingly positive response of both Peter Davies and Knopf, for the fourth time in the three and a half years since *At Mrs Lippincote's* had appeared, Elizabeth awaited the reviews with trepidation and indeed with anguish. However thick a skin she had tried to develop, reading reviews was always agony for her. And she was now so well established that some reviewers would sharpen their knives simply out of vindictiveness. As Peter Davies had said, 'It is often noticeable that a certain type of jealous reviewer lies in wait for an opportunity to wound anyone whose work has been much eulogised.'[24] And it is shocking, really, reading the reviews nowadays and imagining oneself in Elizabeth's shoes. (And what are reviews for? And why do they 'go through' the plot in such soul-destroying detail?)

The most interesting piece was by the sweet-natured and incisive Elizabeth Jenkins (who was to write one of the great novels of the twentieth century, *The Tortoise and the Hare*, in 1954). She praised the interesting and sympathetic female characters and the domestic detail 'which she makes glamorous by her original kind of sensuous perception'. Although she felt there was too much description of the painter's vision, and Virginia Woolf's influence hovered unduly, 'her own unadulterated manner is unusually charming and distinguished. Very few writers have so assured a future.'[25] Then there was a review by Richard Church which Elizabeth loved ('it was almost a doctor's diagnosis'[26]) because it wrote about the book's sensuous, almost anaesthesia-like quality 'to compensate for a slight weariness of spirit, a slackening of intellectual vitality, as though [Miss Taylor's] mind is tired and her mental vision blurred by the fog of everyday life.'[27] (It was, to some extent; the review caused her to tell Ray how much she regretted her twenties when she should have been making all her current mistakes. 'I think now that I have passed the time when I should have written a good book.'[28]) There were many other kind reviews, particularly George Malcolm Thomson in the *Evening Standard* (which chose it as its Book of the Month). But there was also John Chandos, a minor critic and writer, on a books programme on the BBC, who plodded through the plot, regretted Elizabeth did not write like Mrs Gaskell in *Cranford* and criticised the men for being implausible. (As Elizabeth would write twenty years hence: 'The reason, they say, that women novelists can't write about men, is because they don't know what they're like when they're alone together, what they talk about and so on. But I can't think *why* they don't know. I seem to hear them booming away all the time.'[29])

In the *New Statesman* Julia Strachey was annoyed by a remark in a Sunday newspaper – 'that so exquisite a writer as Elizabeth Taylor is also "ordinary" is something to be thankful for' – and spent her review demonstrating why *A Wreath of Roses* was so much inferior to Sartre's *The Diary of Antoine Roquentin*. Elizabeth had done

> virtually no 'thinking' in the intellectual sense at all – spiritually her book is a 'pre-fab' . . . Besides the rays of [Sartre's] powerful and adventurous mind . . . Miss Elizabeth Taylor's country cottages and pubs, her artists, discontented wives, and mysterious strangers, seem to dissolve and melt into transparency.[30]

The effect of this piece was to make Elizabeth feel 'bewildered, horrified, singled out . . . I always quite liked her writing. (When I say "liked", I do not mean I have changed my mind, but that she no longer does any . . .*) I can never understand that I provoke such strong feelings.'[31] While in *Tribune* Pamela Hansford Johnson called the novel 'as cold as

---

* Julia Strachey had not published a book since *Cheerful Weather for the Wedding* in 1932.

ice. It is cold because it simply is not true . . . *A Wreath of Roses* is not real love, friendship, hatred, kindliness and cruelty; it is art and intellect arranging selected aspects of these passions to make . . . a devilish clever design.'[32] Elizabeth was corresponding with Robert Liddell by the time this review appeared and we know from what he later revealed that there was much ribald and hostile discussion of Pamela Hansford Johnson in their letters, this being one of the many reasons he destroyed them.

Elizabeth Bowen almost made up for the carping. In an interview in the *New York Times* in March she named her favourite living fiction writers as '(*not* in order of preference) Henry Green, Graham Greene, Mauriac, Montherlant, Sartre, Colette, Evelyn Waugh, Camus, Eudora Welty, Rosamond Lehmann, Ludwig Bemelmans, Ivy Compton-Burnett, Faulkner, Elizabeth Taylor, Elizabeth Jenkins, EM Forster, Frank O'Connor, Sean O'Faolain, Rumer Godden, PH Newby, Dorothy Parker.'[33] Elizabeth could not have been in better company; there would, however, be a great deal of hostility in the future from the writers not singled out (Olivia Manning, Pamela Hansford Johnson etc.). A month later Elizabeth Bowen reviewed *A Wreath of Roses* – she must in fact have been writing the review while she gave the *New York Times* interview – and praised the younger novelist effusively. Because of the novel's 'quiet ordinariness' she recommended two readings, 'then, perhaps, a return'. She admired all the characters (especially the men, and especially the 'light, off-hand, gaily preposterous running dialogue between Camilla and Liz' much criticised by other reviewers) and liked the way Elizab took into account 'the irrational element in people . . . As against that, there is a beautifully concrete *practical* accuracy about her writing.'[34]

Eighteen months earlier, when Elizabeth Bowen had written her very warm review of *A View of the Harbour*, Elizabeth Taylor had written to thank her, and when *The Heat of the Day* came out in early 1949 she was sent a copy, read it 'with wild excitement' and told Elizabeth Bowen that 'you rake up the dead leaves in our hearts and say many things which we did not know how to say ourselves.'[35] Interestingly, even a letter like this was not drafted and then copied out – some of the words are fainter than others and 'many' was 'more' but was scratched out and written over: by now Elizabeth had enough self-confidence to write spontaneously to an older and revered novelist without planning what she was going to say. Yet when she agreed to go to tea at Elizabeth Bowen's house in Regent's Park (at 2 Clarence Terrace) she said self-deprecatingly, 'it would be nice to talk about our books. I am not used to talking about anything but What the Butcher Said, so perhaps I can't. But I should like to try.'[36]

She did try and

that afternoon with Elizabeth Bowen meant a great deal to me. If not a turning-point, at least a steadying-point. It was going into that Regent's Park house from *The Death of the Heart* . . . and her saying, 'You and Virginia would have found so much in common' made me feel dizzy and unreal. I like women to love one another & help one another & I liked to think of those two sitting in that room talking about their work, as we were doing. Both very beautiful and great people.[37]

Although they could not meet over the summer of 1949 because Elizabeth Bowen was at her house in Ireland, by the winter of 1949–50 the two of them felt they had become close friends. It was not surprising – the younger Elizabeth had long revered Elizabeth Bowen's work, the elder one had reviewed her first four books almost rapturously. And although their backgrounds were quite different there were numerous similarities between the two of them: the death of their mothers had been a shattering blow for both; their working methods were similar (they wrote their novels straight through from beginning to end, they did not keep notebooks); and neither had ever thought of doing anything but writing – 'when I have nothing to write I feel only half alive'[38] was Elizabeth Bowen's comment in the *New York Times* but it could have been Elizabeth Taylor's. Although Elizabeth Taylor knew very few of the eminent intellectuals who were part of Elizabeth Bowen's entourage, each considered the other one of her very dearest friends. Elizabeth Taylor's family would say that for her three people could do no wrong: Elizabeth Bowen, her daily help Mrs Howard (who worked for her from 1952 onwards), and her butcher.

One of the reasons that Elizabeth was a little happier with John at the end of the 1940s was that she had now 'got over' Ray: the letters between the two of them virtually stop at this point. From time to time Elizabeth thanked Ray for a book he had sent. But it was over; once, in the mid-1950s, when she in the train from London with the children, she cut him (according to Ray). She did not need him to write letters to because she had Maud and, soon, Robert Liddell in Greece. And in her new role of successful novelist she was able to rely on John in a way she would never have been able to rely on Ray. Once John came with her when she took Ivy Compton-Burnett and her companion Margaret Jourdain out to lunch. 'He behaved very well. I did not meet his eye. He advised Margaret Jourdain about her income-tax, while Ivy and I tore Graham Greene up into tiny, tiny pieces and scattered the remains.'[39] Ray would not have been able to fulfil this role, nor would he have been able to dine with, for example, Blanche Knopf. John, after his experiences during the war, and being comfortably the managing director of a successful business, could hold his own with many different types of people in a way that Ray could not have done.

Elizabeth also played her part as businessman's wife, housewife and mother, and although she was never a part of a literary 'circle', she now had several friends who were writers. Apart from Ivy Compton-Burnett and Elizabeth Bowen, there was Barbara Pym. She worked at the International African Institute and had met Maud through other anthropologists who worked there; the two of them quickly discovered that they both admired Elizabeth's novels, and early in 1950 Maud introduced Barbara to Elizabeth over tea at Fortnum's. After that they kept in touch, sometimes meeting for lunch or going together to evening events at PEN (the writers' club, affectionately satirised in Barbara Pym's 1953 novel *Jane and Prudence*). The two novelists' writing styles were very different,

BY AIR MAIL
PAR AVION

William Maxwell Esq;
The New Yorker,
25 West 43rd Street,
New York 18, U.S.A.

and in any case Elizabeth was an unabashed atheist, but they tacitly accepted this and remained on affectionate terms until Elizabeth's death.

Now the literary friendship that would mean most of all to Elizabeth was about to begin. In the summer of 1948 she had read a novel called *The Last Enchantments* in which the author Robert Liddell* 'describes some apparently half-mad but utterly convincing people in Oxford: scholars, minor writers, their servants and landladies, and university hangers-on . . . The talk of Oxford tea parties has never been so brilliantly captured.'[40] The book owes something to Ivy Compton-Burnett, of whom Robert Liddell was a great admirer. He would say later that he thought Elizabeth first decided to write to him because of a reference to Ivy in his book; her letter 'didn't say much, but that the book might have been written for her, and that she had laughed and cried in the right places.'[41] She told Ray: '*The Last Enchantments* by Robert Liddell is a fine book. Certainly made me cry. I don't think we should approve of him as a person though. Ivy is in his blood . . .'[42]

When Elizabeth first wrote to Robert, he had just left England** for Cairo. He realised, or hoped, that it would be a

---

* 1908–92

** He was never to return, since for him England would forever be associated on the one hand with his hated stepmother and on the other with his beloved brother, killed in the Normandy landings: 'For Robert the death of his brother was devastating . . . it made him feel he could never return to live in England' (*The Times* 7 August 1992). Also, he was homosexual.

regular correspondence and kept her letters. However, in 1953, he was away when Nasser took over and the anti-British riots began, and he went to Athens; he never returned to Cairo to recover his possessions, and although he kept Elizabeth's subsequent, twenty-two years-worth of letters, these were then, with the exception of her letters about Ivy, deliberately and 'most scrupulously'[43] destroyed by Robert at her insistence. 'I had them on condition that they should not be kept, so what could I do? Various dishonest courses were suggested: "deposit in a Library" and so on. But they would not do. And yet she was (I think) the best letter-writer of the century.'[44] (It is still just possible that Robert did not in fact destroy the correspondence but embargoed it for fifty or a hundred years, or at least until all the neighbours in Penn, and the contemporary writers who were vile about Elizabeth's work, were no longer alive.)

The two of them, who were not to meet for ten years (since Robert never came to England), sent each other two or three pages every three weeks or so, although Elizabeth probably wrote more often. This is because her letters to Robert began at exactly the time her letters to Ray stopped and it seems likely that again she used them as a diary, as a way of thinking aloud, as a writer's notebook. Robert's great attraction as a correspondent was that he too was a writer, and one that she admired, indeed loved: she told him, 'when I have read your books I feel more loving, and it is no use being alive if one doesn't feel that.'[45] The love she had felt for Ray for fifteen years, and had put into her letters, could be transmuted into the love she felt for Robert's work, for his 'writerly' perceptions and, eventually, for himself. There was no sexual element (Robert was homosexual) and he was blessedly far away and with no intention of ever returning.

They used to write about anything that interested them and even looked for copy. She was

> wonderful about local bores (and that I promised to destroy, and most regretfully did) – as good as Mme de Sévigné about Breton neighbours. Of course we became such intimate friends that sometimes we poured out some of our troubles – but if there were 'painful' letters no other eye will see them. We were reasonably fortunate people – knowing only too well where our next meal was to come from, having usually cooked it. But we had our troubles . . . I daresay she needed to write – not always having the right people to talk to.[46]

Elizabeth did not have the right people to talk to: letters were a substitute and became her talking. During the last twenty-five years of her life, when she was a successful writer, there was this perception that she was deeply private and deeply shy – she refused to give talks, was monosyllabic on television, and so on. But she had not been so shy in the '30s. What happened was that she was wounded almost in a physical sense by (some) people's hostility, particularly that of reviewers; and, as well, she never found anyone with whom she could have the kind of conversations she had had with Ray and with Maud. Letters became not just a substitute for friendship and companionship but they *were* the friendship. This is why she was so emphatic that her letters to Robert should be destroyed; that she destroyed Maud's letters to her and hers to Maud when they were returned to her; and that she presumably can have had no idea that Ray had kept her letters or she would have made efforts to destroy them. A letter was, for her, an almost profound expression of self, of her personality, of a reaching out to the other person. When her friend Herman Schrijver* died she said how much she missed him, 'especially when there are amusing things I want to tell him about. I wish one could write letters to the dead.'[47] The last remark was not merely frivolous.

Apart from being private, a letter embodied good or bad manners. Elizabeth cared about good manners very much indeed and would have been mortified to have been considered rude to anyone. In late 1955 she wrote a preamble to one of the (preserved) letters about Ivy:

> I would not like to think of myself as a little Boswelly person, and my mother brought me up so much better than I have turned out. To abuse hospitality was the most horrid thing; worst of all, I often think how she would despise me when I am driven by curiosity to ask the children what they had for lunch when they were invited out. Loving does not cancel out such bad manners or excuse them, and she would not think so either.[48]

---

* an interior decorator, 1904–72; he wrote *Decoration for the Home* in 1939.

As Robert was to write, 'I think one of the uses our correspondence was to her was that she could say what she liked about people without feelings of treachery or abuse of hospitality.'[49]

Yet even Robert betrayed her in a very small sense. The preamble above about not being a little Boswelly person turns out to have a pre-preamble in the original version of the letter (which survived because it describes a visit to Ivy). This reads, 'Dear Robert, If you were sitting here with me I would make you cross your heart and swear that no temptation would ever make you divulge the following disloyalties & indiscretions. How can I make you swear, unless by return of post. Or would you rather throw this straight on the fire?'[50] When one rereads the letter that follows (it is reprinted in full on p 55 of Robert Liddell's *Elizabeth and Ivy*) it seems that Elizabeth's dread was that the letter should fall into Ivy's hands (Robert, after all, was a close friend of hers as well). In this respect he was only a little indiscreet; the 'lunch with Ivy' letters were not published until Ivy had died and Elizabeth herself had given permission for them to be shown to her biographer, Hilary Spurling. And when Robert published his own book he used these same letters and no others.

It was because of her friendship with Robert that Elizabeth agreed to go again to lunch with Ivy. She had not enjoyed herself the first time and when she received another invitation, in July 1948, she told Ray, 'I am bidden again to luncheon with Ivy. Command performance. I cannot go.'[51] She did go, and the reason was that knowing she would be able to tell Robert about every detail of the occasion (she used to write in the train going home or in her armchair the next morning) made it less intimidating. In any case their feelings about Ivy were mutual. Robert would write: 'Our common devotion to Ivy made us like two siblings or cousins, drawn together by our feeling for a beloved aunt. Loved, indeed, but not blindly.'[52]

Since 1932 Ivy had lived with the furniture historian Margaret Jourdain in a gloomy flat in Braemar Mansions, Cornwall Gardens, off the Gloucester Road. Here she gave small lunches and teas at which conversation consisted almost entirely of fairly malicious gossip and complaints about the difficulties of post-war Kensington life; the male guests were mostly homosexual, the women were almost all successful writers such as Kay Dick, Kathleen Farrell, Olivia Manning, Theodora Benson and Elizabeth Sprigge.

Entranced by what she observed at Braemar Mansions, Elizabeth did not mind her relationship with Ivy being almost entirely one-sided; for, not only was Ivy a supreme egoist, she was one of those women who, although childless and undomesticated herself, did not hesitate to advise about children, housework, cookery or to lecture Elizabeth on subjects such as getting up in the night to go to the bathroom ('put on your stockings *and* your knickers'[53]). The compassionate, which Elizabeth believed Ivy to be and hoped she herself was, would say that these remarks were kindly meant and a convoluted way for the inhibited to express affection. Nor did Ivy much respect the work of any living author apart from herself, with the possible exception of the early novels of Elizabeth Bowen. All in all, her flat was a court, where guests visited the 'fabulous monster in her ogress's den'.

Here Elizabeth was happy to be a courtier, not because she saw herself as Boswelly (she did not), but because she admired Ivy's novels so deeply. And, in her quiet way, she promoted Ivy's career. She had suggested that Blanche Knopf add her to her list. And then, when asked to write a piece about Ivy for *Vogue* she most unusually agreed, and even agreed to Robert's suggestion that she turn it into a talk at a British Council Summer School in Oxford in the late summer of 1952. She began the article by mentioning *Darkness and Day*, the newest addition to the list of those 'bi-nominal titles' which Ivy had made her own: '(So much her own that, reading in the most dull of Parliamentary Reports the words "Landlords and Tenants", one feels a momentary lift of interest and anticipation, at first hard to account for).' And she went on to give some reasons why Ivy was a great writer, 'one of the greatest of our times', and to make a few points that, perhaps, would have interested *Vogue* readers: that evil can be committed within the close ranks of the family ('devilry can suddenly develop on page one as they all sit down to breakfast'), that Clemency in *Two Worlds and Their Ways* is tormented by the other girls at school because of her party-dress 'and with it the background, the parentage, the life which they believe it to suggest.'[54] Although Elizabeth would never change her mind about Ivy being a great novelist, 'the only great writer',[55] her point of view was hardly universal: more typically, Jocelyn Brooke told Olivia Manning that 'Ivy Compton-Burnett is one of my blind spots. I can see she's very good, and the stylised dialogue is great fun for a few pages, but then I get bored.'[56]

In the early summer of 1949, by which time *A Wreath of Roses* had sold 15,000 copies in Britain and 6000 in America (it was eventually to sell 26,000 in Britain) Elizabeth began what many, this writer included, consider her masterpiece (and what some consider her last great novel), *A Game of Hide and Seek*. The opening sentence is of poetic beauty: 'Sometimes in the long summer's evenings, which are so marked a part of our youth, Harriet and Vesey played hide-and-seek with the younger children, running across the tufted meadows, their shoes yellow with the pollen of butter-cups.' (We must imagine Elizabeth sitting on the floor, in a wide skirt characteristic of the late 1940s – she rarely wore trousers – reading this sentence aloud to herself; and wondering whether she should dare put in the second phrase or whether 'critics' would be annoyed by the reprehensible – or is it? and if so why? – authorial voice.)

This, her fifth novel (her fifth to be published, but might have been her twentieth or even twenty-fifth to have been written), is about two 18-year-olds, Harriet and Vesey who, naturally without knowing it, are in love. Vesey, who is bored and difficult, wants to be a writer: 'At school, he had often turned to the index of a History of Literature and in his mind inserted his own name – Vesey Patrick Macmillan – between Machiavelli and Sir Thomas Malory.' Harriet, of course, has no envisaged future apart from marriage. Vesey goes to Oxford and becomes an actor, Harriet, her heart broken by Vesey, meets Charles. He is not unlike an earlier Charles, Charles Bovary, being steady and kind; although when he plays the piano Harriet, ominously, 'had not imagined that the playing of Chopin could be turned into such a Caesarist display'. By marrying Charles and living in Jessica Terrace (the name of the street where Elizabeth's schoolfriend Josephine Bales had lived in Reading), Harriet moves into a world of au pairs and drinks trays, where 'white lilac was arranged against the red damask curtains; the white kitten slept on a crimson cushion'; Vesey, who 'never threw out fastening tendrils such as letters or presents or remembrances',[57] remains oblivious to the tidy, the respectable, the bourgeois. (And yet the red and white are potent images of something more primeval.)

When Harriet and Vesey meet again after twenty years she is very much in one 'camp', as Ray would have put it, he in another; and she has to decide whether to run off with Vesey or stay with her husband and daughter. The ending is indecisive because it is not clear whether Vesey, who is ill, is going to get better. This was to annoy American critics in particular, who demanded the neat tying up of ends even more than their British counterparts and seemed to have no conception of Chekhovian subtlety: *A Game of Hide and Seek* is Elizabeth's *hommage* (conscious or, more probably, unconscious) to 'The Lady with the Dog'. Yet none of the reviewers ever mentioned Chekhov; even that great critic David Cecil wrote Elizabeth a fan letter but said that he wished the ending had been more clear-cut. 'Do you mean us to think that Harriet eloped with Vesey, or just started the affair again on the same terms, or had come to take her last farewell?'[58]

For this is Elizabeth's most flawless, most nearly perfect novel. None of the incidental characters are bores (as, alas,

Mrs Bracey and Iris can be in *A View of the Harbour*); there are, for example, the women she works with at the dress shop who are good to Harriet (her 'virginity they marvelled over a great deal. It seemed a privilege to have it under the same roof. They were always kindly enquiring after it, as if it were a sick relative') and educate her ('Lilian watched her daughter growing day by day more colourful from all the beauty hints Miss Lazenby gave her. Her finger-nails, at first timidly pink, soon grew rosier, her eyelids bluer'); Betsy, Charles and Harriet's daughter, is one of the most memorable of all the memorable children in Elizabeth's novels; and Vesey's aunt and uncle, the once-bohemian and now merely vegetarian couple at the beginning of the book, are admirable in their easy-going friendliness, their belief that spaniels should be allowed to flop on beds, in Hugo Macmillan's 'type of masculinity now perhaps vanished to the world; the walking-tours in perfect spring weather, Theocritus in pocket: an aesthetic virility.' (Yet even he has fossilised: 'His old-fashioned liberalism now contained elements of class-hatred; his patriotism had become the most arrogant nationalism.'[59])

Another influence on *A Game of Hide and Seek* was the film of *Brief Encounter*. Elizabeth had seen it not long after it first came out, in the early spring of 1946, and told Ray that it was good to have the particular made general: although she never referred to it as such, it must have been a crucial film for her. There was, to start with, the coincidence (as she must have thought when she saw it) that parts of the film had been shot in Beaconsfield the previous year, just before she started going shopping there; Celia Johnson was filmed coming out of the International Stores, now Elizabeth's grocer, and a scene was shot in the Five Ways Café where she had begun to go almost every week with her friend Gerry from Penn. In fact Elizabeth and Celia Johnson were not unalike in looks or voice; and when the critic CA Lejeune remarked that Celia Johnson's voice has 'a peculiar sort of intimate appeal to the spectator, whispering directly and persuasively to the individual rather than speaking to an audience as a crowd', she might have been describing Elizabeth's writing voice. One of the reasons the film appealed to its audience was because there has rarely been such a match of character and actress – Celia Johnson *was* Laura Jesson. But Elizabeth was both of them.

Although it has been observed that *A Game of Hide and Seek* 'seems in its use of dirty trains and railway stations at dusk deliberately to echo *Brief Encounter*'s *mise en scène*', this was not deliberate in the sense that Elizabeth thought, I will refer to *Brief Encounter*; it is more that adulterous love of the kind she was writing about, or Rosamond Lehmann or Graham Greene wrote about, used trains and station buffets and seedy hotels as the kind of places where lovers might plausibly meet. When Alec and Laura wanted to meet more often than by encountering each other in the High Street, then – if they wanted to be unobserved – they had to resort, very much like Harriet and Vesey, to the station buffet or a café or a borrowed flat. It was all very un-French, very English in the lack of glamour, and indeed the film (which begins with the sentence 'It all started on an ordinary day, in the most ordinary place in the world'[60]) is about the kind of Englishness that stresses behaving sensibly, not hurting people, being considerate rather than giving in to emotion. When Laura thinks about her husband 'and oh my dear, I don't want you to be hurt', this is very much what Harriet thinks about Charles. Both wives are loyal to their husbands and fond of them; it is just that they are not in love with them as they are with Alec and with Vesey.

At Mrs Lippincote's had been semi-autobiographical because Julia Davenant was so like her creator; *Palladian* because it was her girlhood; *A View of the Harbour* because she was another aspect of Beth the novelist; and *A Wreath of Roses* because it expressed some of her deepest beliefs about life and art. Now here was a novel about a love affair, one that would be seen by some as one of the great novels about love in the English language. No one would assume that Elizabeth had never *been* in love. But what would anyone think who met John? One reason Elizabeth dreaded reviews was that her books exposed her self. There might come a time when no one would believe her any longer, as she kept declaring to interviewers that she only used her imagination; it would be with unusual self-revelation that she would write to Blanche Knopf, after a batch of hostile reviews of *A Game of Hide and Seek*, 'I suppose it was a fore-doomed book, and had not the authority of being untrue'.[61]

Elizabeth started writing with *élan,* and then 'a great darkness has come down in the middle of it: it has cracked in two with a yawn.'[62] As she would write in *Angel* five years later: 'She had reached a desperate, claustrophobic stage of being imprisoned halfway in a novel; there was too much behind her for her to retreat and not a glimmer of light ahead.'[63] This can indeed be seen in the abrupt transition between Part One and Part Two, twenty years on.* But if one thinks of the conditions in which Elizabeth worked it is hardly surprising that a book would occasionally crack in two; it is miraculous that it did not happen more often. In *A View of the Harbour*, five-year-old Stevie comes home and her mother (the novelist) looks up:

> 'What is it,' she asked suddenly, sharply . . .
> 'I am home from school,' said Stevie simply.
> But with the dying child still on her mind, Beth could not bring herself to welcome this living one.
> 'Then run and wash your hands,' she said.[64]

This is not, apparently, what Elizabeth would have done, for she claimed in every surviving interview and written comment that the children always came first. Yet it seems unbelievable that she could produce a masterpiece in such difficult working conditions (sitting in an armchair, having to cook lunch, the vacuum cleaner being pushed around by the daily). It was her choice; but when Elizabeth Bowen told the *New York Times* that she worked 'from 9.30 to 1, 2.30 to 5.30 . . . My room should be a silent room. A large writing table . . . Ideally,

---

* The cracking in two, the abrupt transition, exemplifies Elizabeth's almost obsessional avoidance of 'those banal links and explanations: "Many years had passed, and the pretty little girl had grown into a beautiful woman." Not for me, I think.' ('The Short Story' in *The Kenyon Review* Issue 4 1969 p 472).

nobody coming near me, no calls to the telephone. Ideally no social engagements before 6.30. After that a drink, a bath, a dress that's fun to put on, and a little gaiety'[65] Elizabeth Taylor, if she had read the interview, must have wondered . . . And may have thought of the review quoted in the 1948 *Current Biography* in which Elizabeth Bowen observed that Elizabeth Taylor's fragmentary style was well suited to an age when 'life is an affair of snatches and moments, of combinations of oddly assorted people.' And ruefully accepted that writers who are mothers *can* only write in snatches and moments.

CHAPTER NINE

PENN COTTAGE 1950−53

She had seemed to wed also a social order. A convert to it . . . she had pursued it fanatically and as if she feared censure. No one had entertained more methodically, or better bolstered up social interplay. She had been indefatigable in writing letters of condolence, telegrams of congratulation; remembered birthdays and anniversaries; remembered bread-and-butter letters and telephone-messages after parties.[1]

Elizabeth's stories for *The New Yorker* would appear at steady intervals. Between 1949 and 1969 she not only wrote six novels but thirty-four short stories,* so that for the first fifteen years of this period *The New Yorker* consistently published somewhere between one and four stories by her every year. Two was the average, but it all depended on whether she was writing a novel, since she found it almost impossible to write a short story if preoccupied with a book. In March 1949 'First Death of Her Life', the story about a girl coming in from the snow to be at her mother's hospital deathbed, appeared (see p 60). 'The Beginning of a Story', which came out in October of the same year, was also about a woman

* although may have destroyed countless others

dying, and Elizabeth was worried that the two stories were too similar; but the tone is so different (in the second story a young couple long for the mother to die and thereby release them for life), and the interval between them long enough, for *The New Yorker* not to mind.

Another story, 'After Hours of Suffering', was rejected by *The New Yorker* for being too subjective; it is indeed hilariously autobiographical in its description of Elizabeth/the heroine lying in bed (she has backache) and being clumsily but well-meaningly looked after by Renny/her son: '"Chanel," he read off a bottle, pronouncing it Channel. He shook it up as if it were medicine and then dabbed it liberally behind his ears. "That will fox them at school," he chuckled.' 'He ranged round the bedroom, picking up jars and bottles, looking along the bookshelves. "*Do* people have their own books in their houses?" he asked, uncertain if my self-effacement were enough. "Who's to stop them?" I asked, a little nettled.'[2] American *Vogue* liked the personal element and published the story.* 'A Different Climate' was also rejected and has not survived unless, as is possible, it was given a new title and published in Elizabeth's first short story collection (the 1954 *Hester Lilly*) as 'Shadows of the World' (see p 184). It is about Ida on the day the family cat has four kittens and is set in a house very like Penn Cottage ('"I don't call this the real country," she said. "People only *sleep* here"').[3]

---

* In England it appeared in *Woman and Beauty*, who paid 18 guineas (£500 nowadays) for it – American *Vogue* paid the equivalent of £75 (£2000).

In November 1949 'Nods and Becks and Wreathèd Smiles'
was published. *The New Yorker* editors were delighted with
what they must by now have thought of as a typically wonderful Elizabeth Taylor short story, about four women who meet
for coffee. They begin by discussing childbirth: '"I was *hours*
with Jennifer," Mrs Miller said . . . "I thought neuralgia was
worse," Mrs Graham forgot herself enough to say. At first,
they were too surprised to speak. After all, *men* could have
neuralgia.' It was the most mature, most accomplished, story
Elizabeth had yet written for *The New Yorker* and was also the
funniest. One can imagine the laughter in the office when
they read about Dolly

> groping tragically before her, like Oedipus going into
> exile . . . a bandage over one eye, her hat crooked . . .
> 'Conjunctivitis,' she said faintly . . .
> 'Wherever did you *pick that* up?' Mrs Miller went on,
> and her voice made the affliction sound very sordid
> indeed.
> 'I've been run down,' Dolly said.
> 'You don't get it from being run down. You pick it
> up.' Mrs Miller spread margarine over half a scone and
> popped it into her mouth.'[4]

A Game of Hide and Seek was finished in March 1950.
Everyone at Peter Davies loved it, and Brandt & Brandt, her
American agent, told Knopf 'they think it is the best thing
she has done.'[5] However, Knopf was disappointed. Herbert
Weinstock liked the parts about Vesey and Harriet but was
bored by Harriet's life as a shop-girl before her marriage to

Charles, by Charles himself, by the scenes involving the au pair Elke (some of the funniest). What he admired most was the atmosphere of a Buckinghamshire town, its streets, pub, shops, and he thought the character of Harriet 'clearly conceived and beautifully built up scene by scene . . . The book has a solid air of reality.' A colleague of his at Knopf, whose first Elizabeth Taylor novel it was, loved the style and 'the magnificent touches' but was bored when the action veered away from the central theme – he wanted more plot, more tying up of the ends.[6]

So Blanche wrote to Elizabeth saying she liked the book very much indeed but asking her to revise it placing all the focus on Harriet and Vesey – which 'to my mind would improve it and its chances over here greatly . . . But, naturally, if you feel that you do not wish to make any changes, you have only to say so.'[7] Elizabeth did say so. She offered to cut bits out for the American readership (this would have meant the loss of all the scenes when Harriet works in a shop, all Betsy's life at school and her crush on her teacher Miss Bell, all the domestic detail about Harriet and Charles) but said she could not rewrite; while she was working on a book she corrected a great deal 'but once it is done it is so lost to me that I can't see it any more, & would not know how to change it.' Nor did she think that people alter books for the better once they are written (here she was echoing Peter Davies's words when she was threatening to destroy *A Wreath of Roses* – 'I am myself not at all in favour of extensive alterations and re-writing'[8]) and she concluded humbly, 'so I think it is the whole thing that is wrong. I expect it was something I could not do.'[9]

Meanwhile, Elizabeth sent the manuscript to Elizabeth Bowen, who read it quickly 'in bed in the early mornings' in Ireland. She wrote a four-page letter saying:

> This is the book of yours I like best . . . It has a really awe-inspiring internal sureness . . . and an authority which rather puzzles one – what is the *source* of the authority! Quite apart from what I feel, I *know* it is a good book. Your best, which is a lot, in the qualitative sense . . . I have tried to see what Blanche Knopf can possibly mean, but I simply can't . . . Anybody who had anything like a true feeling for your writing would have been waiting, unconsciously, for you to write *this* book . . . You have written something tremendous.[10]

This was overwhelming. 'Your letter was like the vision of Mrs Ramsay [in Virginia Woolf's *To the Lighthouse*] sitting at the window – part of your perfect goodness to me.' Elizabeth said that she did find criticism very hard to bear and admitted that 'I was more stunned than I can say by [Blanche's] coldness . . . But I do myself, since your letter, feel free again and peaceful.'[11]

Then, apparently (because the correspondence is missing from the Knopf file[12]), Blanche capitulated. But two small but crucial mistakes were made: Blanche claimed to have had second thoughts – 'the more I think about that novel, the better I like it' – and said that if Elizabeth did not want to make any revisions it was fine with her; but she said this to Elizabeth's American agent rather than writing directly to her to make up. Secondly, Knopf offered less than they had for *A Wreath of Roses* ($1500 instead of $2000) and then belatedly raised it to the earlier amount 'in order to show Elizabeth Taylor to some degree our great confidence in her as a writer.'[13] But the damage was done and thus the relationship between novelist and publisher was slightly but fatally wounded.

Knopf's original criticism, and their failure to put it right, also reaffirmed Elizabeth's latent scorn of Knopf's readership and of America in general. This was one reason why she never went there until, in 1970, she was forced to go for a week by the terms of a course for writers with which she had become involved; another reason was that her membership of the Communist Party would have debarred her from entry during the McCarthy era; the main reason was that she was simply not a traveller and although she developed a great love for Greece, and enjoyed family holidays in France, she never wanted to go anywhere else. She wrote delightful letters thanking for the gifts of ham, beef, rice and so on, sent over by both Knopf and *The New Yorker* ('I get so moved by all your kindness. You are a generous country'[14]); but there is an undertone in her thank-you letters which hints at her ambivalence at accepting handouts from America.

However, if she had mixed feelings about most things American, there was one haloed exception – *The New Yorker* and William ('Bill') Maxwell.* Bill took over the full-time editing from Katharine White in 1950 (although she stayed

* 1908–2000

on informally for another decade) and from the moment he did so became a revered figure for Elizabeth. (Well, he is a revered figure for this writer.) To read his 1987 *Writers at Work* interview or his obituary, or to read his novels and short stories and correspondence with other *New Yorker* writers such as Sylvia Townsend Warner, is to be sure that one is reading about one of the most brilliant, kindest, most modest figures in twentieth-century letters. Normally when an obituary writer, as the *Guardian*'s did in 2000, tells one that the subject's home was 'an oasis of beauty and serenity' and that his and his wife's lives together 'almost constituted another art form' one calls for the sick bag. Not in the case of Bill Maxwell. The obituary writer went on:

> They were people whose souls were in their eyes. As Bill once wrote: 'As a rule, when I am being introduced to a man or woman who interests me, I am so intent on searching the eyes I don't even hear what they are saying.' To spend time with the Maxwells was to feel light and fancy free. Neither suffered pretension or grandiosity gladly and clichés made them wince. But if you were their friend, they would forgive your occasional lapses. Above all, to be with them was to feel safe, protected, accepted, respected and loved.[15]

It is rare to know people like this, and now Elizabeth did (she felt that she knew Emily Maxwell as well and met her once or twice when she came to Europe). Bill was the university education, the encouragement, the understanding that she would always have liked; especially the encouragement. Once, when one of the other *New Yorker* editors had used one of Elizabeth's stories ('Hare Park') 'as a kind of test for job applicants', Bill told her that 'he had it copied and the applicants were given it to edit and if they touched a hair of its head, by God, they were no editors.'[16]

A whole book could be written about Bill Maxwell's editing technique. Unsurprisingly, he worked on instinct, or feel – he *knew* a perfect sentence when he saw it. And it was all in the sentence. As he said in his *Writers at Work* interview:

> Something that is characteristic of the writers who appear in *The New Yorker* is that the sentence is the unit by which the story advances, not the paragraph, and the individual sentence therefore carries a great deal of weight and tends to be carefully constructed, with no loose ends. And style becomes very important.[17]

Surprisingly, this is something that is often overlooked and is one of the reasons Elizabeth Taylor was a writer of genius. It is her style. Critics may say, to take a germane example from among Elizabeth's contemporaries, that the reason Barbara Pym is an outstanding writer is 'the originality of her mind. She knew she saw life from an unusual angle.'[18] And, as well, Barbara Pym could put sentences together with the distinction of someone who had been at Oxford; but she could not write a sentence that would pass Bill Maxwell's inspection. After Elizabeth died he wrote John a condolence letter. He said that he had opened one of Elizabeth's books at random.

'*The Blush*. And the first sentence I read was "In the morning, Charles went down the garden to practise calling for three cheers" and instantly I remembered the excitement, the bliss, of reading that sentence for the first time, in a manuscript that had arrived on my desk from across the ocean.'[19] If an editor can see that this sentence is written by a great writer; and if he can understand that most people could not write it; he himself is an editor of genius. (Elizabeth would have been embarrassed by all this talk of her sentences. She wrote to Barbara Pym after a PEN meeting where her work was mentioned, 'I was dreadfully confused when that Indian woman talked about my *prose*.'[20])

It was Bill who was responsible for a small triumph in Elizabeth's deteriorating relationship with Knopf: almost as soon as he had read the manuscript, he decided that the entire first chapter of *A Game of Hide and Seek* should be published in *The New Yorker* and it appeared in August 1950.[21]* Elizabeth knew well what an honour this was, since it was extremely rare for a part of a novel to be published in this way; but one reason it could be done was exactly because it had 'cracked in two with a yawn', the first part having a self-contained unity.

In June, John and Elizabeth went to France again on holiday; they had been with the children to Brittany the previous August, but this time it was just the two of them.

* She was paid £1261.0.2, about £30,000 in today's money. In total for *A Game of Hide and Seek* she received £3650, about £90,000 nowadays.

They were not often on their own without a background of domestic life or the possibility of a neighbour calling round or one of the children telephoning from school; the unusual feeling of closing a bedroom door behind them and there being nothing except themselves, their couple-ness, inspired the story called 'Gravement Endommagé', about a husband and wife on holiday in France just after the war. 'What Richard needed was a holiday away from Louise, and what Louise needed was a holiday from herself, from the very thing she must always take along, the dull carapace of her own dissatisfaction, her chronic unsunniness.'[22]

Bill wrote Elizabeth a three-page letter about this story. For various reasons, to do with the *New Yorker* house style, he asked her to cut the reference to the setting being France immediately after the war, and also asked her to cut 'the matter of the wife's having been interned in a Japanese concentration camp'. Elizabeth agreed: 'I have instead bombed her house & removed her to the country for the duration.'[23] It is interesting that she agreed so meekly, where she would not have done for Blanche Knopf, since the changes weaken the story in one crucial respect: they make the couple's sour relationship depend entirely on themselves, on their claustrophobia with each other. What Elizabeth originally meant to explore was two people's readjustment after both have been through unimaginable trauma. Can one rediscover passion, or at least tenderness, or even be mildly content, after going through so much? And was the wife's misery and foul temper a result of, even perhaps justified by, her experiences? In that respect she had meant the story to be more profound than the more ordinary 'personal relationships' story into which Bill turned it. (He also ignored the title, which means 'gravely damaged': to what was it referring if Louise had not had an appalling war?)

It was at this time that Elizabeth also wrote 'The Idea of Age', which evokes a child's relationship with an elderly woman who goes to a guest house like the one at Naphill. She goes here 'to rusticate (a word she herself used, which put a little flushed constraint upon the ladies who kept the guest house, who felt it to be derogatory).'[24] The story (which began by being called first 'Mrs Vivaldi', and then 'I Dropped Off') was a forerunner in miniature to *Mrs Palfrey at the Claremont* twenty years hence.

A Game of Hide and Seek (in its entirety) came out in England six months later, in February 1951. Elizabeth Bowen's review was long and lyrical:

Two masterpiece love stories in our language, *Persuasion* and *Wuthering Heights*, have been written by women, but long ago: they await successors in our day. Still more, they await a successor; a single book which shall merge the elements in those two. To suggest that *A Game of Hide and Seek* fills this gap might both embarrass the author and by making an exaggerated claim for it, injure the novel. Soberly speaking, however, it is not too much to say that *A Game of Hide and Seek* has something of the lucid delicacies of *Persuasion*, together with, at moments, more than a touch of the fiery-icy-strangeness of *Wuthering Heights*. The characters are of less high voltage than Emily Brontë's, on the other hand, they dare and envisage much that Jane Austen could not.[25]

Marghanita Laski thought that Elizabeth's style had now reached full maturity and praised 'writing of the very highest quality. Her genius – and this is a just word – lies in her discriminating observation of the exact comment, whether her own or quoted from her characters, that will most immediately and economically evoke the full picture she seeks to convey.'[26] And Richard Church thought *A Game of Hide and Seek* confirmed the promise of *At Mrs Lippincote's* and that now Elizabeth 'is assured of recognition as an artist whose qualities are absolutely distinct. The steadiness and integrity of this writer's observation of the workings of human nature cannot be too highly praised.'[27]

Otherwise there were the usual comments that Elizabeth's books lacked construction, that she was all style and no content. And although Robert Liddell thought (correctly) that she had 'never been so "powerful" before, Olivia [Manning] (sick, I fear, with envy but you mustn't say so),' he told Barbara Pym, 'wrote about it so bitterly.'[28] It was the start of 'The Lady-Novelists Anti-Elizabeth League', as Robert called it, whose founding members were Kay Dick, Kathleen Farrell, Kate O'Brien, Pamela Hansford Johnson,* Stevie

---

* Elizabeth's only book to be a Penguin was *A View of the Harbour,* in 1954; on the inside cover, opposite the last page, were advertisements for two of Pamela Hansford Johnson's novels, the two

Smith and of course Olivia Manning. The latter was so notorious that even the blurb of her recent biography mentions 'her tendency to be mean-spirited to those writers who happened to be women and whom she regarded as having received more fame than herself.' And one might have expected better from Stevie Smith, yet she too thought Elizabeth wrote no better than several other 'less garlanded' women writers who also 'see life in terms of the daily domestic round, the children and the washing-up and the clock ticking in the hall . . . How unhappy everybody is in this book!'[29]

There were various reasons why these writers disliked Elizabeth's work with such passionate intensity. They were snobs, and mocked Elizabeth being married to a sweet manufacturer; they thought her work was merely derivative; they did not see that *A Wreath of Roses* had addressed important issues to do with women and writing, condemning it as trivial; they disliked her tone of voice – Bill Maxwell once told her that 'everything of yours that I have ever read has been identified as yours . . . There isn't a moment when it doesn't *come through*';[30] they derided the attitude defined in the 1953 *New York Herald Tribune* interview when Elizabeth said that 'nothing sensational, thank heavens, has ever happened' and that she preferred 'the days . . . to come round almost the same, week after week'[31] (p 208) – it made her sound so *dull*

novelists being thereby bracketed together in a way that must have been painful for Elizabeth, despite her smile in the picture on p 260.

and also it identified her so much with the feminine.* As Robert Liddell would put it, remembering the time when 'Elizabeth's growing reputation began to attract the envy and malice of reviewers. "Feminine, feminine!" cried the manlier sort of lady novelist. But we may be glad that she decided to be feminine, as thus she was made.'[32]

Finally, and crucially, the members of the League all lived in London and egged each other on over South Kensington drinks trays. Elizabeth once told an anecdote about Ivy dining at a friend's house.

A fellow writer was sitting on her left and at last she turned to him and asked, 'Where do you live?' 'In Kent,' he said. 'No, I didn't mean your country house. I meant where do you live in London?' 'I *don't* live in London.' 'Ah!' she said, after a pause. 'I believe that some writers can't stand up to the rough and tumble of London literary life.'[33]

Elizabeth was one of them, and the League despised her for it. But because it was cruel to her, she retired into herself

* 'Gravement Endommagé' appeared in *Woman and Beauty* in 1951 and 'Plenty Good Fiesta' in *Housewife* in September 1953, the month before the *New York Herald Tribune* article: 'She's just a woman's magazine writer,' the League must have sneered, her work having become tainted by being popular with women. They had forgotten, or probably never knew, that Katherine Mansfield's work also appeared in 'women's magazines'; and of course *Good Housekeeping* published writers such as Virginia Woolf and Vera Brittain.

hurt and never had the courage or the arrogance indeed to emerge. So she never reviewed, never went to literary events unless accompanied by an ally such as Barbara Pym, never lunched with literary editors, never did the kind of things which should not make a difference to a writer's career but invariably do. When she became a Fellow of the Royal Society of Literature in 1966 (Robert had become one the year before and must have put her name forward) a tiny part of her must have wondered why the honour did not come fifteen years earlier.

These English women novelists were not the only ones who got out their knives. Bill Maxwell wrote to Elizabeth: 'The reviews I have seen of *A Game of Hide and Seek* have been so wide of the mark that I haven't had the heart to send them along to you, while feeling that it was too much to hope that others would spare you likewise.'[34] Elizabeth wrote back: 'No one could ever have felt so giddy with success as I have felt with failure';[35] and after she received a letter from Elizabeth Bowen, praising the book again and exhorting her to be proud of it, she thanked her for being

> wonderfully comforting. Especially after a spate of bad I mean unfavourable reviews. They do inspire terror, and come in such a headlong downrush. However often beforehand one says it will be thus & that one does not mind – one does mind and it seems the end of the world. Very isolating, like being bereaved. One feels the little glances of people who wonder how one is *taking* it.[36]

Years later, the novelist Elizabeth Jane Howard, with whom Elizabeth would become friends at the end of her life, told Elizabeth's daughter, after reading the reviews of *A Game of Hide and Seek*, 'I was very much struck about how these complacent, often well-meaning people get things *wrong*. The only person who understood that novel was Elizabeth Bowen. It is, of course, a work of art, and that is what most of those journalists find so difficult to recognise.' And she added, 'I felt, after reading the reviews, that never again should I care what *anyone* – excepting serious professional colleagues – ever said about anything I wrote. Rather cheering, really.'[37]

Bravely, Elizabeth wrote to Blanche Knopf, apologising in advance for the bad reviews that she felt would be forthcoming in America and telling her, unguardedly, 'whatever happens in America, I cannot cry any more. I am simply through with weeping. It has made even my ears sore. I do not cry often, so the tears do not know which way to run and unaccountably get into my ears . . . I am very sorry.'[38] But Blanche did not reply to this for six weeks and when she did it was to send a batch of reviews with no comment except 'the fiction market is not good and you must not feel too unhappy.'[39] What Elizabeth needed was kindness and reassurance and this Blanche did not have the psychological insight to provide. When Knopf criticised Elizabeth again she would have had enough.

Before beginning a new book Elizabeth sent three stories to *The New Yorker*. 'Plenty Good Fiesta' was about Antonio who stayed with the Taylors in 1938 (see pp 89–90). Bill asked for a lot of clarification of the detail and Elizabeth, apologising, said that 'the trouble is caused by writing about something true. One doesn't start from scratch',[40] a disingenuous remark but with this story Bill knew it was indeed based on truth whereas he only suspected it with the others. (She also told *Housewife* magazine when it was published in England that 'this is a true story, one of the few things I have ever written from life'.[41]) 'Oasis of Gaiety' describes a family on a 'Sunday Afternoon' – the original title – whose youngest son Thomas* comes over from Aldershot to see them. But he was 'of a more serious generation and seemed curiously practical, dis-abused, unemotional. His military service was a life beyond their imagination', preoccupied as they are with golf and roulette and having a good time; for 'in some of the less remote parts of Surrey, where the nineteen-twenties are perpetuated, such pockets of stale and elderly gaiety remain. They are blank as the surrounding landscape of fir-trees and tarnished water.'[42] In fact by now Thomas and his family lived in two irreconcilable worlds. The focus of the story is Surrey, a county so close to Penn and yet spiritually so far. 'I love to gaze over at Surrey,' Elizabeth would tell Katharine White, 'and feel thankful I'm not there – a bit of England that depresses me.'[43]

The third 1951 story was turned down by Bill. It was called 'A Ceremony' and was almost certainly the typescript called 'A Responsibility' that Elizabeth preserved among her papers and was eventually published in 1995, in a new selection of

---

* Thomas and his friend Syd were to reappear as Len and Laurence in *The Sleeping Beauty*.

her stories. It is about a barmaid called Jessie who has been asked to be godmother to Gwen's baby; Jessie is approaching middle age and Gwen is nineteen. The other godparent is a man that Jessie had been courting and as a result the ceremony is infused with her wounded feelings. The nub comes after the four of them return to the little flat above the butcher's. While Gwen and Jessie put the baby in his cradle 'the men lolled in their chairs, their arms trailing over the sides as if they were drifting in a punt on the river.' It is the most magnificent, classical image of male arrogance and indolence and Jessie comments:

> 'A pity if either of you over-taxed yourself. You want to take things quiet at your age,' she said. The other three could see the reason why she had never married, and, a second or two later, she saw it herself, looking at Gwen complying for all she was worth handing them cups of tea, perching on the arm of her husband's chair in a grateful way.[44]

Jessie has never married because she is sharp and hostile; Gwen complies for all she is worth and has been snapped up by the complacent Nicky. But, Elizabeth is asking, should life be like this? Should a married woman have to comply? Should Jessie be condemned to loneliness because she refuses to? Why is society organised so that men can loll in chairs trailing their hands over the sides as if they were in punts and women make the tea? Should women put up with it? And yet, apart from a sexual revolution, what was the alternative?

Read fifty years later, this is one of Elizabeth's most accomplished stories. And yet Bill turned it down and it was not published elsewhere. We do not know why, except it was not 'right' for *The New Yorker*. Bill tried to define why and wrote to Elizabeth saying, 'I felt very bad about the last story . . . I've tried since to formulate in my mind some kind of definition of the too-English or too-French-for-the-New-Yorker story but of course it isn't a matter for definition but for conversation.'[45] Bill must have thought this story too English. But why it appeared more English than any of the others is a mystery.

In the summer of 1951 Elizabeth began another novel. *The Sleeping Beauty*, unusually, has a man as its central character. Vinny is a Lloyd's underwriter in his late forties who lives with his mother. He comes to stay with the recently widowed Isabella to try and help and console her, since helping and consoling is his mission in life. He is an earlier, male version of Flora in the 1964 *The Soul of Kindness*, believing that he is 'good' at people, drawn to disaster because his sympathy is 'professional in its skill; yet adept, exquisite . . . His letters to the bereaved never expressed inadequacy on his part: they seemed simply to be the reason for his existence.' He does not see that quite quickly people find his kindly efficiency cloying, if not creepy.

Vinny falls in love with Emily, who has been in a car accident which left her unrecognisable: when she first looked in a mirror, 'until then, however in pain, bandaged, in darkness, despairing, I had been myself. But in that looking glass there was no vestige of me.' Because of this, she has withdrawn from the world, and from reality, to look after her sister's child. The prince decides to awaken the sleeping beauty but asks anxiously why she loves him. "'Oh, I am nothing without you,'" she said. "I should not know what to be. I feel as if you had invented me. I watch you inventing me, week after week.'" Yet it turns out that Vinny is married already, that his sympathy was both dishonest and illegal. When Isabella tries to confront him with this he misunderstands her and thinks he had failed to realise that she herself is in love with him; the scene between them has echoes of the farce Elizabeth had appeared in twenty years before, *Take Two from One*. "'It is your guilt,'" she said in an astonished voice. "*I* have done no wrong." "I must ask your forgiveness." "I could not forgive you,'" she said in alarm; for she thought that bigamy was more a matter for the Quarter Sessions.'[46]

The fairy-tale ending is not such a happy one – when is it ever? – and, as in the play, and characteristically of Elizabeth's novels, the conclusion is left open-ended, both practically (we do not know if he will go to prison) and morally (if Vinny does have another wife, but has done a noble thing in rescuing Emily, should we take the moral high ground?). Some months later there was a proposal to make a play out of *The Sleeping Beauty* and the ending was changed (presumably Vinny goes to prison). Elizabeth thought it made the book 'pointless. I wanted the conclusion to be that people commit bigamy and get away with it.'[47]

The bare outline does not make it sound anything much. As so often with Elizabeth's work, there is room for half a dozen short stories within the one book (and in the case of *The*

Sleeping Beauty she might have written six stories of genius rather than one good enough novel: the necessity of constructing a plot on which to hang her art often reduces the novel to bathos in description and exposition (one reason the hasty reviewer, skim-reading through to the end, so often did not 'get it'). One story could have been the subtle irony of the hero-prince turning out to be a bigamist; another the reaction of the cold, brisk, opinionated sister, Rose, to her sister's marriage; a third could have been the widowed Isabella's dreams that it was her Vinny might marry, and her very funny disillusion. And so on.

The very best thing in the book was missed by most reviewers. The description of middle-aged women in *The Sleeping Beauty* is, as Bill Maxwell put it, 'classical: my God those women are funny . . . as a little boy I wandered in and out of bedrooms with more freedom than is permitted me now, and I remember it all, the sense of spreading flesh, the retreat into the peignoir, the whole hopeful-despairing milieu.'[48] The life behind closed doors was one of the things at which Elizabeth excelled. Yet what critic, what academic, has ever perceived artistic brilliance in the description of middle-aged ennui, despair and bulging flesh?

But the critic Susannah Clapp has commented perceptively: 'The irony of Isabella and [her friend] Evalie's position is that, though they have no real purpose in their community, they are what could be called its pillars. Isabella has sat on many platforms, "holding bouquets and smilingly looking down at her little feet"; Evalie organises the Moral Welfare bazaar.'[49] And it is true that what Elizabeth is writing about (a theme to which she would return in *In a Summer Season* in five years' time) is the menopausal woman. Do they, should they, have a role in life? Is there any point in their visits to the hairdresser and the massage parlour, the almost reverent smoothing of mud-packs onto their faces? How should Isabella and Evie get through their days? Or should they shrug off angst and simply enjoy themselves studying form (see pp 301–2) and, as it were, eating chocolates?

In 1952 the 'Anti-Elizabeth League' sharpened their knives again. Olivia Manning was asked by *Harper's Bazaar* (in Britain) to write about 'the talent of some contemporary women writers'. In a piece called 'The Facile Feminine Pen' she said she did not wish to reassess established novelists such as Virginia Woolf, Ivy Compton-Burnett or Elizabeth Bowen but to consider 'a notable few whose reputations have been slower in the making.' She then picked out for praise Julia Strachey ('among her gifts is the rare one of genuine comedy'), Viola Meynell, Stevie Smith, Elizabeth Jane Howard, AL Barker, Emma Smith and someone called Celia Buckmaster. Elizabeth was accused of writing too much. 'Her last two novels have lacked any real substance. Reading, as I have lately done, a number of her books together soon leads one to suspect that the impulse behind her work comes less from the necessities of genius than from a clever eye for the way in which the model is made.' She then told her readers that, try as she might, she could not find any 'startlingly exact descriptions of human behaviour' and instead quoted from Julia Strachey.

As if this was not wounding enough, Olivia Manning (who was refused an interview by Elizabeth) sneered at her because she had decided to send her children to boarding school whereas 'a woman like Betty Miller, whose children are at day schools, can write only by the most jealous guarding of her very limited spare time.' And she falsely quoted Elizabeth as having said that she thought the interruptions of domestic life did no harm to a writer and that she 'could not see "what harm it can do for young writers to take another job and write at night."'[50] Olivia Manning claimed, untruthfully, that when she herself worked in a pub for three years and wrote at night she brought herself to a state of physical collapse.

The article should have been too absurd to worry about. But Elizabeth did worry. She could not understand why anyone would want to be so vile to her or why Olivia Manning disliked her work so much. And she knew that every time she published a book in the future the League would collectively spit. The thought was unbearable. She wrote to Patience Ross about the article by 'that shocking Miss Manning . . . I did not realise that what I did not tell her she was going to make up. I can do nothing about the untruths; but it is shocking that one writer will betray another in this way out of pique, or for a guinea or two . . . I am so tired of writers' griefs & grumbles. To refuse to join in the dirge lays one open to charges of arrogance & lack of sympathy & immense wealth.' It *was* shocking and Elizabeth was terribly hurt. It was also difficult for her that she was deeply fond of Robert Liddell as a correspondent and as a friend, but he was also the confidant of many of the women in the League.

The Sleeping Beauty took a year to write and was finished in the summer of 1952. Elizabeth had misgivings, telling

Patience Ross: 'I am not happy about that book. I think – to avoid repetition – I cut out too much. Would it not be better to have it back & think about it again in some months' time?'[51] She tried out a new ending but still felt that it spoilt the book. We do not know if she did rewrite, or put material back, but Knopf were sent the manuscript in the autumn. Almost at once they wrote and said they did not like it. Elizabeth was never allowed to see their letter, but what Herbert Weinstock said was that even if changes were made this new novel still could not be sufficiently improved to be worthy of *A View of the Harbour* and *A Wreath of Roses*. He thought the book un-attractive, with uninteresting characters who 'have some emotions but no ideas',[52] and objected to important state-ments (Laurence saying he had left his father to drown, Vinny saying he was in love) being made too baldly. He could not see that Elizabeth was implicitly saying to the reader, you know and I know this is only a novel and therefore I am giving you this bit of plot detail offhandedly, almost flippantly, because they do not matter, what matters is the characters and what I am telling you about them. Perhaps Weinstock was not a Forsterian.

The ensuing correspondence has disappeared, all we know is that Elizabeth told Bill that 'Madame Knopf' had called her 'intransigent. (The word rankles.)'[53] Yet Bill, rather mysteriously (can he really have thought so?), wrote to her to say that he thought *The Sleeping Beauty* was

the best of your books, and that you have clearly outdone yourself . . . it is, as a novel, so good that I feel

compelled to ask *Are you all right?* and to say anxiously, *You will be careful crossing the street, won't you?* Because works of perfection that are at the same time an unclouded demonstration, sentence after sentence after sentence, of the writer's pure identity, are not written out of an ordinary state of mind and being . . . be happy in this enchanting accomplishment.[54]

'How kind of you to write that comforting letter!' Elizabeth replied. 'I am still in the state of bliss of believing it – although I know that I shall not for long. For adverse criticism is the only kind which *stays*.'[55] It did stay, and having thought about it over Christmas, in the January of 1953 Elizabeth broke with Knopf.

The real reason for the break was that they had criticised her too often. But although she professed not to 'quite know who has divorced whom',[56] what she told Blanche was that she did not want them, for a second time, to publish a book of hers in which they had no confidence, nor could she do rewrites which changed the book's nature. 'Bad though [the novel] may very well be, I am afraid that it is the best that I can do; and this is from some lack in me, which no outside person can make good.'[57] Blanche did not give up at once, writing to say that she would rather have published the novel as it stood than let it go to another publisher; but before her letter arrived Peter Davies advised Elizabeth to go to Viking, and this is what she did. Blanche came to London in February. She demanded lunch, Elizabeth refused; in July she again asked for 'a long, long talk . . . [however] if she so badly needs to have the last word, she can write it on a piece of paper and send it to me, but I can never face her again.'[58]

Fifty years afterwards it is difficult to decide whether Elizabeth was right or wrong or what they really objected to ('was it bigamy, I wonder . . . [that] Knopf took issue with?'[59] Katharine White would inquire, having no idea either). It is true that Knopf had never handled her tenderly enough and that she was poised to leave them even before Herbert Weinstock disliked *The Sleeping Beauty*, true as well that they had failed to see the brilliance of *A Game of Hide and Seek*. But *The Sleeping Beauty* is not one of Elizabeth's best novels and some rewriting might have improved it. On the other hand, Bill Maxwell *claimed* to like it best of all the books she had written so far and it would have been impossible for Elizabeth to ignore his opinion – well, why should she since it was so positive? What Elizabeth really wanted from her publisher was to be left alone but cherished *when necessary*. She wrote to Patience Ross: 'How exhausting & emotional publishers are! I mean in America. I am most grateful to Peter [Davies] that he does not keep bursting into tears. His rather disabused feelings about his profession are very calming.'[60] And she told Barbara Pym, who had evidently been invited to a publisher's party, 'Peter Davies never gives parties and hates parties, authors and nearly all books. The literary world makes him shudder. He scorns his profession – saying he is a cross between a midwife and a commercial traveller.'[61]

When the notices came out many were positive, but in a slightly lowering way. John Betjeman called Elizabeth 'a fully equipped novelist in the best feminine manner. I rank her with Elizabeth Bowen and Christine Longford* and Elizabeth Jenkins. Her work may not now be startlingly original, and it does not climb to the cold heights of the literary and experimental novel. It is warm, humorous and ingenious . . . '[62] Peter Quennell called *The Sleeping Beauty* 'witty and acute with occasional flashes of poetic insight.'[63] John Lehmann said that Elizabeth's 'sense of the femininity of women together, gossiping in a Turkish bath or daydreaming or secretly betting on horses without their husbands' knowledge, is acute and entertaining; but too much of the novel is on this low voltage when it should be on the much higher voltage her conception postulates.'[64]

There were fewer women reviewers in the 1950s, but even if there had been more this might not have helped Elizabeth, since 'the League' was mostly female. Yet not entirely. Robert wrote to Barbara Pym, 'it's odd how some people hate her – dear Olivia, Mr Walter Allen,** my correspondent Miss Kay Dick'[65] (she told him that Elizabeth's work 'made her sick. Why? I think she likes women to write manly novels'[66]). Walter Allen's review in the *New Statesman* must indeed have made Elizabeth feel he hated her. He began by mocking her

* now best known for the 1931 *Making Conversation*. This was reprinted in 1970 after Pamela Hansford Johnson wrote a panegyric about it in the *TLS* (28 November 1968), calling it 'an English comedy classic' like *Cold Comfort Farm*. It has now been reissued by Persephone Books.
** Walter Allen would write a book about the novel in 1964, and the short story in 1981, but disliked Elizabeth's work so much that he did not mention it.

delicate/exquisite sensibility/wit/humour etc., conceded that she had ingenuity, real ability 'and a vein of delicate/exquisite grotesquerie', but then put the knife in. 'And what does it all amount to? It seems to me, in spite of the undoubted felicities of expression and description, almost nothing.' He then twisted it further by saying that although Elizabeth had 'looked very hard' at the novels of Virginia Woolf, Elizabeth Bowen and Rosamond Lehmann, 'there are precious few indications that she has ever looked at life.'[67]

Very much upset, Elizabeth told Katharine White that 'it has been a day, for me, of being bludgeoned by bad reviews. I tried to remember the lines Mr [Adlai] Stevenson quoted – about being too hurt to laugh, and too old to cry.'[68] One can sense the tears close to the surface, tears that were still there four months later when she explained to Bill that her writing was going slowly because of 'a dreadful pressure of anxiety from all those bad reviews; lack of confidence. I cannot get angry as you suggest. I just believe them.'[69] Ironically, many dazzling reviews of *The Sleeping Beauty* arrived from America later in the year. Diana Trilling in the *New York Times*, for example, must have given Herbert Weinstock a shock when she called Elizabeth

a writer of the most serious account . . . Among living novelists it is EM Forster of whom Mrs Taylor most reminds us . . . She has the same gentle worldliness as her older compatriot, a similar undemanding love of people, a similar wit. And also, like Forster, she knows what is, after all, the secret of fiction's continuing moral appeal for us: she understands that good and evil are not white and black but various enticingly confusing shades between these two extremes. Not only is she telling us that things are seldom what they seem. She is also, like Forster, enjoining us against moral absolutism.[70]

And one of Elizabeth's most perceptive reviewers, the critic Arthur Mizener,[71] praised her skill at letting her characters speak for themselves and quoted Vinny's thoughts about Isabella: 'He had seen too many mothers like her . . . to wonder how she had ever come to have a child. He took that miracle for granted, supposing that everyone has his informal moments.' And:

'How nice!' Isabella said. 'We will all have a little drink. I feel rather gay tonight. I can't think why, but I expect because the boys are here. This doesn't look very nice whisky . . . so much tartan all over the label. Oh, I always wanted two sons, and a daughter too; but after Laurie there was all that bother with my Fallopian tubes, whatever they may be. I am so sorry there's no soda water.'[72]

With writing of this kind, Arthur Mizener observed, a review was completely redundant.

The sadness for Elizabeth was, as she often said, that she believed the bad reviews but not the good ones; and that there was not enough armour in her past or her present to allow her to withstand the shock, and the hostility, of the bad. When she wrote to Bill, thanking him for sending Diana Trilling's 'heavenly' review, she told him how pleased she was that 'there was also some criticism in it and that is more than ever I hoped for.' She meant serious criticism, serious lit crit. For, she added, 'I do not get anything but a kick on the shins in England. I should find that painful enough – but most of all loathe the spiteful shriek that goes with it – "And you can take that, you little copy-cat." '73

This is a remark of unusual and deep feeling. And of course, not everyone kicked her on the shins and a few suggested solutions. JB Priestley, for example, wanted Elizabeth to give up writing short stories. 'She is still only in her early forties, but she must not waste time and energy on sketches for *The New Yorker*, tempting though the dollars are. She must settle down to an *opus* that might put her at the head of the procession of post-war novelists.'74 Elizabeth would have been annoyed by this, as are those of us who consider short stories to be works of art in their own right. Indeed, some of Elizabeth's readers may feel that after she had written her first five (published) novels, after – say – the publication of *A Game of Hide and Seek* in 1951 and the beginning of her close relationship with *The New Yorker*, that her greatness lay in her short stories (which is why *The Other Elizabeth Taylor* describes each one in detail).

Yet Priestley meant well. He wanted Elizabeth to emerge from the constraints of Buckinghamshire and make some friends – writers or otherwise – with whom she could discuss her work; he wanted her to have a room of her own (which she could easily have done, it was her choice to sit in an armchair and put her work away at the approach of the milkman or John home for lunch); he would have liked her to win prizes, be elected to societies, be sent to villas in Italy for a month's retreat. He would have liked her to have more *amour propre*, rather than retire hurt when a review was crushing. He would have liked her to do much more than smile sweetly and go on being grateful that she was allowed (courtesy of the sweet manufacturer) to sit in her armchair, lunch tidied away and *Woman's Hour* over, and scribble in her notebook. Indeed he would probably have preferred her to spend more money on herself. When, after her death, her will revealed that she was worth £75,000 (half a million pounds today), if Priestley had seen it he must have wished that 'you can't take it with you' had been a precept she believed in.

Finally, readers of this biography might say that they would have preferred Elizabeth not to be so self-effacing. For some will conclude that after the mid-1940s, and her momentous decision to stay with John on his terms, she changed personality. It could be argued that this might not have been so and that we do not have letters or diaries to dispel this assumption. But it seems, with no evidence to the contrary, that in some respects she gave up on life. Why did she prefer the local Penn gentry to people at the PEN (writers) club? Why did she always refuse to go to America to do a publicity tour? Why did she drink more alcohol than was good for her? Why did she go on giving disingenuous interviews (except nobody thought they were disingenuous, they described how she had become) delighting in the fact that nothing ever happened to her? Why did she not take herself off to Paris or to Tuscany rather than going on rather prim holidays to Greece or Normandy? (The answer to the last question is that she went away for a holiday but not to do 'research', once agreeing with an interviewer that she found it very strange that Graham Greene went to the Belgian Congo to gather material: 'Somerset Maugham says a travelling scholarship polishes things up . . . I often wonder what they did . . . You can't do that. Having a notebook, working things out.'[75])

They were her choices and we must respect them, of course we must. Nobody, certainly not a biographer, must criticise what other people choose to do. It is just that one wonders whether it *was* a choice, whether a determination to stick with the conventional, with John, with Buckinghamshire, with being a good mother (above all else a good mother), was gradually crushing her personality and her writing. It was almost as if she was in shock; as though the loneliness of the war years, combined with the loss of Ray as her best friend, lover, psychiatrist and correspondent, and John's ultimatum (a kind, forgiving ultimatum, but that is what it was) led her to dread the idea of a room of one's own and of the courage needed to go into it and close the door.

Fifteen years after Elizabeth's death the novelist AL Barker suggested in an introduction to a Virago reprint that when she wrote 'about tyranny of the self, the hopeless longing to break out and be different, be someone else, someone successful, loved and envied – young . . . I think she was writing *herself* out, taking her own nature as far as she cared – and did not care – to go. In a sense, these stories [in *Hester Lilly*] are her autobiography.' [76] This was a profound point about Elizabeth's personality (that perhaps only a fellow writer could make), the crucial phrase being 'did not care'. Elizabeth chose the last thirty years of her life. She chose to live in the society she did, and she chose not to leave. And she did so because of her writing. In this respect she was no different from Jane Austen, and may consciously have seen herself as the inheritor of Jane's mantle. In 1940 she could have read an essay in *Scrutiny* by DW Harding, a psychologist, called 'Regulated Hatred'. 'The stress of his argument,' observes the critic John Wiltshire in his recent book about Jane Austen and her biographers, 'is on Jane Austen's novels as a mode of reconciliation to the social environment, not expression of her antagonism towards it.'[77] Harding wrote:

> To her the first necessity was to keep on reasonably good terms with the associates of her everyday life; she had a deep need for their affection and a genuine respect for the ordered, decent civilisation that they upheld. And yet she was sensitive to their crudenesses and complacencies and knew that her real existence depended on resisting many of the values they implied. The novels gave her a way out of this dilemma.[78]

And John Wiltshire concludes that 'the writer Harding found was no genteel satirist, pandering to the comfort of middle-class readers, but one whose work displays a sophisticated negotiation between solidarity with the society that nourished her (and would buy her novels!) and intense critical scrutiny.'[79] The same should be said of Elizabeth.

CHAPTER TEN

PENN COTTAGE 1954–56

I only want to write of things as they are. There is unreality &
that is photography, for it ignores the essence of a thing. And
there is reality, & that is Van Gogh painting a chair or a tuft of
grass. The ony time painters and writers seem to touch hands
is in Impressionism. This is why I understand and delight in it
. . . Impressionism catches and pegs down a mood. So does
poetry. This is not a superficial thing to do. It is slight, but
great in its own way. We cannot all be monumental.[1]

Elizabeth's self-esteem had been badly battered. Nevertheless, in 1953 she wrote a novella, a *conte*, *Hester Lilly*.
Whether she decided to experiment with the form or
abandoned a novel a third of the way through is not known.
But she sent it to *The New Yorker*, thinking perhaps that if they
had published a long extract from *A Game of Hide and Seek*
they might publish a novella. They turned it down because
'though the story stands alone, and is complete, it doesn't
necessarily have to stop where it does.'[2] This is true; yet
Elizabeth must have wondered exactly what was really wrong
with it. She told Bill Maxwell, 'My novels are too short. I
believe there is a thing called a *Conte*, but it is hardly a useful
thing.'[3] Paradoxically, *The New Yorker*'s financial 'generosity

sets up such a guilt complex that I become over-anxious'.[4] She exaggerated, but was conscious of their large cheques – they were now paying, in today's terms, £10,000 a story. If Elizabeth had only ever written short stories she would not have suffered financially – few of her novels can have earned what *The New Yorker* paid for a single piece.

Hester Lilly has a familiar theme, being about Muriel, a headmaster's wife, whose husband's young cousin Hester comes to stay and thus changes the dynamics of their marriage. It is rather as if Cassandra in *Palladian* had arrived as a guest instead of a governess: because Hester has nothing to do except feel grateful for being looked after, she is bored and resentful and inevitably thinks she is in love with her cousin Robert. In Elizabeth's accumulating gallery of vile women, Muriel is one who has no redeeming features at all; by crassly, deviously fighting for her husband she destroys any affection he had for her: '"If I can never love her again," he thought, "why is it Hester's fault? It is she, Muriel, who destroyed it, let it slip from her and then, in trying to have it back again, broke it for ever."'[5] Having innocently put a wedge between her cousin and his wife Hester is manoeuvred by Muriel into marrying a young schoolmaster whom she hardly knows – perhaps the cruellest of all the cruel things that Muriel does – and thus the novella ends, for 'I had really only wanted to describe the dissolution of love and was not much interested in What Happened To Hester.'[6]

The other short stories Elizabeth wrote at this time included 'Spry Old Character', inspired by a blind man whom she had seen on a bus. He lives in a Home and is patronised by

Matron, who, like his sister (now dead but with whom he had been happier) 'used no tact or Montessori methods on him', as well as by the Home's visitors. He is made unexpectedly happy by the kindness of the bus conductresses and bus drivers – 'the first pride he had felt since his blindness, was in distinguishing Fred from Syd or Lil from Marg.' At the end Fred and Vi take Harry to the fair and make him throw balls at the coconut-shy. 'Only by pleasing could he live; by complying – as clown, as eunuch – he earned the scraps and shreds they threw to him, the odds and ends left over from their everyday life.'[7] It is hard to think of another writer who has entered with such compassion into the mind of the blind man or woman, or into that of the old and abandoned; the story is another forerunner to *Mrs Palfrey at the Claremont*.

'Swan-Moving' is about a swan who lives for six months on the village pond. Then the water level drops and the villagers 'went off on their bicycles to look for better accommodation for the swan, who seemed too negligent to do so for himself.' Ceremonially he is moved. And as everyone crowds happily into The Stag and Hounds the swan 'made a great commotion with his wings and . . . flew on, away from that countryside for ever.'[8] And later that spring, 1954, Elizabeth wrote one of her greatest stories, 'Goodbye, Goodbye'. It describes a man who lives abroad going down to the sea to see the woman he loves who is on holiday there with her children: 'A girl leaned from an upstairs window and called down to him. "Do you want mother?" Hit by the irony of the words, the shock of seeing Catherine's eyes looking down at him, he could not answer her at once.'

What is unforgettable is the depth of emotion and the descriptions of the children; and the humanity. Peter is still deeply in love but, understandably if ignobly, 'had always refused to see [Catherine's husband] as anything but a monstrous begetter of money and children, and showed himself up in contrast – the bachelor beyond the gates, without home or family, whose schemes came to nothing as his love-making came to nothing, neither bearing fruit.'[9] Bill told Elizabeth: 'When Mr Lobrano [the *New Yorker* chief editor] finished reading the manuscript he said that the story could go into the magazine just as it was, without editing. I don't ever remember his saying that about anything before.'[10]* When this superb story appeared in *Woman and Beauty* in the spring of 1955, the League's earlier condemnation of Elizabeth for being a woman's magazine writer was presumably reinforced.

Yet the hostile reviews were mostly of Elizabeth's novels and when *Hester Lilly and Other Stories* came out in 1954, no one attacked her (although she cannot have been too happy about John Betjeman saying that 'she can get under the skin of all sorts of unconsidered people . . . with an understanding which reminds me of Monica Dickens at her best'). The *New York Times* pointed out that critics used simply to compare

* 'Goodbye, Goodbye' appeared in *The Vintage Book of Love Stories* edited by Helen Byatt. She wrote: 'In many ways [it] is the saddest story told here. It is the kind of short story that comes nearest to how VS Pritchett defines one, as something "that tells only one thing, and that, intensely."'

Elizabeth Taylor to other writers but the novelist Eudora Welty had 'put a happy stop to it by recognising her as an individual not a gifted pastiche: "Her sensitivity of spirit, excellence of mind, subtlety and wit of perception are unlike anyone else's."'* Then the reviewer added endearingly, 'personally, I was not exactly headstrong in recognising Mrs Taylor's ability. Now I'm on the bandwagon.'[11] And the *New York Herald Tribune* said that although Elizabeth only wrote about a circumscribed milieu she did so 'with a touch of genius'.[12] Gratifyingly, Bill wrote to Elizabeth to say that he 'growled' that 'Taking Mother Out'[13] (about a flashy, cynical young man called Roy whose doting mother unwittingly humiliates him) had not appeared in *The New Yorker* (they rejected it), nor had 'A Sad Garden' (written ten years before, see p 140), and that he hoped *Hester Lilly* 'will be recognised instantly for what it is – one of the best collections of short fiction that was ever published.'[14]

Apart from the misery of bad reviews, of knowing that Olivia Manning and her ilk disliked (indeed loathed) much of what she had written, and being upset by what she saw as Blanche Knopf's disloyalty, the early 1950s were, as Robert Liddell put it, 'on the whole happy years for both of us.'[15] Elizabeth's life was indeed contented. She saw a great deal of other Penn couples such as Jon and Veronica Walley and Barry and Gerry Ercolani, the children went back and forth from school to home bringing their friends with them, John ran the business. It was a life of dinner parties, cats, dogs,

* Elizabeth Bowen brought Eudora Welty to tea at Penn in 1954.

au pairs, holidays in County Cork, Brittany or Dorset, trips to the Grand National, art exhibitions or, once, the Fourth of June at Eton (with Peter Davies), some of it lovingly described in *In a Summer Season*. These were, on the surface, the most important elements in Elizabeth's life. Privately there was her writing, but this was something she never talked about with her friends in Penn – unless, that is, they had been invited round to enjoy meat sent by *The New Yorker*. She told Bill Maxwell in 1951, thanking him for another American parcel:

> Round here writing is not thought to be much of a job. It would not be taken any more seriously than making lamp-shades in one's spare time. That one is paid for it is nothing, because quite often one is paid for these hobbies; but when meat arrives from friends one had made via writing, it is another matter. It raises literature itself to something not respectable, but respected. And then, one's hospitality has the extra charm of offering what cannot be offered back, trying to be casual, but suddenly blushing in the midst of the amazement.[16]

It was around this time, the mid-1950s, that Elizabeth was drawn by the artist Rodrigo Moynihan. A few years before 'a friend said, "I want to take you to see some paintings which remind me of your writing"' and she had gone into the Leicester Galleries in Bond Street and bought a painting of some boys on a breakwater which she could hardly bear to leave until the end of the exhibition. It was by Elinor Bellingham Smith and over the next twenty-five years Elizabeth was to buy five more of her paintings. She would write to Elinor: 'I feel such a curious affinity with your painting, and your pictures give me pleasure every day – I sometimes look at them – the word is, almost *watch* – for a long time, and seem to go deeper and deeper into them.'[17] Elinor had studied at the Slade under Henry Tonks (one of the best-known art teachers of his generation) and married Moynihan, a fellow student. Before the war she did fashion illustrations for *Harper's Bazaar*; but after Moynihan was appointed Professor of Painting at the Royal College of Art she turned to painting full-time. In 1959 she had her fourth exhibition at the Leicester Galleries: *Tatler* magazine's verdict was that 'there is surely no better living woman painter of English landscape than Elinor Bellingham Smith.'

She also painted children with sad, beautiful, pale faces set against veiled light and drifting skies and frosted fields, the canvas equivalent of Elizabeth saying: 'Our winter here has started early with the ponds frozen, the leaves rimed and a furry and romantic fog over all . . . I love the English weather – doting on fogs, and those mild, drizzly days so good for the complexion.'[18] Elizabeth often saw herself as a painter who could not paint: Elinor was the painter she might have been if she could not have been Gwen John or Vuillard, her other two favourite painters. And at the end of her life Elizabeth would pay homage to Elinor's work when, in *Blaming*, a symbol of Martha's so-called extravagance is that she buys 'a very beautiful painting of rimy branches by Elinor Bellingham

Smith which hung frostily above the gas-fire, and had cost, he knew, two hundred pounds.'[19]

When, in 1949, Elizabeth went to the Royal Academy Summer Show and bought a painting by Rodrigo Moynihan called *The Sleeping Soldier*, he wrote to her and said: 'I always like selling pictures, but this sale pleases me particularly because you already own a picture by my wife . . . Both of us would greatly welcome the opportunity of meeting you.'[20] They met, and thus Elizabeth became a friend of both the Moynihans; and at their house in Old Church Street in Chelsea, Rodrigo drew a pencil sketch of her.

Most of Elizabeth's friends at this period were in Penn. Alas, in 1955 it was convulsed by the most dramatic and appalling event in its rural, undramatic history: in the spring of that year a young man who lived there was murdered. His name was David Blakely and he was murdered by Ruth Ellis, the last woman to be hanged in England.

David's Irish mother, Annie, had been married to a doctor in Sheffield who was attractive to women and often succumbed – hence David's childhood was dominated by his parents' rows. They divorced in 1939 when he was nine, some-thing so unusual that every one of David's contemporaries mentions this as being something that singled him out, and his mother married Humphrey Cook, a well-off ex-racing driver. David went to Shrewsbury, did his National Service and lived with his brother in the family flat in Mayfair.

His stepfather had hoped that he would work in the hotel business but his only enthusiasms were racing cars and having a good time. In the early 1950s, by which time David had inherited £7000 (£150,000 nowadays) from his father, the Cooks bought a large house at Penn, The Old Park, where they 'maintained an almost Edwardian taste for tradition and comfort. Each week a watchmaker came in to wind his clocks whilst a cobbler visited regularly to go through his shoes.' We can imagine that Annie Cook would have been one of the people who kissed Lady Curzon; Elizabeth, meanwhile, called her Mrs Cook not Annie.

At Penn, David had his own flat, worked at a local engineering firm called Silicon Pistons, and divided his time between Mayfair, where his life was that of building his own racing car, hard drinking and fun, and Penn, where he was looked after by his former nanny, was charming to his parents' guests and played for the Penn cricket team. But he led a double life emotionally: although he became engaged to a stolid, exemplary young woman from Yorkshire, he had begun an affair with a 29 year-old night-club manager called Ruth Ellis.

David, who was 25 in 1955, was immensely popular with women but men often thought him a 'good-looking, well-educated, supercilious shit.'[21] The superior air was skin-deep; a Shrewsbury contemporary suspected that the women who were charmed by him were 'naïve in the face of his charm; and responded maternally to his apparent need, since I suspect that beneath the surface he was a rather lonely, insecure individual.'[22] But his family loved him very much: after he died his brother Derek would write to the *Evening Standard* protesting at the writer F Tennyson Jesse's reference to him as 'a lamentable specimen of humanity'. 'Those of us, and there are many,' he wrote, 'who knew and loved David for years wish to register our protest at these remarks.'[23]

Five years after his death Elizabeth would write *In a Summer Season* and create Dermot, who has many of David's characteristics.* He is 35, half-Irish with a 'broguey voice' and ten years younger than his wife Kate (the original draft of *In a Summer Season* had the sentence 'in the year when she left school he was born', but seventeen years younger might have seemed implausible). Dermot has no direction in life and is aimless apart from wanting to be with Kate; he likes driving fast but it is only the driving he likes, not the cars. In many ways he is reacting against his father's almost neurotic sense of order: Humphrey Cook's wound clocks and mended shoes become, in the novel, 'his shoe-laces ironed and his pocket-linings taken out and laundered every week'.

Sometimes Kate senses her husband's restlessness, especially in the early evening: 'He had had too many years of pubs and clubs and pleasing himself' to be satisfied by the ritual gin and tonic before dinner. Often they go to the pub. 'His drinking evenings had the same pattern always, as she knew. Caution, exhilaration, aggressiveness were followed by the diminuendo of face-saving, self-reproach, reproach, attempts at recovery, back to caution again.'[24] Alcohol and

* Elizabeth Taylor's daughter has commented: 'Most of what Nicola has written is untrue and the rest hurtful to many people. David was certainly not the person Dermot was based on. (The real person was very different.)' However, the author has not been told who the real person was.

sex fuel Dermot's existence, as it certainly fuelled David's relationship with Ruth Ellis. 'Resentment, jealousies and violent drunken fights between Blakely and Ellis were commonplace.'[25]

Yet there was another side to Dermot; he loves Kate deeply, indeed 'his love for her was his chief pride',[26] and the reader concludes that his inertia and drinking are in part his mother's fault; this is not to exonerate but to explain him. One side of David was also kind and loving, and he was remembered by the girl to whom he had been engaged as having a wonderful sense of humour.[27] Elizabeth, too, saw a quite different side from the public perception, telling Patience Ross:

A dear young man . . . whom we all loved very much became caught up in a strange net of ugliness & fear, living this double life; mostly here, but then – as another personality – going to London to a very frightening sort of woman . . . It is so difficult to cling to the idea of the real David, who was so kind & gay . . . & was so adored by Joanna & his little niece, so doted on by his old Nannie whom he used to take to the cinema and for drives in his car.[28]

Ruth, the 'frightening sort of woman', was violently possessive by temperament and thought she had reasons for being jealous of her lover: she believed that 'what she called "the attraction" was a very good-looking married woman' of about 30, an actress, married to a serving officer, who lived at The Old Vicarage (which is what the house is called in *In a Summer Season*). Once Ruth confronted her; she invited Ruth in for coffee and explained that David had spent the night innocently on her settee because 'he is not very happy at home'.[29]

Elizabeth, too, would have been sympathetic to David's impatience with the values of The Old Park and it is possible that she felt something of a *tendresse* for him. Robert Liddell, planning to write his book *Elizabeth and Ivy*, did not destroy the letters about the famous Ivy Compton-Burnett ménage at Braemar Mansions and allowed Ivy's biographer, Hilary Spurling, to see them before they were expurgated. In a 1955 letter Elizabeth told Robert that '[Ivy] suddenly asked: "What about that murder? I saw the young man lived in Penn." '[30] In the surviving copy of the letter a section has been cut out with scissors; but Hilary Spurling saw it before the lines were cut away. These were: '"Did you know the family?" I wondered what would happen if I suddenly said: "Yes, I was in love with him although I was nearly twenty years older." '[31]

This may not have meant more than Elizabeth ruefully admitting that she enjoyed David flirting with her, that she was ashamed to confess that he made her feel young. In *In a Summer Season* Kate's daughter wonders whether her mother had been in love with Dermot before her first husband died because 'she always seemed excited and laughed a lot when Dermot came to the house.'[32] Here Elizabeth is perhaps castigating herself, and other middle-aged women, for their foolish flirting with younger men in pubs.

Yet, whatever her true feelings, we know from another source that when, on Easter Sunday 1955, Ruth shot David outside the Magdala pub in Hampstead, Elizabeth was greatly upset: the date of the trial having been originally set for 11 May but postponed until 14 June, she wrote to Elizabeth Bowen and asked if she could go and stay with her in Ireland for a week from 13 June. 'The idea fills me with happiness,' came the reply. 'Bring what you're writing, and I'll get on with mine, and in the evenings we'll walk and drive about the country. I am deeply sorry you should have had this distress. Talk to me – or don't, as you feel, dearest Elizabeth, when you're here.'[33] And so, for a week:

> By day, we had agreed to work – she in a room upstairs, while I chose, because it was perfect weather, to sit on the steps in front of the house. At twelve o'clock, she would come down to the library for a drink – 'for my brains'. After lunch, we would often resume our labours, and by tea-time, her room upstairs was thick with cigarette smoke. One might have cut it with a knife, if a sharp enough one were handy.[34]

Afterwards, Elizabeth Bowen wrote to say that she had been honoured – 'that's really the word I mean' – by Elizabeth wanting to be with her in Ireland. 'I don't think it was cowardice – very much not & I think you showed very great courage.' In the end the trial was delayed by a week and Elizabeth was after all in Penn during the day and a half when it happened. But 'I was glad for you that it was over so quickly. Also, nothing horrible about David. I wish I had known him.'[35]

There was enormous controversy about whether or not the death sentence should be carried out; but Ruth Ellis was executed by hanging on 13 July. Fifty years later, it seems unbelievable that at the trial so little could have been made of the mitigating circumstances: the times when David hit Ruth; her miscarriage two weeks before the murder (possibly caused by David hitting her); her two young children; and the fact that it was a *crime passionel* and, as later emerged, that her 'alternative' lover, Desmond Cussen, gave her a gun and showed her how to use it.

To have been even tangentially involved in a murder would have been traumatic for anyone, and for Elizabeth, who shied away from any kind of publicity, from any kind of violence, the episode must have been an almost insurmountable shock; in the months following David Blakely's death her equilibrium was destroyed. The sweet, even rhythm of her days, with the bus journey into Beaconsfield (past the drive leading to the Cooks' house), the Friday appointment with the hairdresser, the short walk along the road to The Crown at six o'clock, John playing hockey on Saturday afternoons while she worked, 'Sunday evenings with *Grand Hotel* going on & on is a very good time for work, I find',[36] all this had been disrupted by the image of Ruth Ellis's neck encircled, primitively, with a rope. And would have been disrupted whether or not she was personally involved. Ten years before Renny and Joanna had asked to go to London to see William Joyce (the traitor) being hanged. Elizabeth was appalled. She remembered that 'when some woman (I believe, Mrs Thompson) was to be hanged, I lay awake almost the whole of her last night weeping

& so terribly present in my imagination in the condemned cell that I can never contemplate anything remotely connected with it without being made ill.'[37]*

In early 1955, Renny had been at home for a long time with pneumonia; one of the people who had helped his recovery was David, who 'sat with [him] for hours'. When, after many weeks, Renny was better, Elizabeth tried to return to the novel she was writing. It is not clear whether this was the one she would eventually finish late in the following year, or one she then destroyed, but she had barely restarted when David was murdered. She told Patience Ross in May that 'for weeks life [has been] too much of a novel itself to tempt me to write one as well. A Graham Greene "entertainment" – full of horror and squalor.'[38] Then in the autumn she was in bed for a week because, as she told Barbara Pym,

> I am ill, but not so very . . . I have just had a miscarriage though it was so early a one that it is technically known as an abortion which can give a very wrong impression. In view of my great age I am made to stay in bed – and in fact do feel fagged and peevish. I pretend to the children that I have a chill, otherwise they might be scandalised, or laugh at me.[39]

However, by the end of the year she had managed to write a short story about the day a stately home named Hare Park (the name of a racehorse, she told Bill) is open to the public

---

* This would have been 1923.

and the effect on the over-protected, isolated son of the house when he encounters one of the visitors; it was in a small way a dry run for her next novel, which was also to be set in a large country house and to be about somebody over-protected who has no contact with reality. She also wrote 'The Ambush', about a girl who goes to stay with the woman who would have been her mother-in-law if her fiancé had not been killed in a car accident. There is another brother but, we conclude, his affections are for his friend Freddie; he is the only obvious homosexual in Elizabeth's work.[40]

In January 1956 she began *Angel*, a novel that was to be so different from her other books that many would agree with Robert Liddell's friend Mark Ogilvie-Grant when he called it 'a good book, but she didn't write it'.[41] It seems very likely that she consciously decided to write an escapist novel, something historical, something about people and events that, for the first time in her writing career, did not ostensibly bear much relation to her own life – partly perhaps as a way of escaping the unkind reviews of *The Sleeping Beauty* and her memories of the events of 1955. The crucial element of verisimilitude lies in the heroine, Angelica Deverell, being a writer, and a determined and single-minded one at that. Elizabeth had more self-knowledge, more kindness, less egoism, but she had the same single-mindedness, which is why *Angel* sometimes reads like a savage, self-destructive caricature of herself.

The seed of *Angel* had been sown the year before when she had been driving back from the Cheltenham races with David's brother Brian:

I went one morning to a place called Paradise – or was going to, but the lane down to the valley was blocked by a cart . . . .We left the car & went into the pub called suitably The Adam and Eve. When we had finished our drink, the cart was still across the lane and Brian asked the landlady if it was worth waiting to go down the valley. It had looked so beautiful in the sun & embowered in autumn trees but she was very scornful. 'There's nothing to see, nothing down there but Paradise House and that's all overgrown.' I had an extraordinary feeling of excitement, promise of enchantment. 'Then we won't bother,' Brian said. When we left the pub, I saw that the cart had gone, but Brian began to drive . . .[42]

Even though Elizabeth never saw the house the imagined 'grey, Italianate façade with a broken balustrade . . . became a symbol of envy, attainment, decay.'[43]

Angel is about Angelica Deverell, who has been named after 'Madam's daughter' at Paradise House where her aunt works and to which she is meant to aspire, and to revere. Instead she plans to be a writer. At first her teachers at school refuse to believe her essays are not plagiarised (see p 22) but soon Angelica insists on leaving school and devoting herself to her writing. To begin with her manuscript is returned; then she receives a letter from Gilbright & Brace in Bloomsbury offering her £30 (it is 1902 and this is therefore £2500 in today's money). Angel goes up to London to see Theo Gilbright and, in the funniest scene in the book, resists his attempts to get her to make changes. ' "For instance, we cannot have a character called the Duchess of Devonshire as there is one in . . . in everyday life; if a duchess's life could ever be so described . . . I don't know much about grandeur, and great establishments, but I thought we might cut down and manage with one butler, eh?" '

'Angelica Deverell' becomes a hugely popular novelist and eventually falls in love. Yet Theo

> could not imagine any brightness or ease ahead of her. Her sternness, the rigorousness of her working days, her pursuit of fame, had made her inflexible: she was eccentric, implacable, self-absorbed. Love, which calls for compliance, resilience, lavishness, would be a shock to her spirit, an upset to the rhythm of her days. She would never achieve it, he was sure. For all the love in her books, it would be beyond her in her life.

Angel marries Esmé, an ineffectual painter, and they stay together in a semi-detached fashion until his death. (Unlike her mother. 'Mrs Deverell's own married life had been short and flawless in retrospect. Her husband had coughed his way through only a year and a half of married bliss.'[44]) Angel lives out her days in a bubble of her own illusions, vanity and absurdity. She continues to write until the public grows tired of her work, becomes increasingly lonely, and dies in the arms of her only friend, her sister-in-law.

Elizabeth modelled Angel's life on that of Marie Corelli, a famous romantic novelist, using as her source Eileen

Bigland's 1953 biography. The similarities between Bigland's Marie Corelli and Angel are numerous: both writers, having sent their first novels to a publisher, wait anxiously for the postman's knock 'unaware that various readers . . . were engaged in writing vitriolic reports on her work'[45]/'Gilbright & Brace had been divided, as their readers' reports had been.' Marie was offered £40, Angel £30. Angel has a 'delightful sensation of being lifted up'[46] when her novel is accepted, Marie's novel was initially called *Lifted Up*. Both writers, who confide only in their publishers, settle down to the life of the reclusive, vain, difficult, bestselling writer with their life-long female companion (Marie's is Bertha, Angel's is Nora), few other friends, and a dog called Czar. Nora writes a poem called 'La Princesse Lointaine'; the frontispiece photograph for the biography shows Marie Corelli dressed as 'La Princesse Lointaine'.

Another real-life model Elizabeth used for *Angel* was the novelist Amanda McKittrick Ros, whose biography was published in 1954. She was the author of a book Elizabeth had loved during the war, *Delina Delaney*; it was first published in 1902, then became unobtainable and much sought-after, and was reissued by Chatto & Windus in 1935 and again in 1936.* Ros, who considered Marie Corelli the greatest writer of all time, had herself been described as 'The World's Worst Novelist' but in her case it was not so much her life that contributed to *Angel* as her prose style, with its romantic flourishes, its almost demented alliteration, its unconscious

---

* It is now unobtainable again.

absurdity. Here is the moment when Lord Gifford, of Columba Castle, first escorts the 16-year-old Delina home to Erin Cottage and her mother comes to the door:

> A flash of the young nobleman's eyes convinced the poor woman that deep affection lay buried in their unseen background, causing her to form a resolution to exercise a stronger rule over her daughter in future lest her simplicity might be spotted out as a mark for his untrusted worth to bruise the bloom of a rose of fate whose oily essence might drip with awful odour over its stained prey.[47]

(Lest the twenty-first century reader should conclude that the awfulness of this sentence is something to do with its being written in 1902: only three years later EM Forster was to begin *Where Angels Fear to Tread* with the beautifully simple words, 'They were all at Charing Cross to see Lilia off . . .')

Finally, Elizabeth – ironically, and savagely – used herself as a model. She knew that despite the public persona of the well-behaved housewife to whom not much ever happened, she had a streak in her, indeed more than a streak, of the angry, obsessive, ruthlessly focused egotist. Privately, she may not have set herself apart from Ruth Ellis the year before: one of the reasons for her anguish may have been that she thought, there but for the grace of God . . . *Angel* is a satire about the lady novelist leading another life, about Elizabeth's doppelgänger. Perhaps the novel she would have liked to write would have described the bad luck and the weakness and the chance that made Ruth Ellis become the last woman to be hanged in England. Instead, she described a novelist given much the same background as herself who then turned into the devilish Angel Deverell.

Her usual dislike of narrative and summary was an especial problem with this book. She told Robert that she did not know how to deal with it. 'I just love to write scenes, but how can I cover fifty years like that?'[48] As in her other novels, she gave clues. Thus on page 45 of *At Mrs Lippincote's* the lilac trees are in bud and on page 62 'the air glittered in the heat'. At the point where *A Game of Hide and Seek* divides in two Harriet thinks, 'after nearly twenty years, I have had my dance with Vesey',[49] telling us what we need to know. But in *Angel* something made Elizabeth be much more obvious. This may simply have been having two biographies at her side; whatever it was, the 'chronology' sentences do not suit her painterly style which made her 'hate the sound of "the hotel at Paignton where they first met" – it is that stuffy, pedestrian kind of writing I dislike so much'[50] (and which may spoil *Angel* for those who dislike it too).

An extra difficulty with *Angel*, for devotees of Elizabeth Taylor's work, is that many of them cannot see the point of it. 'No sense of humour,' the aficionado snaps back, and it is true that Elizabeth meant the book to be funny and that many of her readers do find it funny; as did the committee (consisting of Elizabeth Jane Howard, Richard Hoggart and the industrialist Peter Parker) which, in 1984, chose the thirteen 'Best Novels of Our Time' for a Book Marketing Council promotion and included *Angel* among them. The other novels, or

series of novels, were *Take a Girl Like You, Herzog, The Sea, The Sea, Lord of the Flies, Manservant and Maidservant, Lolita, The Honorary Consul, Sword of Honour, Catcher in the Rye, A Dance to the Music of Time, The Raj Quartet* and *Staying On.* Claire Tomalin, then the literary editor of *The Sunday Times,* was astonished by the choice of *Angel.* It was, she said, 'the portrait of a monster, and traces her obsessions, with a house where her aunt was a ladies maid, and with a well-born painter who marries her for her money. It is a delicately crafted but a very slight book.'[51]

Yet the novelist Paul Bailey, who was to write several prefaces to Virago editions of Elizabeth's novels, believes *Angel* to be 'in some ways her boldest conception . . . [she] is drawn with a sharpness that never becomes derisive or satirical.' And he claimed that this is because Angel has 'a truly desperate sincerity',[52] she is an original, has been influenced by no one and rarely reads ('"I quite liked Shakespeare . . . Except when he is trying to be funny"'[53] she tells Theo Gilbright). However, those who disagree must concur with a recent *Times Literary Supplement* critic who believes that '*Angel* has neither the psychological precision nor the human warmth of Taylor's other fiction: it is at best a lively *jeu d'esprit,* at worst a sterile exercise in improbabilities.'[54] The 2007 film of *Angel* by François Ozon has divided critics in the same way, with Philip Hensher in *The Independent* declaring that he would not be going to see it in case it spoilt 'an almost perfect novel'[55] and the reviews turning out to be almost absurdly divided as to whether the film was a successful blend of pastiche and irony or an over-romanticised bore.

Traumatically, at around the time Elizabeth was finishing *Angel*, when she might have thought she was beginning to recover from the shock of David's death, the news came from New Zealand of the death of Maud. She and her husband Bill Geddes had stayed on in England for a year after their marriage, living in a flat in Highgate. Then, in February 1949, Bill went to Sarawak in order to study the Land Dayaks and was on his own in the village of Mentu Tapuh until 'for five months in 1950 my wife joined me, and it is to her that I owe the friendly relationship which I established with the most important part of the community – the children.'[56] He wrote in his 1954 monograph *Land Dayaks of Sarawak*:

> In the longhouse form of dwelling the people are together. They are a very close neighbourhood, always on one another's doorsteps, constantly mingling by chance . . . . The Land Dayaks have solved a great human problem – how to be independent and yet never be isolated. It is no wonder that none of them commits suicide. In the longhouse it is possible to be an individualist and yet lead a cosy life of company. If one is shamed or angry, one can sulk and yet never be forgotten.[57]

This was republished in 1957, in a version called *Nine Dayak Nights* meant for the general public. By then Maud was dead. She had killed herself.

She was not unhappy on Borneo, where she taught the local children and took photographs. However, she caught a parasite, could not get rid of it and became thinner than ever. When, in 1951, Bill was appointed as lecturer in Auckland, Maud, who was not suited to being merely a faculty wife, could not find anything of her own to do – she could not find a way to be 'independent and yet never be isolated'. In addition, she was beginning to lose her hearing in one ear (perhaps through tinnitus, a most dispiriting condition whereby the sufferer cannot hear because of a constant buzzing in the ear-drum).

In the autumn of 1956 she flew to London to consult a doctor about her hearing and her lingering parasite. 'But they were brutal to her,'[58] according to her friend Heather Sutton, and callously told Maud that her hearing loss was incurable. She was in London for only three days; then flew back to New Zealand without seeing Elizabeth or Heather or Mrs Hayek, her former landlady. Bill was away giving some lectures, Maud told him she would stay with a cousin, but she took an overdose of sleeping pills one weekend in October.

In some respects it was not altogether surprising that she took her own life – her fine, vulnerable, other-worldly temperament meant that things were always going to be difficult for her, and when her melancholy became deep depression, this, combined with her loneliness, her deafness and the lingering effects of the parasite (loss of appetite and anorexia are well-known causes of depression) made her not want to live any more. She killed herself a decade before Hannah Gavron did the same thing in Highgate: she wrote *The Captive Wife* in 1966, describing the difficulties of the female graduate who is left stranded – educated but bored. Children were the answer for many (although they did not help poor Hannah Gavron) but Maud, despite having once had a miscarriage, did not want to have them. '"Perhaps I should tell you," [Martha in *Blaming*] said, frowning. "I don't want, I'm afraid . . . to have children." "Oh, children would be out of the question for many years," [Simon] said quickly. "I meant I don't think I want to have them ever," she muttered.'

Elizabeth's posthumous novel *Blaming* is based on what actually happened to Maud. In the novel Martha gives Amy an early painting by Amy's husband; Maud gave Elizabeth a drawing by Whistler, because she knew she loved his work. Martha gives Amy a cheque for £200 (£1250 nowadays), '"My escape money. If, or when, I need it, I shall let you know,"'[59] and Maud, too, gave money to Elizabeth ('all that embarrassing complication about the money actually happened'[60]). Martha has premonitions of her death because she asked Amy what she would do if she had a short time to live; Maud discussed Virginia Woolf's suicide with both Elizabeth and Heather Sutton. Then Martha leaves.

> There were longer gaps between Amy's letters to Martha than Martha's to her . . . [Martha] was unhappy. She found that she could not finish her novel about London . . . She went nowhere; saw no one. She was not asked to lecture on English literature, or on anything else. . . . And she had constant headaches, but could not afford the special medical treatment

she thought she needed. Simon was, on the whole, both kind and considerate; but his work came first . . . New Ludlow had no art gallery, no old buildings, nothing beautiful or interesting . . . [Amy] sat down, with Martha's last letter before her, and began to compose her piece. She was sorry this; she was sorry that – sorry about the headaches and the ugly town, and the loneliness.[61]

Thus it was for Maud. And we can imagine that the sentence that gave Elizabeth the greatest grief to write was: 'She was sorry this; she was sorry that'; we can imagine her, in the summer of 1956, preoccupied with her latest novel, 'getting over' David Blakely, not having seen Maud for six years, writing as one does to a friend who is no longer an integral part of one's life – 'I am sorry about this, I am sorry about that . . . ' (In the same way, soon after she met Maud, Elizabeth had castigated Frances, the painter in *A Wreath of Roses*, for writing to Morland while he was a POW 'with enquiries after his health, hoping this, hoping that',[62] all rounded off by a few remarks about the weather.)

In *Blaming* Martha asks Amy to use the cheque for £200 to send her a single ticket to London and then to put the rest in her old Hampstead bank account. 'Unless Amy cared to meet her plane at Heathrow, she would write to her, or telephone, as soon as she could give her new address.' This was the cry for help. But Amy did not care; nor did Elizabeth. '"It would mean taking a taxi all that way, and you know how expensive that would be,"' says Amy, as she also wriggles out of having

Martha to stay. Then she waits 'but with no great impatience, to hear from her at her new address, complacently imagining her in some, but different, bed-sitter in the Hampstead area, writing her novel, booking up her lecture engagements for the beginning of the season.' She does not hear, and 'had to admit that with every day that passed her guilt grew deeper.' Then Martha's husband writes to tell her that she had died of an overdose of sleeping tablets 'taken at an hour of depression, of pain, of loneliness and futility; of, worst of all, she said, of having let him down.'

Maud, in fact, did not kill herself in London but flew back to New Zealand and died there. Later Bill Geddes came to London to talk to Elizabeth, as Simon talks to Amy after the funeral in the book. And it seems likely that the appallingly painful incident when Simon returns the money for the air-fare really happened: Maud gave Elizabeth a lot of cash before she left London and Elizabeth may not have wanted to tell Bill that she had done so. In the book Martha told Simon that Amy had lent her the money, but Amy lies and says that in fact Martha had been given the money by her grandmother. ' "I can see now how I failed her," Simon said. "She kept this money a secret from me. She thought I was ungenerous about the way in which I arranged our affairs." '[63]

As we read this page, and the two final pages of the novel, it is almost unbearable to think of the remorse Elizabeth would feel for the twenty years after Maud's death. Whether she was as much to blame as she believed no one can say; we have all written letters saying 'I am sorry', failed our friends when they needed us. If she was to blame for her small lapse –

then we are all to blame, every day, for similar failures. What Elizabeth is saying in *Blaming* is that Amy, while pretending to be kind, unselfish, courteous and so on, was in fact as selfish and unheeding as any of the women Elizabeth had ever satirised; and we must all look into our hearts to see that we are not behaving like Amy. She was to blame for Martha's death, Elizabeth thought she herself was to blame for Maud's – and who is to say whether she was or not?

CHAPTER ELEVEN

GROVE'S BARN 1957–59

I wouldn't describe anything that was not what I had gone through and understood myself – in my experience or out of my imagination, and other people's words wouldn't do.[1]

In 1956 John and Elizabeth decided to move. They had not been restless, but their friends Jon and Veronica Walley who lived in a large house across the road decided to sell their barn and the Taylors bought it as a bare shell and did it up. The house, Grove's Barn, would be bigger but the garden smaller; passers-by, and cars, would not be so close to their sitting-room window. 'It has a very small garden and a tiny courtyard with a fine view across Windsor Castle to the Surrey Hills'[2] and 'the Thames Valley lying below and in the distance the gas-holder at Staines, the grand-stand at Ascot' (see p 181).

So, in the early spring of 1957, they left Penn Cottage and the small panelled sitting-room with a fireplace and a bow window in which Elizabeth had written five novels and more than twenty-five short stories and moved their furniture over the road, helped by eight men from Taylor's who, feudally, all had a special lunch in the bottom bar at The Crown. Elizabeth was immensely happy about her new sitting-room, which she thought one of the most beautiful rooms she had ever seen. Not long after they moved in she allowed photographs to be taken and an article to be written in the local paper. She was now indisputably one of the English middle classes whose houses appeared in magazines, gave dinner parties for friends, had their hair done in Beaconsfield or in London, had a dog, a drinks tray and a daily – and went, appropriately dressed, to the races.

Horse-racing had long been an important part of her life: she quite often went to watch it (for example, at Killarney, in 1957, before visiting Elizabeth Bowen), frequently placed bets (having had an account at a bookmaker since the 1930s) and once told Bill Maxwell, 'I have also had a bad flat racing season'[3] and that she had bought her evening paper from 'my usual street-seller who gives me such dubious racing tips.'[4] On the back of a 1953 letter from Peter Davies she scribbled: '2.00 Fiery Torch, 2.30 Fur Baby, 3.15 Wait and See [Quite Naturally was crossed out]. 3.30 Llanstephan, 4.15 Millionaire'.[5] It annoyed her to go to races and see young people throwing their money away, she told Robert. 'Had their parents never taught them to study form?'[6] Sometimes she used form as an image, thus when Oliver in *At Mrs Lippincote's* does sums set for him by Eleanor 'occasionally, he had a right answer, in much the same manner as when one backs a horse a great deal, now and then one of them comes in for a place.'[7] And in *The Sleeping Beauty* Isabella and Evalie studied form 'industriously . . . jockeys' names became as familiar to them as their own relations': secretly (for their husbands would have disapproved), they progressed from little flutters to a cool and steady daily appraisal of all the runners and riders.'[8]

Another thing that the middle classes did at this time was to travel, and from the mid-1950s Elizabeth started going regularly to Greece. The first time she went was with John and Joanna (then aged 15) when they decided to go on a cruise in April 1956. The boat would visit Rhodes, Kos, Santorini, Naxos and Delphi and 'EM Forster is going to Greece on the same boat,' Elizabeth told Bill, having seen the passenger list. 'Everything comes at once – to see him and the Parthenon.'[9] The family memory is that Forster asked to be introduced to Elizabeth, although a fellow passenger had the impression that he did not know Elizabeth's work.[10] (A few years before, Elizabeth had written: 'I always have felt that he is one of the few whose opinion about my writing I would accept. If he said there was a grain of goodness in it, I would be quite overjoyed. And if he said, "No good; pack up", I would be downcast indeed. But I wouldn't pack up and I wouldn't believe him.'[11] Alas, he never did give his opinion.) Elizabeth was teased by John and Joanna for her reverence for Forster, for the way she dived to pick up his glasses case. 'He is absolutely *sweet*,' she told Renny. 'A many-splendoured thing. His fluffy hair blows about his balding (Time magazine word) pate. He has little tin spectacles.'[12] Once 'they ate their hard-boiled eggs together, sitting high up in the theatre at Delphi "on the prompt side". "Salt is essential with eggs, I think," Forster remarked.'[13] Robert found this funny, or at least touching, and so did the Taylors; ever since, the family have ritually said the same thing when cutting the tops of their soft-boiled eggs or peeling a hard-boiled one. The biographer can only feel frustrated that Elizabeth did not mention her books. She and Forster met physically; if only they had met mentally, even for an instant. But to see him was enough. She stuck a photograph of him in her scrapbook and wrote beside it (presumably her own words): 'In appearance I see in him a mixture of owl and kitten. In profile, however, he takes on a cosy, rodent-like look. Most astonishing is his utter lack of a sense of his own importance and his willingness to indulge in small talk. A curious and alive man, he asserts, outside the restless worlds, the calm of his personal vision.'[14]

Elizabeth had taken Robert's *Aegean Greece* with her but although he was in Athens, the two did not meet; nevertheless 'I think of you wherever I go,' she wrote to him, 'all made lovelier by what you have written, in books or letters'; and she (apparently) described everything she saw, for example, 'in a café in Rhodes, three Englishwomen walked in wearing the most outlandish holiday clothes and panama hats, with lots of raincoats and cameras and walking-sticks and rucksacks. They stood looking about for a waiter and one said in a loud voice: "How do we attract attention?"' One of Elizabeth's most distinctive qualities was that, like Julia in *At Mrs Lippincote's*, she never stopped looking at things as though she was seeing them for the first time. It was this sharp, almost naïve, watchfulness that made her family love and admire her so much: they never knew what she was going to say next, just as Ray or Robert never knew what she would write about in her letters. But she was miles away from being outrageous like Jean Rhys or Julia Strachey, was never unkind, and her pose of the country housewife who did nothing more exciting than buying chump chops at the butcher was of course a disguise, behind which she could more easily observe what was happening. If it did not sound sentimental she would have said that everything was an adventure, even a bus journey, because you never knew what you might see or overhear.

Greece was a great adventure because everything was so new; overwhelmingly so, she told Robert. 'Sometimes I feel frightened and sometimes tired from walking on a knife's edge, and also from seeing too many beautiful things.'[15] And once she woke up at dawn to find the boat entering the bay at Santorini but 'the effect was too dramatic for me. I felt quite panicky'.[16] She was not exaggerating: Elizabeth's perceptions were sensitive in the extreme. Again, this was all disguised by her pose, her poise. Some assumed she was tough. She was not.

The winter after this first visit to Greece she wrote 'The Letter-Writers'. It is about Edmund and Emily* who have been corresponding for ten years (as, by now, had Robert and Elizabeth) but have never met; Edmund does not live in England 'from old vexatious associations' but likes 'to have some foothold there' and his letters from Emily help to

* This story was in part a tribute to Leslie Yates, a poet whom Elizabeth had encouraged and to whom she wrote letters, who died in a hospital in Istanbul in November 1943. 'I had letters for a very long time from a man I had never met and one day he asked to come to tea . . . It is a dreadful experience to be going to meet someone one has written to for years' ET to Katharine White 27 April 1953 *The New Yorker* Papers.

give it to him. She is not the novelist he had at first assumed, 'then he realised that letter-writing is an art by itself . . . and one at which Englishwomen have excelled.'

Through the letters Edmund gets to know Emily's neighbours and people whom she had loved but who are no longer alive. Then he decides to visit her. '"He knows too much about me, so where can we begin?" she wondered.' And indeed the visit is a failure, ruined by the cat eating the lobster that Emily had so extravagantly bought and by a visit from a neighbour who was funny in Emily's letters but was not in real life. At the end Emily sits down 'and wrote, in her fine and flowing hand, her address, and then "Dear Edmund."'[17] 'After that story,' Robert Liddell commented, 'I dare say [Elizabeth] felt that we could meet – for though it had not been "taken from the life" it had, as Elizabeth's very solid stories were to do, taken on life. It had happened – and nothing worse was likely to happen – and it had done no harm.'[18]

So in 1959 Elizabeth went to Greece by herself. This is not something that her neighbours in Penn would have done: they would not have wanted to travel alone, and in any case they would have found 'the facilities' much too primitive and disliked 'the frustrations and misunderstandings about the language. And sometimes the food . . . and having no water all that time.'[19] And when Elizabeth told Robert 'I am not very good at travelling on my own. I am always punctual and on the platform in plenty of time, but it is seldom the right platform',[20] she did not admit that she had in fact never been abroad without a companion. But she flew to Athens and stayed in a hotel which would inspire the short story 'The

Voices' in 1962. This is about Laura overhearing the conversation between Amy and Edith in the room next door to her. Laura is on her own and less energetic than her neighbours; she very much enjoys hearing them talk about their expeditions to Delphi, their postcard-writing, the oily Greek food. Then one morning she sneezes. 'There was a deep, long silence in the next room. She imagined them staring at one another, hardly daring to stir. It was some time before they began to whisper and move stealthily about the room.'[21]

She went to see Robert straightaway and, unlike Edmund's visit to Emily, their first meeting was a success and Robert thought her 'charming, but painfully shy and sensitive'. She arrived 'trembling and silent, and was gradually restored by ouzo and the view. Then we said some very sharp things about the Snows,* and felt more at home. After two hours she was thawed enough to be taken out to dinner'[22] and 'by the end of the evening we were talking easily, like the old friends we were.' Over the next few days they made several expeditions together. Once they had lunch with 'her other Athenian fan, Mark Ogilvie-Grant, at his pretty house. "You observe," he said, "we are not having lobster."'[23]

After her time in Athens Elizabeth went to Hydra. She knew no one there but 'being on my own will be a relief':[24] she went because she wanted to, and it was the first time in her life she had gone somewhere simply to please herself. It was significant and sad that it was on her own. Fifteen years before, Julia in *At Mrs Lippincote's* has a vision of happiness,

* CP Snow and his wife Pamela Hansford Johnson, both novelists.

seeing 'herself beneath a striped awning, at the edge of some pavement . . . On the iron table a glass was still clouded with some frosted drink, there was the smell of sun-baked foreign newsprint; warmth, leisure, delight, relaxation . . . ' This was France not Greece, and the image ends with someone leaning forward to lay 'a hand over her hand on the iron table';[25] but the 47-year-old Elizabeth (but is 47 after all so old?) had given up on this kind of happiness, would *au fond* always be alone. She was, however, idyllically happy in Greece; and perfectly content on family holidays in France, although in a different – domestic, maternal, uxorial – way.

Angel had been finished in the autumn of 1956 and published the following summer. Iris Murdoch's review in the *Evening Standard* was headed 'This Angel is a bit of a bore', the general, although not universal, view in England. She thought, however, that 'the dreary gas-lit poverty of the grocer's shop is described with a sort of picturesqueness which marks Angel out, for better or worse, as a true heroine of romance', loved the descriptions of the dogs and cats, 'of which there are a splendid and increasing number as the book goes on', and was moved at the end by 'the picture of the decayed and deluded old lady living in the wreck of the great house she had dreamed of in childhood.'[26]

In the *Spectator* Kingsley Amis, who was consistently to champion Elizabeth's work for the next twenty years, approved of her trying to extend her range and wondered why she received excellent notices yet in surveys of the modern novel never seemed to find a place. The reason, he decided, was that Elizabeth's work superficially resembled the library, or woman's, novel frequently vilified (though rarely read) in literary circles. 'Her favourite subjects are indeed domestic and true to life as it is lived by large numbers of people, neither eked out by odd bits of murder or incest in the Compton-Burnett vein, nor veneered with trumped-up sensitivity after the manner of – quite a few other writers.' Although her characters tended to be mothers of young children who have difficulties with the char, 'such a world is as valid as any other, and more valid than many, for exploration by the serious novelist.'[27] Twenty-five years later Amis defended *Angel* for being included in the 'Best Novels of Our Time' promotion: 'Read properly it stands out as a powerful story about a violent and hysterical egotist, a character deeply seen into and judged with scrupulous fairness, all done with triumphant narrative skill, a wonderful eye and ear and unfailing humour.'[28]

The American reviews of *Angel* a few weeks later were mostly far better than the British ones, the *Time* magazine reviewer concluding that Elizabeth had 'magically managed to write a brilliant and extremely funny book,'[29] *The New Yorker* calling it expert, funny and pitiless, and Alice Saxon in *The Commonweal* also finding it funny, but being conscious that some would not. 'The earlier a reader catches the tone of this book,' she declared, 'the sooner he may start enjoying it. He may well bumble about at first while the delicate humour seeps unhurriedly out of the seams of a disarmingly familiar literary setting.'[30] For fifty years *Angel* has been a novel that divides Elizabeth's readers into two camps. There were many appreciative reviews; yet, as Elizabeth told

Patience, 'I only wish it were not so despised a book. People here treated me as if I were deformed.'[31]

The following year four stories by Elizabeth appeared in *The New Yorker*, a record. These were 'The True Primitive', 'The Rose, The Mauve, The White', 'The Blush' and 'You'll enjoy it when you get there'. The first describes an intellectual lock-keeper and his son's girlfriend, who is bored by his interest in art and in 'Cicero and Goethe, Ibsen and Nietzsche and a French poet, one of his specials, called Bawdyleer.' 'The Rose, The Mauve, The White' evokes three young girls going to their first dance, their preparations: '"What a lovely smell. It's so much nicer than mine," said Frances, dredging Katie [with talcum powder] as thoroughly as if she were a fillet of fish being prepared for the frying-pan.' And: '"I hate my bosoms," she suddenly said. "They are too wide apart." "Nonsense, that's how they're supposed to be," Katie said, as brisk as any Nannie.'

This is the story that begins: 'In the morning, Charles went down the garden to practise calling for three cheers.'[32] As Bill Maxwell understood (see p 243) there is something classical, and classically Elizabeth Taylor, in this sentence's simplicity, beauty, understatedness and subtlety. The story would appear (next to a story by Dorothy Parker) in the 1960 anthology *Stories from The New Yorker 1950–60*; it will be handy for a potential dissertation-writer working on Elizabeth's stories because the differences between Bill Maxwell's version and the English version (published in *The Blush* in 1958) are evident from the first page. For one thing, in the first sentence in *The New Yorker* Charles is Charles Pollard; most obviously,

Bill excised many commas. Elizabeth disliked her words, her vocabulary, being changed, but ostensibly did not mind Bill editing her grammar and indeed would apologise jokingly to him about her lack of understanding about commas; she would always say that all she minded about was that the sentence sounded right in her head.

She admired William Strunk's *The Elements of Style*, revised by EB White and extracted in *The New Yorker* in the late 1950s, yet would generally follow her instinct rather than a rule. Thus Strunk/White say that you should 'enclose parenthetic expressions between commas', and 'place a comma before a conjunction introducing an independent clause'.[33] Bill did this. Elizabeth did not – to the extent that although she asked if she could dedicate *The Blush* to him, when he received a finished copy he realised that none of his changes had been incorporated. The saintly Bill wrote a good-humoured letter about it:

> Like Galileo I have a secret that I whisper to myself from time to time, and it is this: Authors like best what they wrote; otherwise they wouldn't have written it that way . . . Your having the new collection made up from the carbons without benefit of all that conscientious scrutiny made me burst out laughing with pleasure and pride in our profession. Nobody is ever really going to succeed in making us write perfectly or do anything else that is irrelevant to our original intention.[34]

Elizabeth replied saying that she had not been able to find spare *New Yorker* copies to send to the printer (which in pre-photocopier days may have been true) and that she had spent 'hours and hours making them tally with the corrected *New Yorker* ones.'[35] This was not true, or rather her corrections were selective; as she put it disingenuously, 'I'm afraid much may have escaped me.'[36]

'The Blush', chosen for the title story for the entire 1958 volume, is about the meek and sadly childless Mrs Allen ('Something had not come true; the essential part of her life. She had always imagined her children in fleeting scenes . . . The years passing by had slowly filched from her the reality of these scenes'). Her daily help, the fecund Mrs Lacey, uses her employer as a cover for enjoying herself in the evenings, a fact that Mrs Allen only finds out when Mr Lacey comes round; '"You may or may not know that she's expecting"' he says, asking her not to keep his wife late clearing up after cocktail-parties and endlessly babysitting for them. It's a story about loneliness (Mrs Allen 'had her own little ways of cosseting herself through the lonely hours'[37]), deceit and the dynamics of village life; and it is a sharply observed portrait of Mrs Lacey. Another 1957 *New Yorker* story was 'You'll enjoy it when you get there'. It describes a young girl accompanying her father to a banquet; Elizabeth alleged that it was partly based on her own 'humiliation' when she went with John to a confectioners' occasion and found that she twice asked the Mayor whether he liked cats, in a nervous effort to make conversation – she had not recognised him the second time they talked, after he had shed his mayoral chains. 'It wasn't funny when it happened to me,' Elizabeth told Bill, 'but soon enough became so.'[38]

More profoundly, this story is about the absurd conventions of social life that we are expected to endure; and by making it a very young girl who says the wrong thing Elizabeth adds a critique of social mores – why on earth does the adult world behave like this? – rather than, more simplistically, concentrating on one woman's gaucheness. Finally, there is a tinge, but only a tinge, of rage about the functions to which Elizabeth sometimes had to accompany John. His father had been 'president of the British Federation of Wholesale Confectioners, president of the Southern Counties Wholesale Confectioners' Association, a founder member of the Confectioners' Benevolent Fund, a trustee of the High Wycombe Liberal Club and vice-president of High Wycombe Hockey Club'[39] (wrote the local paper when he died) as well as a town councillor; and John stepped into every one of his father's shoes – the confectioners, the Liberals, the hockey, the local government.

Meanwhile, as John and Elizabeth grew more and more entrenched in Penn middle-class life, as Elizabeth wore a hat and gloves to go shopping and John led the managing director's life, Ray, during the early '50s, was still living at home and still convalescing, both from his four years in Austria and from the ending of his affair with Elizabeth. It must have been appalling, although it is impossible for the biographer to ask, cheerfully, and how did you feel in the late '40s and early '50s as you nursed your broken heart, recovered from your time as a POW, had to accept that you would never make a living as a painter but would have to work in an office, and so on and so forth? This one cannot do. All one knows is that

Lotte Meitner-Graf   London

Ray in his eighties and nineties looked like someone who had not changed very much since he was in his thirties. It was not that he had arrested development. It was that the greatest thing that had ever happened to him had happened, and unless he was inordinately lucky nothing like it would ever happen again.

So he went on with his old life. He never left the Communist Party, and never regretted not having done so; he began working in a design company in London, to which he travelled every day. Then, in 1952, when he was 39, he married a Welsh girl thirteen years younger than himself, whose father was one of the two thousand Welsh miners who had come to High Wycombe in search of new jobs; the two of them met when he was (still) selling the *Daily Worker* outside Woolworth's. (It was in fact partly because of the miners that unemployment remained high in High Wycombe, one reason Ray could not easily find work there.) He and his wife Eunice first lived in the house at Queen's Road; then, in 1958, they asked a local architect, Anthea Hardie, to build them a house at 81 Carrington Road, a street on the edge of High Wycombe to the west; this used to look out over sloping beechwoods although more and more houses were being built every year. Ray and Eunice had a son, Colin, in 1960; by then Renny was not far off having his own children. The Russells lived in Carrington Road for twenty years; when Ray retired, after Elizabeth had died, they moved away from High Wycombe, to Hull.

Ray and Elizabeth kept tenuously in touch until her death; he never fully accepted that she had broken with him. But in fact, although he would obsessively relate an anecdote about her cutting him dead in the train in the 1950s, she was as loyal as she could be, posting inscribed copies of her books, Christmas cards, news, 'hoping this, hoping that' and even sending him a postcard from the Parthenon. 'Picture postcards of the Parthenon have an air of hallucination'[40] she wrote on the back in 1956, alluding obliquely to the day fifteen years before when Ray had sent her one. Even in the early 1970s, when Ray had a hernia operation, he rang to tell her he was all right. John was in the room when Elizabeth answered the phone and she wrote afterwards to apologise for being stiff. Many women would have told their ex-lover to leave them alone. Ray went on wholeheartedly believing Elizabeth when she said that she would always love him, and even though they never saw each other it was as if his heart was across the beechwoods in Penn. A very small part of her may have gone on loving him; she was an intensely loyal person, felt remorseful at having destroyed his chances of marrying before he was in his late thirties, and never tried, as she could have done, to make a final break. She always remained grateful to Ray for loving her, for his kindness, for his interest in her early work, and was always sad about what became of him.

There were four more stories in 1957: 'The Letter-Writers' (about the meeting between Edmund and Emily, see pp 304–5), 'A Troubled State of Mind', 'Perhaps a Family Failing' and 'Summer Schools'. 'A Troubled State of Mind' describes 18-year-old Sophy, home from Switzerland but having to behave 'as if it were a perfectly normal thing for one's father to marry one's schoolfriend.'[41] (Joanna, like Sophy, was about to go to school in Switzerland for a term.) Sophy falls in love with someone of her own age; her stepmother is abandoned to boredom and loneliness and the demands of an elderly husband. *The New Yorker* turned the story down but it was published in American *Vogue*.

'Perhaps a Family Failing' is a marvellous *jeu d'esprit* about Geoff and Beryl who have just been married. 'For weeks, she had thought and talked and dreamt of the wedding, studied the advice to brides in women's magazines, on make-up, etiquette and Geoff's marital rights – which he must, she learnt, not be allowed to anticipate.'[42] At the hotel she spreads about the lacy lingerie with which she had long planned to entice her husband. After dinner she goes upstairs first. But Geoff, ever-sociable, stays downstairs and at the end of the evening drunkenly accepts a lift back home to his surprised parents. The story is like a Whitehall farce in miniature, and yet is deeply funny, and sad, about marriage.

'Summer Schools' is also about a marriage, except that Pamela and her dentist husband are happy together, so happy that when Ursula goes to stay with her old schoolfriend she discovers that: 'It was difficult to find anything to talk about. The books they had once so passionately discussed were at the very bottom of the glass-fronted case, beneath text-books on dentistry and Book Club editions.'[43] Meanwhile Ursula's sister goes on a literature course and decides she is in love with a professor, although he barely notices her; Ursula is fleetingly groped by a friend of the dentist's; for both of them life will never be much more exciting and will go on as it always has done. As Goronwy Rees would observe (in a review of *The Blush*): '"Summer Schools" is at once pathetic, amusing, and horrifying, and it is the combination of these three qualities which gives Mrs Taylor's stories their distinctive flavour . . . One sometimes wonders how Mrs Taylor manages to combine so sensitive an understanding of characters with so merciless an eye . . . '[44]

Both stories show the results (as Robert put it) of Elizabeth having done 'a good deal of fieldwork in the pubs of commuterland'; and he singled out the 'almost "Gothic" horror' of 'Summer Schools': 'Its characters live their absurd lives in a décor that might have been invented by Osbert Lancaster or Sir John Betjeman at their best.'[45] In fact this is wretchedly missing the point of the story. What Elizabeth is asking is – who are we, *New Yorker* readers who smugly think of ourselves as tasteful intellectuals, to criticise the comfortable, nay cosy, worlds described in this story? She herself found the characters' lives 'pathetic, amusing, and horrifying', but she would not have dreamed of calling them absurd. Significantly, neither of these two stories sold in England; they must have been thought too sharp, too critical, and, by the obtuse, too snobbish. But that was not how Elizabeth meant them to be read. She would have liked her stories to be seen as funny and perceptive not scornful or condemning – documentaries, in fact, not critiques, merciless but not cruel.

It was between January 1958 and the spring of 1960 that *In a Summer Season* was written, evoking the relationship between Dermot and Kate (see pp 279–80). It brings on the 'Charles' figure who appeared in *A Game of Hide and Seek* (again he is literally called Charles) who was the husband of Kate's best friend and whom the recently widowed Kate should have married instead of Dermot if she had been 'sensible'. Then it describes the way in which the marriage begins to fall apart: a defining moment is when Dermot says he does not know Mrs Gereth (in *The Spoils of Poynton*) just as Roddy in *At Mrs Lippincote's* had said he did not know Catherine Morland (in *Northanger Abbey*). And the novel ends with Dermot being killed and Charles and Kate getting married. What is unusual is the description of Kate's second marriage (the 'summer season' in between the first and third); it is described with acute brilliance and sensitivity. Elizabeth conveys the sexual attraction between Dermot and Kate in very few words; she creates a cousin figure to stand as comic chorus, as did Eleanor in *At Mrs Lippincote's*; and she evokes the impossibly deadening effect on a marriage if the husband has no occupation, nothing which he cares about deeply ('his love for her was his chief pride'). This, she is saying, is the tragedy of their marriage; and Kate is as much at fault as her young husband for allowing him to live off her and for allowing him to be a malign influence on her son ('Your new husband is a bad example to us young lads' Tom tells his mother).

In a Summer Season is one of Elizabeth's strongest novels, the reason being that, as with *At Mrs Lippincote's* and *A Game of Hide and Seek*, there was a huge amount of herself in it and therefore genuine feeling. Also, in many respects she was by now leading Kate's life and could accurately describe every detail, ranging from the commuter village where men, fetched from the station, 'hurried up the slope towards the line of waiting cars, where their wives, who had rushed out in the middle of peeling potatoes or weeding rockeries, were waiting for them, with their thoughts all back at home where telephones might be ringing or children in mischief or things in saucepans boiling over the stove', to Mrs Meacock the cook who 'had pinned a folded napkin round her head as if she were a Stilton cheese.' '"And what was London like today?" she asked, as if she were enquiring after an invalid' – but a melancholy one. 'Was it what life should be? Kate wondered. It seemed so very little.' Yet, once, her daughter, sitting in the bus, 'felt completely happy, without knowing that to feel so is such a rare experience that it might never come to her again.' By contrast, Kate is unhappy because she has nothing to do, not even cooking. The strongest feeling in her life is sexual desire; but social convention has ensured that this be subsumed by the demands of The Old Vicarage.

There is a strong implication throughout that Kate and Dermot would have had a better chance of being happy not only if he had had a job but if they had only been alone. When they go on holiday to the Cotswolds, 'removed from their watchful audience – the chorus waiting to comment on and explain their downfall – their love stood a better chance.' On the title page of the original draft Elizabeth wrote 'The Chorus', 'Two with Chorus' and 'The Commentators'.* And it is true, Kate's children, Aunt Ethel (who 'had a way of bending her head at closed doors, not listening, as she told

* She also tried out 'A Family Affair, A Thames Valley Story, Return of the Thorntons, The Summer and April and May.

herself, but ascertaining'), friends, neighbours, all pass
comment either openly (Aunt Ethel and her friend Gertrude)
or unspokenly (Mrs Meacock). What Elizabeth is exploring
here is whether a marriage can succeed if it is lived in public,
whether being enmeshed in a social setting/a summer season
is the best way for a couple to live its life. '"We're all of us just
passing time,"' Kate thinks in one of the bleakest passages
in the novel: 'It seemed to her that it was worse for herself,
without religion, to be squandering her life, expecting no other
and chilled by the passage of time.'

This is also, as the critic Susannah Clapp has observed,
Elizabeth's sexiest novel. 'He drew her shoulders back against
him and slid his hands inside her thin shirt' she writes about
Dermot and Kate; and describes Tom dabbing a stain off
Araminta's dress: 'his knuckles brushed against the softness
of her stomach, warm under the thin silk. "My God, she's
got nothing on underneath," he thought, and felt faint.' We
realise that an affair between Dermot and Kate would have
been fulfilling and intensely happy for both of them but a
marriage absurd. Is sexuality ridiculous when the woman is
so *old*? is the question Elizabeth asks. When Dermot makes
love to Kate in the afternoon the whole household senses
it; hurrying from their room to her 'duties about the house'
(he has no duties of course) she is then embraced by him
before dinner. '"It will all begin again," she thought in a
panic, and felt tired and light-headed with desire.'[46] The
'tired' is significant. If the question is – can, should, a woman
have a fulfilled sexual existence once she is over 40? –
the answer, Elizabeth apparently believed, is that she should

not. It cannot happen within marriage: Emily, Harriet, Cassandra, Tory, indeed all the wives in her novels, never marry for sex but for social status, companionship, financial security; and outside marriage an affair ultimately causes grief to everyone.

The love Dermot and Kate feel for each other is set against the unabashed, cold and egocentric sexuality of Charles's daughter Araminta, 'a maddening vision,' in Susannah Clapp's words, 'of icy deliciousness, with her false eyelashes, exiguous shift-dresses, over-candid talk of lavatories, and Continental poise.'[47] Unusually, Araminta had already appeared as Arabella and Mrs Meacock as Mrs Hatton in a short story Elizabeth wrote just before she began writing *In a Summer Season*, 'The Prerogative of Love'. This is about an affluent Home Counties couple who are giving a dinner party – their cook is 'well forward' in the kitchen, Lillah is lying on her bed ('"The heat's knocked Madam," she remarked, and took up some steak and began to knock that'). Lillah's beautiful niece disrupts everything by dropping in unexpectedly. 'I thought you were stark naked'[48] says Richard to the tanned Arabella in her small, white frock, presumably experiencing the same feelings as Tom.

Alas, this short story provides a clear example of poor Elizabeth having no one (a husband, a close friend) to read her work with a critical but friendly gaze except, separately, Bill Maxwell and her publisher: the image in *In a Summer Season* about Mrs Meacock having a folded napkin round her head as if it were a Stilton cheese also appeared in 'The Prerogative of Love'. When, more than ten years before,

Elizabeth, or the 'narrative voice' persona, had observed in *At Mrs Lippincote's*, 'it is seldom safe to confide in lonely people',[49] Elizabeth had been writing about herself. She understood herself then and was not to change; intellectually she was very lonely, and as a result her work suffered, in the tiny details and, much more important, in its broader aspects. Writers are solitary people, but most of them have someone with whom they can discuss their work; that Elizabeth did not was, perhaps, another of the reasons she did not become the truly great novelist she might have been otherwise.

It is curious she did not send her manuscripts to Robert Liddell. Once he noticed that a 'a leg of mutton makes an unexplained appearance' in a vegetarian household (in *Angel*). When he mentioned this to Elizabeth she told him: 'I almost fainted when I read your letter . . . If only you had read it first – at least six people did without realising.'[50] She failed to realise – or perhaps did realise and wanted it thus? – that these six people would have been a publisher in a rush, an agent in a rush, a copy-editor, a proof-reader and so on – but no one with the intelligence and perception of Robert. It was not that it mattered particularly whether or not lamb was served to non-meat eaters; it mattered that a fellow novelist never gave an opinion before the book was set in type.

Not long after beginning *In a Summer Season* Elizabeth stopped writing: in August 1958 Renny, who was then just 21, was nearly killed in a car crash. He had left school in 1955, done two years' National Service and then gone into the confectionery industry, working in different companies in order to learn about the trade from various angles. For the first week after the accident his life was in the balance but then, after many operations, he began to recover. He was in hospital for six months. (This was the summer that Eddie Fisher left Debbie Reynolds for Elizabeth Taylor. It was the real-life soap opera of the decade. But Elizabeth would not have cared.)

Nor would she have noticed the November 1958 issue of the *London Magazine* about post-war novelists. Anthony Quinton began by saying that some critics had suggested that post-war novelists did not bear comparison with the inter-war ones but that this was quite untrue: he mentioned Kingsley Amis, Sybille Bedford, William Cooper, Nigel Dennis, Roy Fuller, William Golding, LP Hartley, Olivia Manning, PH Newby, Iris Murdoch, Anthony Powell and Angus Wilson and asserted that 'neither of the inter-war decades could yield as long a list of thoroughly expert and individual writers.' He declared, bizarrely, that 'the nearest thing to a great novel that I can discern in the post-war years is Hartley's *The Boat*.' And referred to 'a lot of entirely readable stuff . . . that lacks bite, originality, humour and mesmeric verbal skill';[51] but still failed to mention Elizabeth. Lettice Cooper then wrote about Rosamond Lehmann, Marghanita Laski, Francis King and one or two promising novelists such as Elizabeth Sewell* and Julia Birley. Frank Kermode wrote mostly about *Doctor Zhivago* and William Golding. And Maurice Cranston mentioned Elizabeth Montagu, Robert Liddell, Olivia Manning,

---

* Elizabeth Sewell surely shares the crown with Elizabeth Montagu for being the most forgotten of all once-lauded post-war novelists.

William Sansom, Gerald Hanley, PH Newby, Francis King, Iris Murdoch and Emyr Humphreys. The contributors then responded to one another and argued the relative merits of the novelists mentioned. None of them mentioned Elizabeth.

Although Elizabeth had not taken much notice of the publication of *The Blush*, she could not ignore the comments of the critic Walter Allen who declared, 'when I read the chorus of praise from distinguished reviewers that greets her work I can only conclude that Miss Taylor must be one of my blind spots.' He conceded that she wrote well, that her wit was nicely astringent, and that technically her stories were virtually faultless. And then he asked, 'But what do they amount to? I have a terrible feeling I have read them all before, and more than once.'* He complained that he was reminded of too many other women writers – that old jibe again – and, as a final blow, said that he found the stories 'almost impenetrably cosy' and that 'the late Mrs Miniver, I think, would have enjoyed Miss Taylor more than I can.'[52] Elizabeth thanked Robert for his letter of commiseration and said: 'It is puzzling to me when people say that I write like this one and that one and all such different *kinds* of writers and so many of them, and it makes me feel I am nothing in myself . . . I can't think why I call down such savagery. Whatever is wrong with my books . . . I should have thought they were pretty harmless. Walter Allen said almost word for word what Pamela

* This was ironic since five years before, in a review of *The Sleeping Beauty*, he asked: 'And what does it all amount to?' – thereby leaving the reader with a terrible feeling he had read this before.

[Hansford Johnson] had said before. I don't mind, but I find it puzzling.'[53]

She did mind, of course, but luckily, Walter Allen's review came nearly four weeks after a review in the *Manchester Guardian*, in which WL Webb, having praised the stories' stylishness and depth, said that after reading them 'you find yourself wondering for a moment not how she manages to say so much about people in a short story but what there can be to say that really needs the length of a novel.'[54] It was a perceptive comment; despite Walter Allen's absurd remarks, there were evidently some who valued Elizabeth's short stories as highly as, if not more than, her novels. For this was her golden age of short story-writing. Whereas her golden age of novel-writing, it could be argued, had passed: it is a minority view, but a plausible one, that her first five novels, written between 1944 and 1950, were her best. The seven novels she wrote between 1951 and 1975 have such extra-ordinary qualities that it would be grotesque to wish them away. But as works of art the early novels such as *At Mrs Lippincote's* and *A Game of Hide and Seek* were, arguably, never later to be surpassed.

CHAPTER TWELVE

GROVE'S BARN 1960–68

I must soon settle down to work, but luckily haven't yet made the beds – so that gives me another half-hour.[1]

With Mrs Elizabeth Taylor we are safe – safe in the Home Counties somewhere between *Mrs Dale's Diary* and glossy magazines and with Mrs Miniver hovering in the background. We are also invited once again to be lyrical or, if that is too much for us, at least to be sensitive . . . This novel is almost certain to be a success with thousands of readers, but there are really too many clothes and meals, or, to put it briefly, too much 'furniture'.[2]

Thus the *Times Literary Supplement*'s reviewer of *In a Summer Season* in 1961. False as this perception is, it derived in part from Elizabeth's own life – a reviewer's judgement of a writer became bound up with his or her judgement of the book – this is the kind of person the writer is, he thinks, this is the kind of book he will write. And in many ways, it is true, Elizabeth's life was a 'safe' one and had the kind of routine she talked about in interviews ('I like the days to come round' etc.). She had many friends in Penn, some of whom she saw at The

Crown every day at six o'clock and others at dinner parties in large 'Underwriters Georgian' houses. On Wednesdays she still met Gerry Ercolani in Beaconsfield for coffee. She and John had long since settled into an easy, unemotional but friendly relationship and, as is often the case when there has been a rift that then heals, were closer than they had once been; and when he was bad-tempered or rude, as sometimes happened, Elizabeth did not complain. The children were becoming independent and she was extremely good friends with both of them. Grove's Barn was beautifully looked after and Elizabeth was a good cook.

Crucially, she had Mrs Howard, who came three days a week from 9–3 (and the other two went to Gerry Ercolani). In some ways Mrs Howard knew Elizabeth better than anyone else, being deeply involved in the minutiae of her life; but Elizabeth never let her guard slip with her, never showed her melancholy side. Once, in 1958, when one of Elizabeth's short stories ('Plenty Good Fiesta') was read on the radio and credited to 'Eryl Griffiths' she 'flew into a rage: "In all the years I've worked for you," said Mrs Howard (who only sees me on my best behaviour) "I've never before seen you lose your temper."' (Elizabeth then telephoned the BBC and 'filled them with horror and despair'.[3]) Another time, Elizabeth was upstairs working in her bedroom and Mrs Howard was downstairs listening to *Woman's Hour* while Barbara Cartland described lying on a sofa with a hot-water bottle dictating. 'My dear Help,' Elizabeth told Patience Ross, 'listening to this (scornfully) as she did the ironing, found it too much for her. Her voice loaded with sarcasm, she came to me upstairs where I was writing, & said: "I've put on the kettle for your bottle, & I'm just fetching your writing-pad." I thought she had gone off her head.'[4]

In fact, when Robert's book about Elizabeth and Ivy came out in the 1980s, a reviewer sniggered because on one occasion Mrs Howard threatened to leave and in Robert's view '"being without anyone" is far worse for a writer than bad reviews, or a nagging little illness.' Elizabeth would certainly have red-pencilled this because she would have seen how irredeemably trivial it is to say that being without a daily help is virtually the worst thing that can happen to one. Nevertheless, she wrote to Robert, in a passage he did not quote:

> It is kind of you to be so understanding about Mrs Howard's going – only another writer could be. 'You'll have to knuckle to' other people say. They relate experiences of 'being without anyone' for months at a time – as if my position is like theirs, with only the housework to bother me. (I have put this in for Miss Manning's sake, as she will be bound to insert a 'Hear, hear' in the margin.)[5]

This reference to Olivia Manning alluded to the 1952 *Harper's Bazaar* article in which she had criticised Elizabeth for being able to send her children to boarding school; and also to the running joke between Robert and Elizabeth – and one of the reasons she was so insistent her letters be destroyed – that Olivia Manning might be the person asked to edit their correspondence for publication. They therefore did not date what they wrote, in order to muddle her, and – apparently – made frequent little jibes at her expense. 'We also added little notes of great stupidity and insensitiveness that we imagined her as contributing' and 'are trying hard to survive her.'[6]

It was several months after Renny's accident before Elizabeth was able to write again: the mental shock to her had been as great as the physical shock to him. Once he had come out of hospital, at the beginning of 1959, she tried to return to her novel. 'But the dead thing I was confronted with was frightful – gone stale & all the characters frozen in hideous attitudes.'[7] After a few months she decided to scrap it; then Patience Ross insisted on reading what she had done and persuaded her to 'grind' away at it again. Because of the difficulties with her novel, Elizabeth wrote four short stories. The first, 'The Little Girl', was about a child who goes with her mother to a department store. In the lift a woman slaps a man across the face and shouts, '"I have never been so insulted", too angry to see the absurdity of the phrase.' There is a good deal of commotion and in the street the child says that she thought '"that was a horrid lady . . . I pinched her bottom very hard."'[8] Bill turned this down because its twist had been done before, several times, and indeed, to take one example, the novelist Martin Armstrong wrote the very similar 'Cupid in the Lift' in the late 1930s. Elizabeth was not surprised: 'It was a timid essay at beginning to write again'[9] (after Renny's accident) she told Bill, asking him to tear it up; but she never destroyed her own copy.

'The Thames Spread Out' describes a middle-aged woman living in a house by the river who has had to retreat to the first floor because 'every ten years or so, the Thames in that place would rise too high, brim over its banks and cover the fields for miles, changing the landscape utterly.' ('Once,' Elizabeth would write, 'I saw all of that familiar landscape submerged; the smooth lawns and flower-beds and shrubberies had disappeared under the flood water, and the stillness and the silence of that world haunted me.'[10]) Rose is the mistress of the man she used to work for and he has set her up in the house and visits her on Fridays; otherwise she does nothing but wait for the next week and 'survive from year to year'. Because of the flood, two boys row over to invite her to have a drink in their mother's bedroom; it is 'one of the loveliest evenings of her life'[11] and gives her the courage to give up her watery exile and abandon the house and her lover.

Elizabeth next wrote 'A Dedicated Man', which was to be the title story of her 1965 short story collection. Again and again she managed to condense into twenty pages material that lesser writers would spin out into an entire book, and this one in particular would have made a good novel. It is about a waiter named Silcox who, desperate to abandon the vulgarities of a seaside hotel, applies for a job at the Royal George and pretends he is married. He then persuades Edith to say that she is his wife, for she too wants to leave the tripperish hotel.

'The "germ" of this story,' Robert Liddell would comment, 'is the idea (I do not know who first expressed it) that couples of servants who apply for situations as man and wife have often met for the first time in the registry office.'[12] However, everything unravels when 'Mrs Silcox' pretends that a framed photograph is of their son and it transpires that he really is Silcox's son, and his 'wife' takes her revenge. Elizabeth's compassion for hotel staff, and others like them, who have no home of their own is palpable; the tragedy is that poor 'Mrs Silcox' has 'never been so happy'[13] as she was during the few days when she has a son to dote on, a sweater to knit for him and a visit to daydream about.

Finally, 'The Benefactress' is about four widows who 'lived in the almshouses beside the church. On the other side of the wall, their husbands' graves were handy.' Mrs Swan's only visitor is her niece who 'thought so much about herself that it was important to have the thoughts comfortable'; when distracted by one of the regulars at the pub her niece criticises her fickleness.[14] Bill sent a telegram saying, 'Mr Shawn says the Benefactress is a flawless story.'[15]

It was in 1960 that both Elizabeth and Ray went, separately, to the Picasso exhibition at the Tate. She still loved Vuillard, and once bought a little drawing by Gwen John, and still loved her paintings by Elinor Bellingham Smith; but it was the Picasso exhibition that amazed her. 'I felt exhilarated & triumphant when I left – to me there has never been such perfection of composition in any music I have ever heard or book that I have read . . . last night I dreamed the exhibition and one picture after another came to me in dazzling detail. So great, so very very great.'[16] For the rest of his life Ray kept the catalogue of the exhibition on the bookshelf beside the dining-room table (the beautifully-made table which could, in another life, have turned him into a Robin Day figure) and would unhesitatingly talk about Picasso as his favourite painter.

Elizabeth still went to lunch at Braemar Mansions. But now she did not go as often as in the past, partly because Ivy had a new 'adoring courtier', Herman Schrijver, who 'flirts with her and flatters her' in a delightful way; this meant she now rarely saw Ivy without Herman in attendance 'and he is so frivolous and gossipy – which one would love in other circumstances – that Ivy never says anything interesting.' Once the three of them went to a Beckett play together. It was *Happy Days* and Elizabeth admired it enormously: she thought it 'really devastating, and as much as one can bear – a middle-aged woman's gallantry (I see so much of it) signifying the human tragedy – the terrifying attempts at optimism and the Molly Bloom nostalgia.' Herman, as so often, dozed off, and Ivy seemed more interested in chocolates – 'One hopes for a ginger one. I wish your husband would make some good, *cheap* sweets.'[17] (The reference to 'cheap', and hundreds of other complaints about the cost of living and the need to economise, must have been painful for Elizabeth in retrospect: after Ivy died she turned out to be worth over £86,000 – over a million pounds nowadays. Elizabeth would have thought it funny; many of her contemporaries found it rather annoying.)

Elizabeth liked Herman and must have confided in him, even on one occasion about John, since Herman responded, 'I am so sorry that you, also, are suffering from what I call "the horrors of marriage"'.[18] She was to be greatly inspired by the courage with which he faced his death, but never felt quite the same about him after an incident in 1969 when he and Francis King did not arrive for lunch on the appointed day. Herman declared Elizabeth had got it wrong and then sent what must have been a forged carbon copy of his original acceptance card 'proving' they had been due a day later. But Elizabeth, without ever admitting it to Herman or to Francis, had kept his original letter. Forging a letter because Herman 'liked always to be in the right' is the kind of morally reprehensible incident of which Henry James would have made much; he would also have made something out of Elizabeth's being so upset that he did not come (she had cooked pheasant, John drove to the station) and, more interestingly, out of her decision to grovel rather than embarrass, and annoy, Herman by saying, here is the original letter, why on earth did you pretend to send a carbon? She knew, of course, that Herman would never forgive her if he was humiliated; anxious to continue the friendship with him and with Ivy, she instinctively grovelled rather than challenge him. Francis King said recently that he was not surprised that she did this: it 'might have been because she felt that this is what a "lady" ought to do in such circumstances. I think my mother, for all her toughness, would have done likewise. There is also the consideration that Elizabeth shrank from scenes and embarrassments. What could be more embarrassing for both parties than for her to tell Herman "I'm afraid I have a letter which shows that my date was the right one?"'[19]

It was now, with the publication of *In a Summer Season*, that English reviewers started to be more and more patronising about Elizabeth's work. In general it was only the Americans who observed, for example, that the plot of *In a Summer Season* may be frail, 'but who thinks of *Pride and Prejudice*, *Emma* or *Mansfield Park* in terms of plot?'; who compared Aunt Ethel with Miss Bates; and who wrote: 'Those who have been grateful all their lives to Jane Austen (and there must be countless thousands) must not at any cost miss this reincarnation of her at her best.' The reviewer (in the *New York Herald Tribune*) concluded, 'this book is a delight from the first sentence to the last, its perplexity and its pain both relieved and heightened by its humor and its almost careless insight.'[20]

Yet it was at around this time that the *Guardian* was imploring 'save me . . . from the wise, witty, sensitive, accomplished, charming female novelist',[21] the *New Statesman* was confessing 'a brutish dislike for gracious upper-middle-class charm, at least in novels'[22] and *The Critics* on the radio were suggesting that Elizabeth's books were not really serious literature because 'we cannot be sure that she herself understands how marginal and decadent this part of English society [she describes] has become.'[23] Unfortunately, these kinds of attitudes would, in the long run, make their impact; for example, Elizabeth, unbelievably, never won a prize in her lifetime (although she was shortlisted once); the obituaries when she died were respectful but cursory; she rarely appeared in companions, dictionaries and works of literary criticism. One has a sense that it was now, in the early 1960s, that Elizabeth began to despair of the literary establishment ever taking her to its heart.

In the year *In a Summer Season* was published she wrote both 'Girl Reading' and 'In a Different Light'. The first is about Etta, who goes to stay with the Lippmanns in a large house on the river, abandoning her mother (in a town very like Reading, hence the punning title) to her sewing machine; when she comes to fetch Etta she is wearing 'a navy-blue suit which looked as if it had been sponged and pressed a hundred times – a depressing process unknown to Mrs Lippmann.'[24] At the end the Lippmann son writes Etta a letter and the 'belonging' she craves seems possible. It is her mother we feel for – she will be left on her own when Etta is subsumed by the way of life of the Thames Valley. And it is the river which is the focus of the story, the river which, as Elizabeth would write in a non-fiction piece called 'Setting a Scene, 'rarely enchants me. It simply has a banal reality, which disturbs me. In some lights and conditions I find it depressing, and sometimes the smooth affluence of river-bank life oppresses me.'[25] Bill Maxwell read 'Girl Reading' and told Elizabeth that *The New Yorker*'s editor, William Shawn, 'was holding you up as a model to every writer he could think of, and they, fortunately, were not present.'[26] Bill's flattery, *The New Yorker*'s pride in her work, had become like a drug; pessimistic as she was about her work, she had begun to depend on it.

'In a Different Light' (which was originally called 'A Feeling of Affection') is set on Paros, where Elizabeth had spent a week on her own in May 1961, and was written almost as soon as she arrived home. Barbara has come from England to be with her sister, whose husband has died. The two of them make friends with an Englishman having a holiday on his own: 'They saw a great deal of Roland, as it was natural to do in that small village – meeting at the *taverna*, the café, the bathing-place below the rocks.' Soon 'it was life in Hampstead that had the look of strangeness about it now – the little dinner parties with the lace mats set out on the polished table . . . listening to records while he stuck his holiday photographs in an album.' Barbara and Roland return to England and mistakenly she invites him and his wife to Sunday lunch. They are smugly childless, have an appalling chow, and are snobs both socially and intellectually. He, poor man, listens to his wife 'with an attentiveness he must have wisely acquired to make up for everyone else's lack of it.' Barbara thinks kindly: 'These weeks, since his return from the island, must have been worse than hers . . . as the rest of his life would be worse. His experience must have been deeper, his brief escape desperately planned and wearily paid for. It was something for [his wife] to deride along with the other things.'[27] After they have gone, Barbara and her husband sit in the garden and wonder companionably if the others are back in Hampstead yet and have finished dissecting them.

The novel Elizabeth began writing in 1962 was *The Soul of Kindness*; unfortunately, it would have been a superb short story (or *conte*, were such things allowed) but is too long as a novel. It focuses on a young woman who 'has so much, and always wants more' and complacently lives her life cocooned 'under an anaesthetic'.[28] Flora is meant to be the portrait of a supreme egoist (like Rosamond in *Middlemarch*, as one reviewer pointed out) who assumes that everyone loves her and that she is good to everyone around her – to her friend Meg, her mother, her gruff, prickly painter friend Liz (yet another one). In fact Flora is 'really awful', as Brigid Brophy said in the *New Statesman*, going on to observe that 'the heart of the book, however, is much more grave. Here Flora is unimportant, a mere blonde sun round which the others revolve, a dance of failed relationships.' She concluded: 'The book itself fails, I suppose, as a whole – no doubt through its split intention; even so, it fails interestingly; and, above that, I value very highly indeed the considered and considerable despair at its heart.'[29] While Jocelyn Brooke in the *Spectator* called the novel a 'study of self-love and self-delusion, and Miss Taylor carries it off splendidly.' She 'analyses Flora's personality with great deftness, and the subsidiary characters are also excellently drawn. For sheer competence, good writing and psychological insight, Miss Taylor has few rivals.' It was faint praise. But if Elizabeth had been allowed to be a Constant or a Maupassant, if she had been allowed to pare *The Soul of Kindness* down to the length of *Adolphe* – what an extraordinary *conte* it would have been! It is in this novel more than in any of her others that she suffered from being forced, according to the conventions of English and American publishing, to spin things out to seventy or eighty thousand words.

Curiously, or perhaps it is not so curious, it was around this time, in 1963-4, that Barbara Pym's latest novel was rejected by her publisher. It would be convenient to be able to link the rather muted reception of *The Soul of Kindness* to what happened so famously to Barbara Pym, but there was never any question of Elizabeth's novels being rejected. Rather, this novel, and the next three, may be deficient in some vital quality because of what was happening in the 1960s; both Barbara and Elizabeth were unable to adapt to a new spirit and their work, instead of being timeless, seemed out of tune with contemporary life. Some of her reviewers tried to define why she was 'greatly under-rated', for example Jocelyn Brooke thought she was

> in the best sense, old-fashioned; that is to say, she writes an elegant, witty prose, has a decent respect for the Queen's English, and is not obsessed by crime, violence, madness or homosexuality. There are a handful of novelists, at the moment, who are considered 'significant'. But I have never seen Mrs Taylor's name included among them . . . .[30]

Elizabeth herself saw that her strengths as a writer were quite out of fashion. The key novels of the 1950s had been Kingsley Amis's *Lucky Jim*, William Golding's *Lord of the Flies*, Iris Murdoch's *Under the Net*, John Braine's *Room at the Top*, Alan Sillitoe's *Saturday Night and Sunday Morning*, Colin MacInnes's *Absolute Beginners*, Stan Barstow's *A Kind of Loving*; some of the key plays were John Osborne's *Look Back in Anger*, Shelagh Delaney's *A Taste of Honey* and Harold Pinter's *The Caretaker*. Elizabeth had been isolated in the 1940s by domestic circumstances; then she had a period when she was a coming writer; but now she was isolated again by being seen as old-fashioned. No wonder, as Brigid Brophy put it, that she wished Elizabeth 'would trust her gift sufficiently to set on it the responsibility of higher artistic ambitions'[31] or as Angus Wilson would comment in (a generally appreciative) 1965 review of *A Dedicated Man*, 'her principal defect as a writer is a certain lack of adventurousness.'[32]

But Elizabeth, miserably feeling out of step with her times, could not suddenly change her style, how could she? She had artistic aspirations, or had had, but it is difficult to cherish them when all around a new kind of artistic excellence is winning all the plaudits. Elizabeth must frequently have thought of EM Forster, who wrote no more novels after he was 45 (which Elizabeth was in 1957) and yet maintained his reputation as one of our greatest twentieth-century novelists. It is one of the great imponderables. If she had stopped writing after *A Game of Hide and Seek* would she have been similarly revered? And yet we would not have had *In a Summer Season* or the short stories in *A Dedicated Man* and *The Devastating Boys*; many would miss *The Sleeping Beauty*, *Angel* and *Mrs Palfrey at the Claremont*. In any case, writing was like breathing for Elizabeth; she could not have stopped.

At this period her novels were not helped by their jackets, which were muted and feathery and thin, or by her blurbs, which talked about characters being delicately drawn and irony light as a feather and deceptive gentleness; it was almost as though she had begun to write out her strength and depth, and pander to her publisher's analysis of her work as gentle, delicate and 'exquisite'. (Once Peter Davies told her: 'Keep your trust in yourself – you have a quality in your writing which is more exquisite than any living writer.'[33] He meant well, but being exquisite was what she was always being damned for.) Nor was she capable of, or interested in, publicising herself. She did not review, go to literary parties or, in general, give interviews; and only twice appeared on television, once in 1958 when she was questioned by the winner of a competition to 'send in the name of the book by a living British author that you have most enjoyed and give your reasons why'[34] and another time in 1961 when she, Susan Hill and Elizabeth David appeared on a programme chaired by Elizabeth Jane Howard. This she found such a frightful experience that she refused ever to do it again. According to Jane Howard her 'impenetrable shyness' meant that the interview was over in less than a minute: her guest sat opposite her, 'her large, extremely beautiful hazel eyes fixed attentively on me each time I asked her a question, to which she answered either yes or no.'[35]

Bill and the other *New Yorker* editors liked Elizabeth's 1962 stories, although the happy relationship was about to wither. They loved 'As If I Should Care'[36] (renamed 'Façade Collapsing' for *The New Yorker*), Bill's customary telegram saying it made him think of Maupassant. Elizabeth had been 'rather haunted by something I read in a newspaper – the teen-age girl telling her mother she must have money – and more and more of it – to go to dances – "and if you don't give it to me, I'll spill the beans to Dad that he's got cancer." I thought I might work up something jolly from this.'[37] The story is about Rita, a hairdresser's assistant who lives with her parents in a town not unlike the Reading of Elizabeth's childhood. She learns she is adopted and behaves brutally to her ill father and to her 'mother', who wearily realises she is turning out just like her sister, Rita's real mother. They tell her the truth at the end; but Rita, who knows it already, will abandon them. The story is indeed like Maupassant in being intensely atmospheric, and depressing.

Bill also accepted 'Mice and Birds and Boy', another study in loneliness describing the brief friendship between Mrs May and a precocious small boy whose fastidious mother then stops his visits because the old lady is '"stark, staring mad and the place is filthy, everybody says so"'. His father feels that '"someone ought to do something to help her"' but his wife's selfishness ensures no one does, and Mrs May remains 'alone . . . except for the birds in the daytime, the mice at night.'[38] The boy was one more variation on Oliver Knox, Renny, Oliver in *At Mrs Lippincote's*; the mother was yet another addition to Elizabeth's gallery of appallingly selfish and domineering women.

Later in 1962 *The New Yorker* published 'The Voices' (about Laura listening through the wall in the hotel in Athens, see p 306) and 'Mr Wharton',[39] which describes a meticulous and trusting mother cleaning the flat in Hampstead into which her daughter has just moved. After she goes back to Nottingham the daughter comes there with her lover: it is yet another story about the young callously abandoning the middle-aged or elderly to loneliness, intent on their own happiness and unable to imagine that one day they too will be old. 'I am staying in Hampstead, settling Joanna into a flat,' Elizabeth had told Bill in 1959. 'I love it. Far below, there is real London, & the dome of St Paul's milky in the misty sunshine.'[40] But what if a 'Mr Wharton' had arrived

1. Farm Cottage
2. Nofr-Martin
3. The Miss Youngs (Connie is thin, the other is Win)
4. Gwen's Barn
5. Cancer woman, I should say Jon & Veronica
6. Old Vicarage
7. Barry & Gerry EvoItani
8. Graham & Yvonne Godwin

Armstrongs
The Green
Pony Church
My Hardynrste

Fields

Here Katharine & Angus was put also her divorce

farm

swimming pool

.... footpath

? Miss Benson stayed at a house down this path. When she was a schoolgirl.

N
W — E
S

Musical Evening

Mrs Jon Walley and Mrs John Taylor
At Home

Saturday, 1st December
at
Grove's Barn, Penn,
Buckinghamshire

7.30 o'clock for 8.0 o'clock

R.S.V.P.

when she left? How well does one know even one's own daughter? Again, this story did not find an English publisher.

Elizabeth had stayed in Athens to see Robert and some of his friends in both 1961 and 1962, before, as she had in 1959, going on her own to one of the islands for a week. Robert told Francis King that she was less shy than two years before and that, out of Muriel Spark, Olivia Manning and Iris Murdoch she was 'the nicest woman of all of them and the best writer too.' (The following year he criticised Francis for having reviewed one of Olivia's novels too kindly. 'I think you don't really do the poor old girl any good service by saying that someone thinks her the best lady novelist – as well as Ivy there are Elizabeth Bowen, Taylor, Elizabeth Jenkins and Elizabeth Montagu for a start. Not to speak of Dame Rebecca.'[41])

But even without Robert, might something else have impelled Elizabeth to Greece? After all, she had also been exceedingly happy during her Greek lessons at school. She was not being frivolous when she told Katharine White, 'I have got to the stage where I don't want to go anywhere else, & leave it in tears.'[42] She could not stop thinking about Greece and over the winter of 1962-3 wrote a non-fiction piece about it called 'Two Islands'; Bill turned it down (it has disappeared).

In the spring of 1962 the Taylors went to Tunisia, where Elizabeth set 'Crêpes Flambées'. A couple return to the hotel where they had had their honeymoon four years before: 'They unpacked happily, looking forward to the drink later, and the welcome they would have in the little garden in front of Habib's café, facing the sea and the mimosa trees. "You remember your birthday?" Rose said to Harry, as she had said so many times.'[43] But they are disappointed, as so often happens when one returns to a place where one had been happy: the weather is bad, they feel exploited because Habib is economical with the truth, and they are depressed and decide to go home early, knowing they will never see Mahmoud Souk or Habib again. However, Bill told Elizabeth's American agent that 'what happens in the second half of the story is pretty much what one would expect to happen, and one waits in vain for the one thing that would make it a story. There is no writer we would rather have in the magazine than Mrs Taylor.'[44]

A year later they went to Morocco. Elizabeth loved the dazzling brilliance of the wild flowers and birds, the drive along the coast, the great square at Marrakesh; John liked sunbathing and swimming, and for this they went to the Miramar Hotel in Mohammedia. Elizabeth wrote 'In the Sun' about their time there. Bunny and Deirdre, who live in Oxford, are dismayed by the hotel because it is so un-exotic: people play tennis, 'scarlet Thames-valley geraniums bordered the drive', and the other English couples are so, well, *English*. The only exotic element is that at the back of the hotel some children are picking over a refuse cart; Deirdre is suitably upset. After dinner the two of them go for a drive in a *calèche* to the old town. '"It is what we came to see," Deirdre said . . . "Not that boring new hotel, not all those tiresome English people. We can have plenty of them at home." "Yet don't," her husband thought sadly': for the truth is his wife is unfriendly to other people and he is lonely. 'It was always the same, Bunny thought wistfully, and without bitterness. She drove people from him, shooed them off, as if he were private ground. Sometimes he longed to have a conversation with someone else . . .'[45]

It turns out at the end that Bunny is a well-known novelist, and back in Guildford one of the guests looks him up in *Who's Who*; he was born on 3 July 1912, like Elizabeth, and had been married for twenty-seven years, like her. Readers of *The New Yorker* would not have known Elizabeth's date of birth; whether the ones who discover it are meant to deduce that she felt isolated by John's protective, exclusive instincts is not clear, but read in a certain way the story could seem a cry of despair. It could, however, be about Elizabeth's longing to go to the pub on her own or, at the very least, to *be* alone; or it could simply be about the tension that all writers experience between the need for privacy and the longing for friendship, between the need to balance gregariousness and privacy in such a way that the writer has time to write but also to be with other people – and to observe other people.

Elizabeth's life became very much more difficult in 1963 because Taylor's, having been independent for exactly sixty years, since John's father began it, was sold to Holland Toffees. At first John remained a non-executive director, driving to Holland's in Southport for board meetings; then, in 1966, it was absorbed by James Goldsmith's Cavenham Foods empire and John retired completely. He was only 58. It was, we can assume, a terrible moment for Elizabeth, although of course she never revealed her true feelings. The solitude which had allowed her to write *At Mrs Lippincote's* during the war and which she had carefully preserved either with the help of a live-in housekeeper, an au pair or Mrs Howard, was now about to come to an end. It was not so much that John would stop her writing. It was that he would be so ever-present. As Elizabeth wrote to Barbara Pym, 'I am trying to get on with another novel but now that John's at home ("For richer for poorer, in sickness and in health, till death us do part – but not for lunch"), and having three grandchildren very near me, and my natural laziness, it is moving slowly.'[46]

Yet her grandchildren were a huge joy, indeed the greatest joy of her fifties. Joanna had been married in 1961, when she was only 20; she had her first baby in 1964 and her second in 1967; he was born a month before Renny (he had been married in 1965) had his first daughter. By the time Elizabeth was 53, she therefore had three grandchildren (a fourth would be born in 1969, a fifth after her death) and although this brought her happiness there were difficulties and a whole new set of worries. As an example: she wrote one day in November 1966: 'Harriet [her eldest granddaughter] has measles badly, and Joanna is pregnant [for the second time] and John has got the sack.'[47] Nevertheless, she was the perfect grandmother, having enormous empathy with small children and, as her former pupil Oliver Knox once put it, possessing the all-important 'gift that often goes with directness, of not condescending and treating everyone, even an 8 year-old, as a grown-up.'[48]

For the publication of *The Soul of Kindness* Elizabeth moved to a different English publisher, Chatto & Windus. The reason was a tragic one: in April 1960 Peter Davies threw himself in front of a train at Sloane Square station. This was not as traumatic for Elizabeth as the death of Maud, but coming only a few years after that terrible event, she felt deeply upset: Peter had been consistently courteous and good to her since they first met in 1945; as the obituary in *The Times* said, his was 'a personality, witty, astringent, with a brilliant and remarkable knowledge of literature, and withal he possessed a deep and kindly understanding of his fellow men.'[49]

The only consolation for Elizabeth was that Peter had been known to be depressed (percipiently, she had told Barbara Pym that he disliked parties and barely liked writers, see p 262). As described in the many biographies of JM Barrie, and with particular insight in Andrew Birkin's *JM Barrie and the Lost Boys*, Peter had lost both his parents when he was a child, and had then had a very odd relationship with Barrie. None of this made for a happy adulthood; but for Elizabeth personally it was upsetting to see the newspaper headlines the day after Peter died: 'The Boy Who Never Grew Up Is Dead', 'Peter Pan Stood Alone To Die', 'Peter Pan's Death Leap' and so on. Significantly, her relationship with her new publisher would be business-like; perhaps she realised that its doyenne, Norah Smallwood, was another Blanche and decided, from the start, to keep out of her way.

The Soul of Kindness came out in September 1964 to respectful if unexciting reviews. And it is impossible not to groan for Elizabeth when one reads something like *The Listener*: 'Elizabeth Taylor is an attractive exponent of what might be called the St John's Wood novel. In this the influences of Jane Austen, Henry James, and Virginia Woolf combine, in gentility of material and setting, an often ironic moral attentiveness and a feminine sensitivity to the elegiac tones in locality and season.'[50] She can only have been depressed by 'gentility' and 'feminine sensitivity' and even 'moral attentiveness' was not very flattering: a novelist would rather be called morally rigorous, for 'attentive' is a slightly patronising word rather like 'noticing'. Nor was it helpful of Brigid Brophy to wish her to have higher artistic ambitions or the *Times Literary Supplement* to suggest that *The Soul of Kindness* 'deserves as big a success as anything Mrs Taylor has written'[51] – it did not, and the reviewer almost belittled in retrospect the greatness of something like *A Game of Hide and Seek*. Yet Elizabeth Bowen, to whom *The Soul of Kindness* was dedicated (as Elizabeth Cameron, to denote a personal rather than just a literary friendship) read it with

immense writer-sisterly *pride* in your power, your style (which as we both know is not just the veneer-thing envisaged by non-writers, but rather a blend of vision and grip) and your penetrating imagination. This is SO GOOD. It's a masterpiece . . . If I were a non-writer, I'd say to you, in good faith, 'How do you know all you know?' As a writer, I know these things are non-accountable for.[52]

This kind of letter made a vast difference to Elizabeth, and so did Elizabeth Bowen's friendship; thanking her after she had been to stay at Elizabeth Bowen's house near Oxford she said: 'Such a lovely time you gave me. I have this feeling of bliss when I am there, & it persists. Coming back on the top of the bus, I felt so happy, & still do.'[53]

That year, and two years later, Elizabeth again went to Greece on her own, staying first in Athens to see Robert and his friends and then, by herself, in 1964 on Siphnos (where 'I have a nice cell, with use of cold water, for 5/- a night'[54]) and in 1966 on Thásos. But she refused to go once the Colonels took power in 1967 and would never go to Greece again. This was a sacrifice for Elizabeth, said Robert, although 'those of us who lived and worked here were grateful to writers who did not join in the boycott [which] punished those whom there could be no intention to punish, and it made no difference to tourism, which boomed during those years.'[55] Luckily for both of them their differing political stance did not spoil their friendship.

In 1964 Bill accepted 'Vron and Willie', which describes a brother and sister coming to live in London and becoming skilled shoplifters until found out; their aunt has brought them up and she has done her best; but alas they have turned out almost completely amoral. Even though this was the only story to be published in 1965, *The New Yorker* went on renewing the First Reading Agreement (whereby they paid Elizabeth a generous fee if she sent her stories to them first) but one senses a change in the letters. Why this is so is hard to explain. In Elizabeth's 1972 collection of stories, *The Devastating Boys*, only two out of the eleven stories were published in *The New Yorker*; and yet they are superb stories (indeed many thought that of the four collections of short stories it was the best) and there is no obvious reason why they should have been considered 'worse' than the stories that had been published for the last fifteen years. But there was a change in the zeitgeist in the 1960s that made the *The New Yorker* look for something different, for contributions of a different nature.

Bill now turned down 'Hôtel du Commerce', a variation on both 'The Voices' (about the two women in the next-door hotel room in Athens, see p 306) and 'Gravement Endommagé' (about the bickering couple in a hotel in France after the war, see p 244). It is about Melanie and Leonard honeymooning in France, with all the attendant aggravations (his thinning hair, her bad temper, mosquitoes); although 'once in bed, they had always been safe'.[56] They wake in the night to hear a couple next door quarrelling and in the morning are barely speaking themselves; then they see the warring couple emerging perfectly cheerfully from their room. Carl Brandt thought 'the tone stronger than anything she's done of late'[57] but Bill disagreed, or perhaps a strong tone was irrelevant to him. It appeared in *Cornhill* magazine in late 1965.

However, he accepted 'Tall Boy', another very sad story about loneliness. A West Indian man lives in a North Kensington bed-sitter, trying to get through a weekend. He valiantly counts his blessings. 'No one here, in England, called him "Nigger", or put up their fists to him.' They are kind to him at work. But 'he had never in his life known such isolation. Back in his own country, home had bulged with people – breadwinners or unemployed, children, the elderly helpless – there was never an empty corner or time of real silence.'[58] A story like this emphasises yet again that Elizabeth's main theme was overwhelming and frightful loneliness, the isolation of the spirit.

After 'Tall Boy' came 'The Devastating Boys', which is also about black boys in North Kensington, but these are six-year-olds. The Taylors had read about a scheme to give London children a holiday in the country and in the mid-'60s began to have two boys called Stephen and Calvin to stay on a regular basis. The short story describes this to almost documentary effect (which is perhaps why *The New Yorker* did not like it). Stephen's father was in prison for stabbing his mother and he lived with an aunt. 'Poor little boy,' wrote Elizabeth. 'How he clings to his virtues from such a background of violence, drugging, neglect, prostitution I cannot imagine. He is so decent and straightforward and with good instincts, kind and polite.' Once, when he was older, Elizabeth beat him at cards, but he simply shrugged his shoulders and smiled; when she said that she remembered that once he would have screamed in rage 'he said, "yes, so do I remember those days." We like reminiscing about his youth.' A year or two later they took him, 'rather a handful', to the pantomime at Windsor. 'He brought with him a note from his mother. "Dear Mrs Taylor, I hope you don't mind if Stephen wets his bed a little." He told me that he was going to have his adenoids out – "then I shan't act so silly."'[59] These kinds of details went into the description of six year-old Sep and Benny in the short story; it is one of Elizabeth's very best, with its accurate but uncondescending description of the two little boys and the reactions of the couple who look after them. But Bill did not want it, nor did anyone in England.

In 1966, as in 1964 and 1965, Bill again only accepted one of Elizabeth's stories and her work was mainly published in magazines like *Saturday Evening Post* and *Homes and Gardens*. By now, although her novels received respectful reviews, the comparisons with the great women writers of the twentieth century were beginning to cease; and since her stories were also being consistently rejected by *The New Yorker* Elizabeth started to feel like a hollow shell. In 1966 she wrote to Bill (who must have written an apologetic letter): 'Of course I am not discouraged with *The New Yorker*. I am discouraged with myself, but this is something I nearly always have to live with. I give myself little talks but they have no effect.'

Bill had apparently sent her several letters. The only one which survives deplores Elizabeth's 'turning away from England in favour of foreign places' and her 'sticking in the company of middle class people when in the past you were found in the company of people far above or else considerably below them in the social scale. Preferably below . . . I see them, the characters only you can deal with properly – the not-respectable, ungroupable, raffish, incorrigible – hanging around outside your house on this marvellous spring day, waiting for you to come out and deal with them, since nobody else can.'[60] She told Bill that she valued his letter very much but he was wrong about 'that crowd of people waiting outside the door. I keep looking, but there is no one there. It is like living in outer space. The more I fret, the worse it is. So write what you will, Bill dear, & I will think about it deeply, but never mention it, for I might drop down dead.' She ended by saying, 'I should be so bad at expressing what I feel about your letters that I shan't try. Change "Charlotte" to "Bill" and it is like the last two sentences of *Charlotte's Web*.'[61] This was the classic children's novel by EB White, Katharine White's husband, which ends, 'It is not often that someone comes along who is a true friend and a good writer. Charlotte was both.'[62] It was one of her favourite books, which she would read aloud to her grandchildren and the devastating boys when they came to stay.

Yet it is true that in some ways Elizabeth was running out of inspiration in the Thames Valley. She refused to draw on material that might have been recognisable, thus wouldn't write about Gerry Ercolani or Veronica Papworth (Walley), 'the career woman' as she called her in her letters to Robert – she worked on the *Sunday Express* – or even Roderigo Moynihan, whom she had particularly regretted not being able to describe when he was drawing her, telling Bill: 'I should like to write the story of the man who is painting a portrait of me, but never shall be able to. To trust oneself as a novelist is making a double demand.'[63] So if she did not write about Greece or Morocco or France, and if not that much happened to her in England and she refused to write about her friends, acquaintances, family or herself more overtly than she had already done – what should she write about?

As distraction, and because, as she once alleged to an interviewer, she felt 'happier and more at ease in writing about children than about anything else',[64] she now wrote *Mossy Trotter*, a novel for children about an eight-year-old boy who is Oliver in *At Mrs Lippincote's* in yet another guise – articulate, independent, liable to get into scrapes, full of life in a way that the adults are not. The plot, such as it is, contrasts Miss Silkin, who is conventional, annoying and obsessed with formality, with Mossy's unfettered interest in the rubbish dump and his grandfather's sports car and everything happening in the garden. His mother is all too human and would have appealed to women reading the story aloud:

> Like many mothers, Mossy's was rather changeable. He could not always be sure where he stood with her. Although she tried very hard never to break promises, she broke threats, which in a way are a kind of black promise. She would send Mossy to his bedroom for having misbehaved and then, in a minute or two, tell him he could come down; or he would be told that if he were naughty, he could not have chocolate cake for tea and be given it for supper instead. It was a shocking way to bring up children, he once heard his father say.[65]

Mossy's mother has a baby, he gets into trouble at school, Miss Silkin marries. The joy of the book is Elizabeth's understanding of Mossy's nature and behaviour – and her insight into the love that a small boy can feel for another child. In a quite unsentimental way she makes it plain that he loves a small girl called Alison and has feelings that are usually attributed to much older children: he thinks she is pretty, feels protective and tender towards her and wishes he could see her again. The ending, where Mossy's mother says briskly that they would not see Alison until the summer and he realises that that is months and months away but tries to look forward to it cheerfully, is unusual for a children's book; it is reminiscent of the love Vesey and Harriet feel for each other in *A Game of Hide and Seek*.

Elizabeth's next short story was 'The Excursion to the Source', which is about Gwenda and Polly in France; Polly falls in love with a local boy but is then killed by stretching over a cliff to pick some flowers. There is something Forsterian about this story, in the unexpected love between Polly and her Jean, and her shockingly sudden death which leaves him distraught but Gwenda 'stunned, rather than grief-stricken.' Alas, Bill thought 'the story contrived and the people not very interesting'[66] and it was not published for five years, when it came out in *Penguin Modern Short Stories* 6. 'Crêpes Flambées' (the story set in Tunisia) was also rejected, as was 'Praises', about a leaving party for Miss Smythe who has spent her life selling 'gowns' in a department store; but the contrast between the busy working life and lonely retirement, encapsulated by the last day at work and the farewell party, had been described by others and Bill turned the story down. It appeared in *Homes and Gardens* in 1969.

He also turned down 'In and Out the Houses'[67] (see pp 177–8) and 'The Fly-Paper'. This last has become one of Elizabeth's best-known stories and was based on the arrest of Ian Brady and Myra Hindley, the 'Moors Murderers', at the end of 1965, as well as on her memories of the Taylors' gardener's daughter being murdered by soldiers during the war. A girl travels on a bus on her own and is abducted. 'I've still got to get home, Sylvia thought in a panic. She stared up at a fly-paper hanging in the window – the only disconcerting thing in the room. Some of the flies were still half alive, and striving hopelessly to free themselves. But they were caught forever.'[68] The story is unbelievably chilling – too chilling for Bill, who wanted to change the last sentence, the one that makes it plain that the couple who had enticed the girl to their house had planned to ensnare someone all along. Elizabeth refused to rewrite it and must have felt a little vindicated a few years later when Paul Theroux wrote in *Encounter*: 'She ends "The Fly-Paper", one of the most horrifying stories I have ever read, just seconds before a girl who has been abducted begins to scream.'[69] (Even her English publisher, Norah Smallwood, accepted that 'I may have missed the point, but I'm not quite sure whether it is all a dream on the part of the child or a story of procrastination, or what'[70] – thus betraying an almost unbelievable innocence. Patiently Elizabeth told her that she meant the story to be gruesome.)*

---

* 'The Fly-Paper' also refers back to Chapter 20 of *At Mrs Lippincote's* (pp172–3) when Julia is visited by Mr Maffick, a curate. 'She was swatting flies, one hand to her breast, the folded telephone directory in the other . . . "Isn't it awful, this stroking movement flies do with their front legs?" . . . "What about fly-papers?" "No, they're so cruel. Imagine it! Striving to free oneself until the legs leave the sockets. This way is bad enough. Contemplating brutality makes you used to it. It's a way of saving our reason – of putting armour over one's nerves. If I really imagined what I'm doing now, I couldn't do it . . . This morning I read in the paper about something vile the Nazis did and I thought: "It's all right. It's not as bad as the atrocity I read about last week." I was very much shocked at myself.' This scene

Between 1966 and 1967 Elizabeth was working, rather painfully, on *The Wedding Group*, which was roughly based on the ménage at Pigotts; it was partly prompted by Robert Speaight's biography of Eric Gill which she was sent at the beginning of 1966. In the novel she imagines what might have happened if one of the daughters had escaped by getting a job in the village and then marrying. The daughter, Cressy, is a rather thin character, and although a child of the '60s she is not as convincing as Araminta in *In a Summer Season*. The most interesting, but most melancholy, character is her future mother-in-law Midge, another in Elizabeth's gallery of appallingly lonely women who have nothing to do all day.

The Wedding Group is also, alas, renewed evidence that Elizabeth did so much of her research in this period in the pubs of commuterland, as Robert had observed so memorably – there are in fact too many pubs and the reader feels, by the end, that the only life she ever saw was at The Crown. There are excellent things in this novel, but perhaps there are not enough of them. As the writer Janice Elliott observed, 'one of Mrs Taylor's greatest skills has always been in taking a lending-library situation and transcending it. This time I am not sure that she has pulled it off.' What she regretted were 'startling and precise illuminations';[71] and it is true, a vital spark is somehow missing.

would have been written in c. September 1944, by which time the world was beginning to realise what was happening to the Jews. See also p 156.

On the other hand Brigid Brophy much admired Elizabeth's 'moral cattiness' here 'deepening into irony': 'What is explicitly exposed is a vision, implicit perhaps in all her novels, of the bleakness of life itself.' She praised one of her 'most perfect moral balancing acts', the portrait of Midge and her son, and suggested that 'the design of *The Wedding Group* is the most deeply ambitious and thoughtful Mrs Taylor has attempted.'[72] Angus Wilson suggested that although Elizabeth was unmistakably a major novelist, 'yet none of her novels, I think, can be judged completely worthy of all that she offers over and over again in particular chapters, particular pages, particular confrontations of characters, particular stories.'[73] However, he was convinced that it was only a matter of time before she produced a masterpiece – although was at a loss to suggest in which direction she should travel.

Finally Paul Scott, while praising the skill and wit of a sentence such as 'At Quayne, that Saturday evening, after beans and bacon, there were stewed windfalls, and a reading from DH Lawrence', wished that Elizabeth would 'come out of her corner and mix a bit'. He suggested that 'only her fastidiousness – difficult, in fiction, to distinguish from timidity – stands in the way of her challenging, say, Spark and Murdoch at their own glittering games.'[74] And he was right.

CHAPTER THIRTEEN

GROVE'S BARN 1969–75

Death does not always give us a chance of tidying up.[1]

John and Elizabeth had a late holiday in 1968, in Malta, and on the way back went to Menton so that Elizabeth could present the Katherine Mansfield Prize to Sylvia Townsend Warner. We can imagine her mixed feelings about this: she and Ray had long ago agreed that they disliked Katherine Mansfield's work because of her whinging, and by now she had come to represent something one rather grows out of (in the 1958 'Summer Schools' Ursula realises she no longer has anything in common with her schoolfriend Pamela; 'finding Katherine Mansfield's *Journal* covered with dust, [she] felt estranged'[2]).

Then in 1969 Elizabeth's father had a stroke and came to stay at Grove's Barn. He had been a widower for seven years, having married (in 1939) a local Naphill woman named Evelyn, a cashier in a butcher's who sat in a little wooden kiosk, discreetly screened from blood and sawdust, where customers presented their money before receiving their wrapped-up meat. The second Mrs Coles had a daughter, Joyce, by her first marriage whom Elizabeth saw occasionally, about as often as she saw John's three sisters Millie, May and

Phyllis, which was infrequently; but in 1962 Evelyn died, suddenly, getting off a bus in Reading where she and Oliver had lived from the 1950s onwards (in a house backing onto the Huntley and Palmer sports ground, since Oliver was besotted by football and also played the clarinet in the Huntley and Palmer band). Now, after spending the summer and autumn with John and Elizabeth, Oliver moved in to the Easton, a home for the elderly near Oxford; here Elizabeth went regularly to see him.

In the same year Ivy died. Robert was one of her six residuary legatees; ten of her friends (mostly writers such as Lettice Cooper, James Lees-Milne, Kay Dick, Francis King and Olivia Manning) received mirrors which had belonged to Margaret Jourdain. Elizabeth did not, which led Robert to surmise that because she was the best-looking of all Ivy's friends she did not need one.

Ivy's last months and Oliver's life in the Easton (as well as some research afternoons at the Royal Court Hotel in Sloane Square) were the direct inspiration for *Mrs Palfrey at the Claremont*, which would become one of Elizabeth's best-known novels, and has recently been made into a film.* Another inspiration was a short story by the novelist Dorothy Whipple, whose novels Elizabeth did not own but which she must have borrowed from the library. (Ivy did the same, borrowing her books from Harrods Lending Library: a friend of hers has described her keeping one pile of books on public display and one hidden; the Whipple novels, of which she was especially

---

* It was shown in America in 2006 and is now available on DVD.

fond, would be on the latter pile.) It is not known where Dorothy Whipple's short story was published, but Elizabeth must have read it because it begins: 'It was astonishing to find anyone so obviously well-off as Mrs Wilmot at the Claremont, one of the modest private hotels in which London abounds. The residents were mostly retired Army officers and their wives, widows, elderly bachelors and spinsters with small incomes.'[3]

In terms of literature *Mrs Palfrey* is worlds away from, say, *A Game of Hide and Seek*. Yet more people have read this, Elizabeth's penultimate novel to be published, than any of her other books, partly because it was the only one of her books to be shortlisted for a prize in her lifetime. It is another study in excruciating loneliness. Mrs Palfrey is a widow, with a daughter who is uninterested in her and a grandson who also never finds the time to come and see her. Elizabeth memorably describes her thus: 'She would have made a distinguished-looking man and, sometimes, wearing evening dress, looked like some famous general in drag.'[4]* This is a compliment in a sense, because Mrs Palfrey had known how to behave as well as any man; in Burma and the other far-off countries to which her husband's job had taken her she was 'brave and staunch'; she was in fact how Mrs Turton and

---

* Originally the sentence read 'like Lord Louis Mountbatten in drag' but Norah Smallwood at Chatto & Windus asked for this to be changed – 'I didn't know about the gossip (we live very quietly)' Elizabeth told her (ET to Norah Smallwood 28 December 1970 Chatto & Windus files, Reading).

Mrs Burton might have been if they had behaved well in India. She is one of only a few female characters (others are Julia, Cassandra and Harriet) whom Elizabeth likes, indeed loves; she may have thought that, one day, Mrs Palfrey *c'est moi*. After all, they looked alike. Once, Bill had asked her 'who is the lady that sits for you when the publisher asks for photographs?' (he was referring to the photograph on p 259) and Elizabeth had replied that she was the wife of Brigadier-General Pomeroy-Thomas (rtd); now she was Mrs Palfrey.

It is because of seeing an advertisement that she comes to the hotel in the Cromwell Road and here settles down to get through the rest of her life. One afternoon, she falls over and is rescued by Ludo, an out-of-work actor who spends his days writing his novel in Harrods Banking Hall (because it is warm, comfortable and free). The relationship between the two of them is touchingly described, and Mrs Palfrey pretends to the other guests at the Claremont that Ludo is her grandson, the one who fails to make the effort to come and see her. At the end she breaks her hip and dies in hospital, her life having been made a little happier by the thought that Ludo had been fond of her.

Mrs Palfrey is 'in many ways the saddest book I have ever read'[5] said Herman Schrijver, echoing the famous opening sentence of Ford Madox Ford's *The Good Soldier*, 'This is the saddest story I have ever heard.' It is, as well, a very funny novel, but also, at times, a cruel one, the only one of Elizabeth's books which strays over the borderline between compassionate observation and almost vicious satire. But it is not Mrs Palfrey who is the object of Elizabeth's critical, painfully objective gaze, rather the other guests at the hotel; for, as Paul Bailey has written about the book, Elizabeth's peculiar gift 'is for noticing the casual cruelty that people use to protect themselves from the not always casual cruelty of others. Her ear for insult is, every so often, on a par with Jane Austen's.'[6] While Elizabeth Bowen thought that she had written a book about grandeur: 'I cannot tell you how much I love and honour it.'

> I think and hope you must realise what you have done. The *surface* lightness, the enchanting scenes of pure comedy . . . makes the deeper-down content all the more telling. The survival of indignity by sheer force of a real dignity seems to me one of the greatest themes one could have . . . One thing, Elizabeth, you did convey in a way which rang an inevitable bell in me: the absolute desolation, the maimed, the amputated feeling of widowhood . . . That you should have perceived through to the core of this is a case of the genius which I do know you have.

And she added that as a work of art *Mrs Palfrey* was flawless, 'luminous from the inside – as your novels are.'[7]

After *Mrs Palfrey* had been published (in its beautiful jacket by the painter Adrian Daintry) Elizabeth met Paul Bailey, an ex-actor who had become a novelist, at a party, one of the rare literary parties she went to, and told him that when his first novel came out in 1967 she had read in a newspaper that he worked at Harrods and had gone up to the magazine department on the fifth floor to take a look at him; she would also have sat for a while in the Banking Hall in which the 'old and frail . . . could snooze for uninterrupted hours,' as Paul Bailey would write, adding that his 'fondest memory of Harrods is of that row of occupied armchairs and its dozing inhabitants, dreaming of more comfortable days maybe.'[8] The dozing old people, all of whom had seen better days or they would not have been there, were one of the inspirations for *Mrs Palfrey*; and Ludo also 'works' at Harrods and, like Paul Bailey, is an ex-actor.

'Sisters', about the woman who is interviewed about her writer sister (see pp xi–xii), was accepted by Bill and appeared in *The New Yorker* in 1969, the last of Elizabeth's stories ever to be published there. Robert would claim that it was about Katherine Mansfield, but Elizabeth told Bill, 'I heard someone say at a lunch party that she had a sister surviving in Knightsbridge, & I fell to musing about her.'[9] However, the same year Bill rejected 'Flesh', and wrote to Carl Brandt to say that 'she had done both characters well, but the story is, alas, familiar.'[10] It is set on Gozo, in a hotel at which the Taylors had stayed (Patience Ross suggested that, to avoid recognition, Elizabeth should be unspecific about the island's real name). 'Flesh' is a gem, Paul Bailey would write, in which Phyl, 'a publican's blowsy wife, who has recently had a hysterectomy, has an enchanted meeting with the newly bereaved Stanley in one of those ghastly Mediterranean seaside resorts from which the natives are wisely absent';[11] and he admired the story for maintaining a balance between the hilarious (their 'wicked adventure' is spoilt by her sunburn and his gout) and the poignant (in another life they would have made a good couple).

It was not only the Colonels who stopped Elizabeth's solitary expeditions to Greece and sent her instead to Cyprus (the 'poor-man's Greece' as she called it) and to Malta, it was John's now full-time retirement; the only time she went away without him was in 1969, when he took his father on a cruise and she decided to go to the Old Ship Hotel in Brighton. She wanted to visit the ex-landlord and landlady of The Crown, who had retired there, and to be on her own to plan *Mrs Palfrey*.* Then, in the early spring of 1970, the Taylors travelled to America, for the first and only time, in order to go to the headquarters of the Famous Writers School at Westport, Connecticut. The justification was that Elizabeth was worried about money because the *New Yorker* cheques were no longer arriving and Oliver was by now in an expensive nursing home; and having agreed to 'become one of the beaks', as the novelist Richard Gordon put it, she had to promise to go to Westport at least once.

All that was involved, apart from an enormous fee, (allegedly £4000 a year, £45,000 nowadays) was lending her name to the Guiding Council, writing one or two short pieces for the instruction manuals,** and spending one afternoon a

---

* Here she mourned *Mrs Dale's Diary*, the last episode of which she missed by being there. 'I feel lost without the Dales . . . No one here seems to care about them,' she wrote to Joanna.

** The first volume was typeset by the Anchor Press, Tiptree, Essex in 1971 as *The International Writers Course – Principles of Good Writing*. It was never published.

month at Brown's Hotel with the other English writers, who included Nigel Balchin, Christianna Brand and Frank Muir. Here they 'got along famously', which was not just Richard Gordon's view: everyone remembered having an extremely merry time round a huge drinks trolley courtesy of the 65,000 Americans currently enrolled at the FWS (annual turnover $48 million, a result of the extraordinary ratio of 800 salesmen to a mere 55 members of the 'teaching faculty'). But the British version of the Famous Writers School was stillborn: that summer Jessica Mitford published a long, debunking article, saying, as Richard Gordon would write in his memoirs, that the American FWS

> existed only on high-pressure advertising and salesmanship, the Famous Writers never read the homework, the drop-outs were 90 per cent, there were no refunds, and the senile and illiterate were pressurised to sign up for a new career as novelists. We felt Miss Mitford was likely to be right.[12]

Elizabeth's agent managed to place the two pieces she had written elsewhere; the worst effect of the whole *débâcle* must have been on her relationship with Bill. She told him she was coming to America on a 'ploy'; when he learnt what this was, he was surely appalled and embarrassed at Elizabeth's naïvety at having anything to do with an organisation notorious in American literary circles for peddling wares not much better than those sold by vacuum-cleaner or encyclopedia salesmen. To mention *The New Yorker* and the FWS in the same breath would have been bad enough; for Elizabeth to consider that she could embody the values of both of them was something that even the saintly Bill would not have been able to comprehend.

But something unexpected happened the following year. In October *Mrs Palfrey* was shortlisted for the Booker Prize. There were fewer prizes then of course, but it still seems astonishing that apart from going into *Who's Who* in 1952 and being elected a Fellow of the Royal Society of Literature in 1966, Elizabeth was given no kind of public recognition. She would not have wanted to be a Dame like Ivy; and she would have said prizes were irrelevant compared with the private joys of writing and family; but her admirers would have liked it, then and now.

The other novelists shortlisted were Derek Robinson, Thomas Kilroy, Mordecai Richler, VS Naipaul and Doris Lessing, and the judges were John Gross, Lady Antonia Fraser, Saul Bellow, John Fowles and Philip Toynbee who, *The Times* told its readers, 'ploughed through' forty-two entries for the prize and passed over 'such established writers as Iris Murdoch, Muriel Spark, BS Johnson and Kingsley Amis.'[13] The chairman of the judges was John Gross and the largest part of the budget for the prize was spent on bringing Saul Bellow over from the States. From the start he behaved rather overbearingly (the other judges had to hear about his irritation that his room at the Ritz did not overlook the park) and he began the first meeting by saying about *Mrs Palfrey*, 'I seem to hear the tinkle of tea-cups'.[14] That settled it. The others knew, according to John Gross, that to persuade

Bellow into a different frame of mind, to choose a delicate, funny, Forsterian, English novel rather than a large-themed, serious, international one, as Naipaul's was, would have taken more energy than they collectively possessed. There was also a general perception that the lukewarm review in the *Times Literary Supplement* (anonymous at the time but in fact by Marigold Johnson) cost Elizabeth the Booker: although 'she has never been better at her gently caricatured domestic details of middle-class domesticity, yet this is somehow a thinner and less satisfying novel than Miss Taylor's best. Slight as it is, there are several repetitious and extraneous scenes . . . '[15]

Elizabeth had expected the prize would go to Naipaul (for *In a Free State*) and this was confirmed just before the prize-giving dinner when 'John, in the john, having a leak, heard it leaked out that Naipaul had won.'[16] It was at the dinner that the poet Anthony Thwaite 'told Elizabeth that she was in his opinion the most underrated and least well-known good novelist and she said that so many people said that in print so often she must surely now be the most celebrated and well-known "least well-known novelist" in the business.'[17]

Inescapably, the Chatto publicity department asked Elizabeth to go through the ordeal of being interviewed. She approached it in her usual manner, telling the interviewer that 'there is not very much to know about me. I have had a rather uneventful life, thank God', that she rarely finished her weekly book from Harrods lending library (a surprising detail as one would not imagine her ever going there except to look at Paul Bailey) and that 'a dreadful thing happened to me about two years ago. [*The New Yorker*] sent back [a story]. I nearly died. It has never happened before.' Bill had not published anything of hers for two years – what can Elizabeth in fact have said about this still bleeding wound? The interviewer probably made this up after Elizabeth told the truth about the lenght of time since they had published anything by her. Perhaps he found it unbelievable.

Almost like a mantra she had told the Booker interviewer that 'her family were very important to her and she did not know what she would do without them.'[18] And it is true that by now she would have been unable to contemplate being George Eliot or Virginia Woolf or Elizabeth Bowen or Barbara Pym and *not* having children and grandchildren. She loved them all deeply, although found it very tiring when she was turned to all the time for advice or was 'lumbered & cumbered with grandchildren'.[19] Never again was there to be the solitude of the wartime years or the days when John was at work and the children at school; with him at home all the time and both the children living close by, with her wanting to be involved in her grandchildren's lives, she never had the solitude a writer has to have.

Her family would not have sensed this craving. They were deeply proud of her but in a rather joshing way, teasing her for being the great novelist in their midst but never actually treating her as a great novelist. This is how she wanted it, presumably, because it is difficult to be private about something and for that something to be treated with awe. But by now, after years and years with no one to talk to about contemporary literature or 'prose' or the zeitgeist, Elizabeth's work was suffering. No different from Jane Austen, she might have retorted. But there *was* a difference: Jane Austen observed her neighbours and wrote about them; Elizabeth, a child of the twentieth century with its easy communications, opaqueness, laws of libel, could not do so. She was forced to opt for reconciliation (and see p 269).

She wrote two short stories in 1971, 'Miss A and Miss M', about the two schoolteachers at the guest house and the death 'by her own hand' of one of them after her companion marries (see pp 32–4), and 'The Blossoming', about Miss Partridge who has been chained to her mother all her life and is bewildered when she dies. Through the kindness of her solicitor, who takes the trouble to bring her a book of wall-paper patterns, she decides to employ two decorators and is tremendously happy bringing them cups of tea and admiring the new wallpapers. At last she realises she is not in fact poor – as she puts a knob of coal on the fire, then another and another. And she has a happy vision of two men in the garden – 'gum-booted, rain-coated, clumping about, measuring, digging, planting, sitting on the old seat drinking pale tea, eating hot scones.'[20] The ending is ambivalent: we can read it as bleak, with Miss Partridge choosing to ease her loneliness by employing workmen and gardeners and simply ministering to men, or we can applaud her cheerful spending of her inheritance.

In the New Year of 1972 Elizabeth wrote 'The Wrong Order'. It is about someone with a terminal illness and, by implication, is about how *not* to behave. At the beginning

Hilda, admiring the white lilac, murmurs, "'I'm so glad it's been good *this* year'".

Oh, God! Her friend, Tom, thought, she is going to say 'As it's my last'.

He got up and went into the kitchen, so that he should not hear her saying it. She insisted on talking about her death, referred to it constantly and casually, as if it were some familiar pet of hers, running always at her heels, like Charlie, her Bedlington terrier.*

How much better, Elizabeth is saying, if 'that damn doctor' had not given Hilda the fatal news; and how much better a death is her husband's when he dies suddenly 'on the first green' than Hilda saying 'softly, as if to herself, "It's not my fault I don't die"' or '"I may be outstaying my welcome."'[21] If fate would not allow Elizabeth to die in an instant on the golf course, at least she would not make remarks that are a shriek for reassurance, help no one except the dying (if they do help), and make the living cringe. (Bill turned the story down.)

The devastating boys came to stay ('almost grown-up now, and so altered'[22]) as did Elizabeth Bowen, for what would turn out to be the last time; she proof-read all eleven stories

---

* The Taylors had a Bedlington terrier called Charlie whom they bought in 1969; after they had been burgled five times the police told them they had to have a dog. They had always had cats and usually a dog; once they had a boxer.

in *The Devastating Boys*. It was published in May to, as ever, mixed reviews: Joyce Carol Oates found 'a distressing similarity' between the stories and thought the people merely 'lightweight, well-meaning, silly, harmless characters'[23] and the *New York Times* thought that 'Taylor is a pastel stylist, a celebrant of delicately-drawn losers'.[24] Finally there was the *Times Literary Supplement*. The reviewer had reservations about Elizabeth's range as a novelist – 'there is an assumption of English middle-class habits, preoccupations and woes which . . . excludes perhaps too much of modern experience to give her broader canvases the significance she herself might intend' – but thought she 'must surely now be among the four or five most distinguished living practitioners of the art of the short story in the English-speaking world.'[25] This was the last review of her work she would ever receive.

Meanwhile, Oliver died, not of another stroke but of a slowly-creeping cancer. Elizabeth could not have been kinder to him, though she knew she could only give him what was in her to give and not what he wanted ('I write to Oliver each day, & can imagine him thinking, "Oh not *another* letter. They're not at all useful or handy, & I can't be bothered to open them"'[26]). After the funeral the whole family went to Brittany, but 'it poured with rain, & to dry the little children's clothes seemed to become the great object of one's existence.'[27] Here, in France, we can assume, Elizabeth decided that on her return she must go to the doctor again. There was a lump in her breast (and a hint in one of Robert Liddell's letters to Barbara Pym that she had been worried for a while, 'she ought to have had the operation four years ago'[28] he

wrote). It was cancer. In July, at St Joseph's in Beaconsfield, a hospital run by Irish nuns, she had a breast removed.

Elizabeth, who had never been in hospital before except to have a baby, was very happy at 'St Jo's' due to the affectionate care she received and the optimistic prognosis. They were 'some of the happiest days of my life'[29] she told Francis King, and wrote to another friend, Janet Fitzgerald, that 'I didn't go to boarding school, & always wanted to, & I felt that at last I had got the sort of institution I had long needed',[30] as she lay in bed surrounded by flowers which 'keep arriving, as if I were the other Liz Taylor. I said to [the doctor] this morning, "Suppose this had happened to my famous namesake." He said, "Well, that would have been a day's work, I'd think."'[31] Her 'world dwindled deliciously, & everything became poignant, or delicious, or greatly funny. What *are* dockers? How much does rumpsteak cost? Ask someone else, for I don't know.'[32]

She very much liked the solitude and, treating St Jo's a bit like a writers' retreat or a women's college, was able to write a short story which Patience sold to *McCall's* in America; it was rather satisfactory, Elizabeth felt, that while she was in hospital she was able to earn £1000 (£10,000 in today's terms). The story was 'Madame Olga' and was about a man named Ronald Ives whose mother has just died; he returns to the sea-side resort, gloomily out of season, where they used to go on holiday, to thank the clairvoyant he once consulted because 'she had protected him from great areas of depression, as when he had thought someone else – young Tarrystone, for instance – would get the branch managership, be promoted over his head.' Madame Olga had predicted he would travel abroad, have a health problem, be promoted, and come into a fortune. All had happened: he had gone on a day trip to France, had had a kidney stone, was now the manager of a grocer's shop – and won £75,000 on the football pools. The story is gentle, melancholy, touching, and ends on a happy note: he asks 'Madame Olga' to have dinner with him.*

What is curious is that Elizabeth would leave £74,800 to John. Once, in the 1930s, she had had her palm read, and was perhaps remembering this incident, and anticipating John's future for, in the story's very first sentence, she says about Ronald, 'To travel first class did not – would not for many years – occur to him.'[33] It would not occur to John who, even with Elizabeth's fortune, was always frugal. Was she wishing she had been better at spending her money? She may have bought good clothes (hats at the same shop as her namesake), sent the children to expensive schools, travelled abroad, placed bets on horses, bought pictures by Elinor Bellingham Smith; but she still had *so much money left*, the kind of amount unimaginable to Oliver and Elsie.

After Elizabeth emerged from St Joseph's, from the little world where she had been so unexpectedly happy ('when I kissed Sister Gertrude goodbye, I had to make a dash for it, with tears running down my face'[34]), she continued with her usual routine of family life, holidays abroad, seeing

---

* Among the Taylor Papers at Tulsa is a script for a play of 'Madame Olga'. It is not clear who wrote this but it has corrections in Elizabeth's handwriting so she must have approved it.

friends and going to The Crown. 'Madame Olga' would be the last story that she completed, and her last published story, however at some point that year she wrote twenty pages of 'The Ghost Story'. This again uses the character of Ludo in *Mrs Palfrey* and begins 'On his way into Derbyshire by train, Ludovic Dymott-Myers tried to do a little work; but his eyes kept straying to the window, & his thoughts towards his destination.'[35] He is met by car at the station and taken to a large house where an elderly rich widow says that she wants him to dress up as a ghost for some visiting Americans; the title is a pun because Ludo assumes he is to be employed as a ghost writer. There are twenty pages of this manuscript, and, three pages before the end, are the words 'Chapter Two'.

A few weeks after the operation Elizabeth and John went on an Italian cruise-liner. Even though, on the way back, the boat stopped at Crete and they saw Robert, it was 'too soon. I kept bursting into tears all over the Mediterranean (every little helps).' But 'there were lovely wild flowers. I smuggled some roots back in my false bra. I always like to turn a mishap into an advantage where possible.'[36] Then, early the following year, a trip to Morocco was marred by the news, just before they left, of the death of Elizabeth Bowen. Elizabeth had been to see her in hospital – she had lung cancer – and her last words were, '"Remember, I love you very much." It was typical of her generosity to send me on my way like that, with a wonderful present to keep for my life-time. But I felt it was a kind of dismissal, too. I didn't see her again.' Thus Elizabeth ended the (unpublished) memoir of Elizabeth Bowen she wrote later that year.[37]

That autumn they handed over a tin of Lyle's Golden Syrup to Robert at Piraeus: they were on a cruise from Genoa to Istanbul and it was the one thing he asked for from England (he wanted to make a syrup sponge). A passenger had died at Istanbul and it is with a death that Elizabeth's new novel, *Blaming*, begins, with Amy's husband Nick, who was a painter, dying on a boat at Istanbul. Amy is helped, both practically and emotionally, by Martha. But once back in England at her comfortable house (based on Zoffany House, on the river at Strand-on-the-Green, which belonged to friends of Elizabeth's, the painter Edna Box and her husband Marston Fleming), Amy fails to be as helpful and considerate to Martha as Martha had been to her in Istanbul.

Elizabeth knew that *Blaming* would be her last novel; thus in some respects it is a coda to her previous books, echoing some of their themes such as death, the art of painting, the loyalty that should exist between friends, egoism, the nearly-old contrasted with the very young, above all the theme of recrimination and remorse, or the lack of it. Deftly she describes Amy suggesting her gravestone should say, 'she meant well'. "But I'm afraid I haven't always'" she adds. There are also sparklingly perceptive observations about other aspects of English middle-class life; for example, Amy is amazed by her son and daughter-in-law's friends because the women have jobs and children and 'also put in hours at family-planning clinics, sat on benches, fought pollution, visited prisons or were marriage-guidance counsellors.' Elizabeth had done none of these things and throughout *Blaming*, one fears, she is censuring herself, as well as Amy, for her selfishness, her inertia, the way she had, she felt, let Maud down; in fact, in most respects she is quite unlike her last heroine.

Then there are echoes of *A Wreath of Roses*, the novel of Elizabeth's in which she made her most heartfelt statements about the art of painting and of writing – Nick's last, unfinished painting is of some old-fashioned white roses against a dark background. And one of the most brilliant elements of the book is the description of Amy's two granddaughters Isobel and Dora. The scene when their mother tells them that Nick has died is a great comic scene, made extra poignant because Elizabeth knew she was dying when she wrote it.

> 'Not everyone goes to heaven,' Dora, who was older said. 'Egyptian mummies didn't go. Or stuffed fishes.'
> 'No, fishes never go,' Isobel agreed. 'Sometimes I eat them. Chickens can't go, nor.'
> 'I don't really know about heaven,' Dora said in her considering way. 'We haven't done that at school yet. But I know they must go somewhere, or we'd be too full up here. People coming and going all the time.'
> 'Being born,' said Isobel.
> 'Well, I'm afraid that you won't see Grandpa again,' Maggie said, thinking that her message was being lost in vague conjecture.[38]

In the autumn of the year, 1973, when Elizabeth began to write *Blaming, Mrs Palfrey at the Claremont* was on television as *Play for Today* with Celia Johnson playing Mrs Palfrey. It was the second time Elizabeth had seen her own work adapted for television (the first had been in November 1969 when *Hester Lilly* was adapted) and although she was pleased and proud, she thought Celia Johnson badly miscast because she was 'quite glamorous & elegant. Obviously not only would her grandson have been on her doorstep all the time, but half the British Museum people with him . . . I had hoped Lord Mountbatten would take the part.'[39]

Then, in the spring of 1974, she and John went with Joanna and the children to a cottage near Ribérac. When they got back to England they found that Renny's wife had left him and gone to live with someone else in Devon, taking the little girls with her. Elizabeth despaired. Not only did she feel desperate for her beloved son, who had lost his wife and his daughters, she could not contemplate that what she had refused to do thirty years before was happening to her family in the next generation. She may have had the moral high ground but this was a private emotion and was trivial compared with the anger she felt with her daughter-in-law.

Later that summer she wrote the beginning of what was apparently to be another children's novel like *Mossy Trotter*. Called 'How Do You Spell Wednesday?',[40] it is about three children whose mother has died, and evokes, very sadly, their life without her; as is evident from one or two notes Elizabeth left, there will be a stepmother in the future, not very happily. She also wrote at this time, commissioned by the editor of a children's anthology called *Allsorts*, a story, illustrated by Shirley Hughes, with the title 'Your Tea Is All About You', which describes three London children staying with their writer aunt in the country and going for a walk on their own. (At the back, the note on the authors says: 'Elizabeth Taylor writes extremely good novels for grown-ups . . . It is a pity that she has the same name as a film star.'[41])

She also wrote another children's story, called 'The Garden's on Fire'; the beginning of a short story about a man revisiting a house, rather like the house at Naphill, where he had lived as a child; and 'The Etiquette of Modern Society', a piece about a book of the same name Elizabeth had found in a second-hand bookshop: to her the word etiquette 'implies something superficial, trivial, meaningless, an unnecessary curlicue to good manners,' whereas to the anonymous author 'etiquette means Life itself – Birth and Death, the Broken Heart, Religion and Morality.' Throughout the book 'he tells us quite simply to be cheerful . . . We should also have Candour, but not too much.'[42]

At this time, in the last two years of her life, something at once cheerful and sad happened to Elizabeth, cheerful because a new friendship brought her tremendous joy, sad because it had not happened earlier. In 1957 Kingsley Amis had reviewed *Angel* most appreciatively and had written Elizabeth a letter; he and his wife, Elizabeth Jane Howard, met the Taylors once or twice over the years, and Jane had interviewed her on television in 1961, but it was not until the last months of Elizabeth's life that they became close friends. 'I do wish we were *very old* friends,'[43] Jane wrote wistfully in April and Elizabeth responded, 'I, too, wish we were *old friends* – before I was sixty & the aches & pains set in, and was in the Prime of Mrs John Taylor.'[44] Jane had a corduroy coat made for Elizabeth and dedicated her latest book, *Mr Wrong*, to her. At the end of July Elizabeth told Patience, 'I am trying to get over a long and boozy day with the Amises, of whom I am very fond. They came to lunch until about 7.30. I know *one* writer who does not drink a great deal, & *have* known two. Ivy was the second.' Then she added an asterisk after '7.30' and wrote, *'Burn at once'*[45] (it was in this letter that she told Patience about the bundles of correspondence in the Bodleian saying 'Burn immediately').

Blaming was finished in May 1975. 'It's called A Fairly Happy Ending. I am trying to type it myself, to save money, & revise for the third time as I go along.' (Other possible titles were Why Did I Do It? and Foreign and Familiar Places.) 'The title is tricky,' Elizabeth said to Patience. 'I want to imply blaming others & the blaming of oneself . . . I can't quite see why, after all these years, Henry Green has the monopoly of all titles ending in 'ing' . . . *Can* I call it Blaming? It really is what it is all about. People blaming others, & themselves.'

Letters to Patience Ross, 1975:

January: 'I am rather living not much in the future at present . . . I have been unwell for about two months – loss of voice. They have found a lump in my throat through x-rays, & the specialist thinks it could be cancer, & to do with my other operation . . . I simply live from day to day, & at present feel OK.'

February: 'I saw the specialist this morning, & he says it is cancer – or, rather, he said, "we have to assume a connection with your other operation". But the last set of x-rays showed a slight shrinkage, so I keep on with cortisone-&-something treatment, & my *morale*. (People always say gin is depressing. I never find it so. I just feel it's rather sordid.)'

March: 'I feel much the same. The steroids I have for treatment make my legs shaky, & upset my balance. Also puff out my face like a balloon. But apart from the continued lack of voice, I feel "all right in myself".'

May: 'It is so nice for me since John retired – not much money, of course – but able to be together . . . J even took me to London to a matinée of *A Family and a Fortune* . . . but perhaps I shan't try London again.'

June: 'Having to be x-rayed for what my doctor calls my "ropey old spine". I can only hobble about, so shan't be climbing the lower slopes of the Vosges. "Probably nothing at all to do with your other trouble" he added. I had never supposed it was."

July: 'Now I have no work on hand. I wish I could write a short story, but my poor head is empty.'[46]

She agreed to go to France with John but knew what was happening and at the Hotel du Champ de Mars at Colmar mostly spent the week away lying on the bed in her hotel room, looking out at lime trees and cobblestones and café tables – facing her own mortality. In mid-June, just before they turned north to go back to England, she told Jane Howard, 'Here, at Colmar, I've decided to turn it in.'[47]

However, she never went in for self-pity. She received a letter from Katharine White in June, telling her about her personal archive at Bryn Mawr; she asked for news of Renny; said that Elizabeth's books were in the living-room next to EM Forster's; and ended her four page letter: 'I still think of the time when I was editing your stories and those of Jean Stafford and Mary McCarthy and Nancy Hale and Jim Powers and O'Hara and dozens of others as the happiest time of my life.'[48] Elizabeth in her reply told her that she too was tidying her affairs, making a bonfire, destroying an unpublished novel without a second glance, that she was sorry Katharine was ill and she was too. Katharine responded immediately, in a kind and sympathetic letter; the part that would have made Elizabeth cry was when she mentioned her five great-grandchildren. She herself would now never be a great-grandmother.

For her sixty-third birthday Joanna gave a lunch party in her garden. 'Beautifully set out under the trees – it looked like that French advertisement for brandy or something. (Shows what a good advertisement it is, when I can remember only the photograph, & not what it stood for.)' From now onwards she stayed in bed a lot of the time, sorting her papers, destroying most of them, and disposing of possessions. 'I sold a faded Julia Margaret Cameron – it was so faded it was hardly there, & disappearing fast.'[49] (It was of Virginia Woolf's mother, she also sold a Cameron portrait of

'Beatrice', May Prinsep; they had been presents from Peter Davies and had hung on the stairs.) And she said goodbye to people like Patience. 'Thank you for your letter,' she wrote at the end of August. 'Curses, indeed! Though I can be much less mild in my language.'[50]

She felt sick all the time for the last few weeks. But she was able to see the Angelica Garnett jacket for *Blaming*. And had an occupation. She knitted a long muffler for Jane Howard. 'It is very ill done, but with love in each stitch one might say.'[51] Jane, in reply, 'felt encircled by your generosity and love' and told Elizabeth that she thought of her nearly all the time and 'can't say what I feel about you. You have done marvellous work – the best of its kind since our favourite novelist. Take a crumb of comfort from that . . . I do love you, darling Liz.'[52] The next day Kingsley also wrote, to say that Jane was delighted with her scarf and that he had asked the literary editor of the *Observer* if he could be allowed extra space to review *Blaming* and do a general assessment of Elizabeth's work. 'It'll give me a chance to say what I've believed for many years, that you're a marvellous writer, among the three or four best of our time, and that your books will be admired and enjoyed as long as people can read our language.'[53] Now Elizabeth could not write back: like Mrs Bracey in *A View of the Harbour*, 'in the things that really matter to us, we are entirely alone . . . Especially alone dying.'[54]

The last time she left Grove's Barn was in early October when she went to see the house in Sussex that Renny was buying with his new wife-to-be. At some point that month she found the strength to write John a letter. It has some of the cadences of Virginia Woolf's last letter to Leonard (she would have read it in 1972, in the second volume of Quentin Bell's biography): 'I just want to thank you for all the lovely times and my luck in having you. I'm sorry it was dreary for you in the end, but my love grew and grew.' And she asked for the quickest possible funeral and specified how it should be conducted ('just simple, over quickly. It has nothing to do with me or my life').[55]

Elizabeth died on her Saint's Day, 19 November.* Two agency nurses had arrived to start looking after her and asked John to go into Beaconsfield to buy something medical. Knowing he was out of the house, Elizabeth turned her face to the wall.

She had asked that at her funeral, at Amersham Crematorium, some lines from Homer be printed on cards and handed round:

As leaves are so are the generations of mankind. As for the leaves, some the wind scatters on the ground, and others the budding forest puts forth when spring comes again. So it is with mankind, one flourishes, and another fades.[56]

It was exactly thirty years since the publication of *At Mrs Lippincote's*; at the end, coming home after discovering that (the oddly named) Mr Taylor has died, Julia has a hot bath:

* St Elizabeth of Hungary, whose symbols are bread and roses

'Oh, death!' she thought, looking down the length of her body. 'For this – so familiar, so reassuring to me, to become familiar and reassuring no longer, to be destroyed!' Cheerless thoughts assailed her. 'I will be destroyed *quickly*,' she decided. 'Not slowly rotting, turning to dust. God don't let me think of it! Cremation. That's better. It's easier for one's friends to contemplate. Over quicker. A simple service and no prayers. A Bach Chorale, perhaps, and some poetry read out – a Chorus from the *Antigone* . . . and a passage from *Ecclesiastes*.' She saw Roddy standing there with Eleanor and Oliver and, strangely, also herself . . . Tears stung her eyes. She felt anxiety, too, thinking that a scratchy gramophone needle, wrong timing with the Greek, would render her funeral bathetic. 'But this,' she thought, meaning her body, 'is reality itself to me. I could not believe in it ever not *being*. That I, too . . . '⁵⁷

After the service (Bach, *Antigone*, *Ecclesiastes*, the lines from Homer read by Kingsley Amis), David Routledge, Joanna's husband, went into the crematorium office to collect the gramophone records. A loudspeaker had obviously been relaying the service to the staff and the girl behind the desk asked, '"Was she a writer then?" David said that she was and the girl answered, "Well, I expect the name helped a lot."'⁵⁸ It was the moment when the children first fully realised that Elizabeth was not there to share the joke.

John Taylor wrote, to the secretary of the PEN club in reply to his letter, 'I of course was proud of her writing but it was nothing to the pride I feel, on reflection, at the courage with which she faced the inevitable . . . From the time of her first operation over three years ago, there was never a word of self-pity or complaint and when she was told just before Christmas last year that nothing could be done, she merely said to the surgeon, "I hope you can keep me alive until I finish my novel".'[59]

Elizabeth, we can be sure, would have found her own behaviour unremarkable. And might have preferred John to be prouder of her writing than of the manner of her dying. But they had known each other for forty years and been married for thirty-nine of those, and although he could be domineering and thoughtless, essentially he was good to her all their life together; he was, after all, the man she chose.

With unbelievable crassness *The Times* obituary said that 'her wit and penetration were seldom in doubt but the true asperities of modern life seemed to elude her.' And that was that.

She left £74,800 – half a million pounds in today's terms. She had earned all of it from her writing.

There was no memorial service, although some would have agreed with Kingsley Amis: 'It is none of my business, but the ceremony [at Amersham] was in no way suitable to the departure of one of the finest novelists of her and our time.'[60]

There were many wonderful letters. The one from Elizabeth's agent Patience Ross – she had been her agent for thirty years, all her working life – was among the most touching. She said to John that 'Elizabeth was never mean or vain or snide or theatrical or self-pitying or phoney or spiteful or unkind.'[61] And she was quite right.

Blaming was published in the autumn of 1976, to generally appreciative reviews. Robert told Barbara Pym that 'Francis King and Lady Wilson [the wife of Harold Wilson] wanted to put *Blaming* on the short list for the Booker Prize – but Walter Allen (always hostile to Elizabeth) said it was "irredeemably trifling".'[62]

John remarried sixteen months after Elizabeth died, in 1977 when he was 69. Suitably, his second wife was a widow who had been a neighbour in Daws Hill Lane in the 1940s. He would live for another thirty-one years after Elizabeth's death, and when he died in 2006 the *Bucks Free Press* told its readers that 'he married Elizabeth Coles in 1936, a popular novelist and writer of short stories.'[63] Elizabeth might have written one about the Beaconsfield ladies going round to the library on a Friday, between having their hair done and going to the Five Ways Café, to ask for a novel by Elizabeth Coles. She would certainly have laughed. We are left wondering, yet again, what's in a name? Might Elizabeth Coles have had the fame of Elizabeth Gaskell? Might DB Coles have had the fame of EM Forster?

In June 1983 the papers Elizabeth chose not to burn appeared as 'The Property of a Gentleman' in a Sotheby's catalogue, flagged up by a recent quotation, 'Elizabeth Taylor wrote about people who are comfortably off and who feel uncomfortable.'[64] In July they were sold, for £5000 (£12,000 nowadays), to an American dealer with a Sevenoaks box number; he sold them on to the London dealer Bertram Rota, and in 1985 they were sold to the University of Tulsa. Mysteriously, a manuscript called 'Mahmoud Souk' (presumably the original title of 'Crêpes Flambées') never got to Tulsa. Well, perhaps it is in a Sevenoaks safe; or waiting for a research student to find it in Oklahoma; or there was a Forsterian muddle . . .

So there the manuscripts sit, nicely air-conditioned, next to the papers of Cyril Connolly, Paul Scott, William Trevor, Jean Rhys, Stevie Smith, Muriel Spark, Rebecca West – and four boxes of Olivia Manning's letters to Kay Dick and Kathleen Farrell. It is a distressingly long way, in every sense, from Penn. But then Elizabeth's modesty would have prevented her from giving anything of her own to the University of Reading, to the Thames Valley where it belonged, or to the Bodleian where the Barbara Pym Papers are, and although she had barely been to America, she might have thought it funny that her life's work ended up there, and certainly would have *been* funny about it; in any case, she would probably not have cared too much.

Nor, apparently, did she care that her letters to Ray Russell, more than a decade's-worth apart from those that were lost, have been sitting in his attic, first in High Wycombe and then, later on, in Hull. Perhaps she knew. Perhaps she hoped that one day the letters would enhance her literary reputation. As indeed this book has tried to do.

CHAPTER FOURTEEN

REPUTATION

Once I worshipped Elizabeth Bowen. 'Here is the great artist:
the impersonal cool one.' I could never have dreamt that one
day she would say a novel I (the raw, stumbling one) had
written had haunted her . . . Then a cold thing happened.
I thought: 'Watch then! You'll see me do it.' Unless I balls-up
badly, I am a better writer than she. I know it in my bones.
I would die if anyone else knows I think this. But I do & it is
no use trying not to.[1]

The reviews of *Blaming* were respectable enough, but
Rosemary Dinnage in the *Times Literary Supplement* was nearly
right when she said that Elizabeth's books were not unlike
Martha's in the novel:

'well-reviewed, and more or less unknown. Without
fretting, she waited to be discovered.' If to some extent
[Elizabeth's] do wait to be discovered, however, *Blaming*
is not really the one with which to make converts. Her
more powerful and concentrated writing is in the
earlier books; in the later ones irony and polish often
take the place of passion.

However, she concluded that 'Blaming now brings to a quiet conclusion a most honourable literary career.'[2]

This was echoed by CP Snow writing in the *Financial Times* that 'it is a pity that she hasn't reached a wider public. Maybe her time will come'[3] (Elizabeth would have smiled wryly). Kingsley Amis reminded *Observer* readers that her 'deeply unsensational style and subject-matter saw to it that, in life, she never received her due as one of the best English novelists born in this century. I hope she will in the future.'[4]

The year *Blaming* appeared Elizabeth was posthumously awarded a Whitbread Prize for outstanding achievement over her lifetime. John went to the dinner to accept the prize and said, with a tinge of understandable rage, 'I just can't help thinking how nice it would have been if my wife could have received this recognition while she was still alive.'[5]

Then, in 1982, Virago began to reprint her books and since then have been consistently promoting them, keeping several in print and periodically relaunching both novels and short stories with new jackets, new prefaces and newly commissioned pieces in newspapers.

After 1984, when *Angel* was chosen as one of the thirteen 'Best Novels of Our Time', opinions polarised. 'Whether discriminating novel readers' attention should be drawn to a book which Elizabeth Taylor once revealed to me as the only one of her works which she regretted publishing, is rather doubtful' wrote Francis King. He went on to explain that alongside the Book Marketing Council list the novelist Anthony Burgess had drawn up his own and that the authors overlapped on both with the single exception of Elizabeth

Taylor. '[Hers] is certainly a fragile talent in comparison with a robust and ebullient one like Mr Burgess's,' remarked Francis King. He added: 'But time often has more difficulty in demolishing the literary equivalent of a Japanese teahouse than that of the Barbican.'[6]

It is surely this fragility which hinders her reputation from being what it should be: fragility, delicacy, allusiveness are not artistic qualities that appeal to the general public. Are Vuillard, Gwen John, Rex Whistler, Eric Ravilious, Edward Bawden, David Gentleman – the kind of painters Elizabeth would have been if she had been able to paint – are they names that drop from everyone's lips? They are not, compared with the Van Goghs, the Sargents, the David Hockneys. As Paul Bailey put it in 1973, 'there is a place in literature, as there is in painting, for the miniature, although the bully boys of lit crit would not have us think so.'[7]

Where the miniaturist is concerned one must remember that for many years Chekhov was principally known as a playwright rather than a short story writer. When AN Wilson invoked him in a review of a selection of some of Elizabeth's stories he could think of no greater compliment when he said that in none of them 'does the comparison with the great Russian [Chekhov] diminish this superb writer who, in her understated way, must be among the English giants of the twentieth century.'[8] (In the context of Chekhov, it would be interesting to know what the American writer Richard Ford feels about Elizabeth's short stories. In a 1998 introduction to some of the short stories he eloquently explained why Chekhov is a genius, yet every sentence he writes could apply to Elizabeth, for example she too sees the importance of the ordinary, writes about 'small issues of moral choice within large, overarching dilemmas', insists 'we keep our notice close to life's nuance, its intimate gestures and small moral annotations'.[9])

If only other critics would start taking it for granted that Elizabeth is one of the great novelists, rather than saying the same thing about her over and over again: John Carey writing in 1986 that 'Elizabeth Taylor is an even more unjustly neglected writer than Barbara Pym used to be' or Anita Brookner beginning a piece in the *Spectator*, 'it is time that justice was done to Elizabeth Taylor, the Jane Austen of the 1950s and 1960s, a writer so beautifully modest that few have taken up the cudgels on her behalf' and adding: 'It has been a matter of concern to see her passed by while lesser artists are promoted and rediscovered.'[10]

Not long before his death Kingsley Amis wrote, indefatigably, about Elizabeth: 'The neglect of her work continues to this day', the reason for the inadequate recognition being that read hastily or superficially her work can seem 'something fit for an old-fashioned women's magazine . . . something trivial. Yes, trivial in the way John Betjeman's poetry is trivial, seen only at a second glance to be concerned with themes like loss, grief, disappointment, loneliness, hope, love, death.'[11] And a few years later Jonathan Keates also expressed his mystification at the eclipse of Elizabeth's reputation, putting it down to Ivy and Elizabeth Bowen having more to offer the sensation-starved whereas 'Taylor's fiction isn't of a kind which draws attention to itself either through stylistic experiment or *recherché* subject matter'. He concluded: 'It's time we Taylorians made a bit more noise.'[12]

Well, we are making as much noise as we can, to which it is hoped this book makes its own contribution. Thus in 2006 Philip Hensher called Elizabeth 'one of the hidden treasures of the English novel' and declared that, although her work had always been admired by the cognoscenti, now it was coming into focus, and the numbers of her admirers are such that her 'reputation seems to be growing beyond anything she knew in her lifetime.'[13] In 2007 Benjamin Schwarz wrote a long appreciation in *Atlantic Monthly*. He began by saying that Elizabeth is best known for not being better known, and went on to list some of the recent efforts to change this; he then had to admit that 'this big push, like previous efforts on behalf of Elizabeth Taylor's reputation, failed to budge whoever or whatever is in charge of canonizing authors.'[14] And NH Reeve recently deplored her neglect by 'the academy' and 'the metropolitan literary world', saying that he had written his critical study 'in the hope of . . . encouraging more readers to explore for themselves a body of work so undervalued and so richly sustaining.'[15]

Even Robert Liddell had written in 1960 (in an article Elizabeth must have read with mixed feelings): 'Great fiction she has not written, and it must be probable that she will not: no living English writer has done so, except Miss Compton-Burnett.'[16] And it is true that for the next thirty years *Manservant and Maidservant* went on being one of Oxford University Press's 'Best Novels of Our Time'.[17] Eighteen years on, however, there has been a change: none of Ivy's novels are in print in Britain (although two are New York Review Books Classics in America) but most of Elizabeth's books are.

It is true, the name did *not* help a lot. But what did not help as well was that Elizabeth's perceptions, her interests, her awareness were essentially feminine; then there is her reticence, the domestic subject matter, the lending-library aura that hangs round her work, the Thames Valley settings, the being married to a sweet manufacturer, the evident affluence, the careful pearls in the photographs, the slightly unmemorable titles, the not having many literary friends, the assumption that her work is predictable when in fact it is full of surprises – one could go on.

And as for her style, although in its pared-down quality, its cinematic technique, its lack of 'and then and then', it was modernist, it was rarely seen as that. Too many reviewers found it too feminine, missed the humour, missed the bleakness, could only see that the subject material was domestic and then condemned the entire oeuvre as minor, certainly incapable of greatness.

Paradoxically, however, Elizabeth's 'range of sympathy and observation is too wide, in spite of the placid Home Counties settings, for preoccupying themes and patterns to be extracted,' said Rosemary Dinnage in 1976. 'Nor does she go in for the kind of "special" passages that are quotable – the texture of her wit is too fine, her irony too lightly and continuously in play.'[18]

Then again, it was not very helpful to label Elizabeth a novelist of manners. The very phrase sounds stilted and old-fashioned; in any case she did not write about manners, although she cared about them personally: she wrote about bad manners, callousness, cruelty, unkindness. And those who thought her 'just another ladylike novelist, writing for a market not far from women's magazines'[19] have, as Philip Hensher points out, badly misunderstood her. The qualities that he values most of all in Elizabeth's work – her unladylike streak of vulgarity, almost sordidness, and the bleakness, the pessimism, of her vision – are the qualities that once prompted Bill Maxwell to compare her to Maupassant. These have nothing to do with the novel of manners and everything to do with 'the quirky underside' remarked on by the novelist Anne Tyler when she wrote: 'Like Jane Austen, like Barbara Pym, like Elizabeth Bowen – soul-sisters all – Elizabeth Taylor made it her business to explore the quirky underside of so-called civilisation.'[20]

And of course Elizabeth never won a prize, never got her name 'known' by reviewing or being the subject of gossip. In fact she 'gave her status no help by having no public life, not being seen on television, not pronouncing on the state of the world and not going round explaining that her under-lying subject was the crisis of the bourgeois conscience'[21] (Kingsley Amis). He could have added, and by not talking about herself.

Thank God for that, she would have said. But, alas, these things do make a difference. The cult of the personality is indeed reprehensible. But fiction readers are, to put it senti-mentally, going on a journey, being taken by the hand by the author: if they have no concept at all of the author, if the novel might as well have been written by someone anonymous, readers have things made very much more difficult for themselves.

And so, although she would have flinched, a biography has been written. Will it make a difference to Elizabeth's reputation? Will critics stop congratulating the reader ('how deeply I envy any reader coming to her for the first time' Elizabeth Jane Howard,[22] 'I envy those readers who are coming to her work for the first time' Paul Bailey[23]) for having discovered her at all, as so many do? Will she at last be bracketed with Elizabeth Bowen and Rebecca West and Rosamond Lehmann as one of the most important writers of the last century, not a consistent genius like Virginia Woolf but with consistent flashes of it? Will the tide turn? I can only hope so.

And one day, when the tide does turn, she will be *the* Elizabeth Taylor.

ACKNOWLEDGEMENTS

The author of this book was authorised by the late John Taylor to write this biography and to quote from all published and unpublished copyright material. She believed, however, that it was inappropriate to publish the book while he was still alive. Following his death, she submitted the manuscript to John and Elizabeth Taylor's son and daughter. They are, alas, 'very angry and distressed' about the book and have asked to be disassociated from it.

The Other Elizabeth Taylor has been fifteen years in the making, during which time many people, including the Taylor family, have been very kind and helpful to the author. But because of the unfortunate situation mentioned above she has decided not to thank anyone by name. However, to every single person who has helped her – and this ranges from the first would-be biographer in the 1970s (whose work was indispensable), to the librarians who answered research queries, to the several friends who read the manuscript – to all these people the author offers her warmest thanks. She will be writing to each of them personally; if she has failed to write to someone who has helped her and is reading this, her thanks are nevertheless very sincere. But there is one person who must be thanked by name: the late Ray Russell.

ELIZABETH TAYLOR'S

PUBLISHED BOOKS

At Mrs Lippincote's (1945)
Palladian (1946)
A View of the Harbour (1947)
A Wreath of Roses (1949)
A Game of Hide and Seek (1951)
The Sleeping Beauty (1953)
Hester Lilly and other stories (1954)
Angel (1957)
The Blush and other stories (1958)
In a Summer Season (1961)
The Soul of Kindness (1964)
A Dedicated Man and other stories (1965)
Mossy Trotter (1967) (for children)
The Wedding Group (1968)
Mrs Palfrey at the Claremont (1971)
The Devastating Boys and other stories (1972)
Blaming (1976)

NOTES

Some points about the notes: Taylor Papers refers to papers in the possession of Elizabeth Taylor's family; the Grant Papers are in the collection of the first would-be biographer, Joy Grant; the Elizabeth Taylor Manuscripts are in the McFarlin Library, Special Collections Department, the University of Tulsa; Elizabeth's letters to Ray Russell are in a private collection – they were dated and numbered by him in the 1970s; *The New Yorker* Papers are in the the New York Public Library; the Knopf Archive is in the Harry Ransom Center, University of Texas at Austin; Elizabeth's letters to Elizabeth Jane Howard are in the Huntington Library, California; Elizabeth's letters to Katharine White are in Bryn Mawr College Library; the Green Notebook is a book into which Ray Russell copied Elizabeth's pre-war letters, but the page references are to the author's transcription of this notebook; if a quotation is not attributed, then it has the same attribution as the next quotation; finally, in general I do not put op. cit. for Elizabeth's novels and short stories.

PREFACE

1 letter to Patience Ross 30 July
1975 Bodleian. The friend was
Robert Liddell. Elizabeth once
wrote on one of her letters to
him, '"burn!" I demurred, as
this is often not practical'
(PEN talk).

2 'Sisters' *The New Yorker*
21 June 1969, *Penguin Modern
Stories* 6 1970, *The Devastating
Boys* 1972 pp 127, 128, 129,
134

3 Paul Theroux *Encounter*
September 1972 p 71

4 John Carey review of Robert
Liddell *Elizabeth and Ivy* 1986
The Sunday Times 19 January
1986

5 Hilary Spurling to author
30 January 1997

6 Robert Liddell to John Taylor
20 November 1975 Taylor
Papers

PROLOGUE

1 interview with Elizabeth
Taylor *The Times* 22 November
1971

2 ET to Barbara Pym September
1953 Bodleian

CHAPTER ONE

1 ET to Robert Liddell
September 1955 Taylor Papers

2 *Angel* 1957 p 49

3 ibid. p 37

4 *A Game of Hide and Seek* 1951
p 118

5 in *A View of the Harbour* 1947,
A Wreath of Roses 1949, *A Game
of Hide and Seek*, *The Sleeping
Beauty* 1953, *The Soul of
Kindness* 1964

6 and there is a Miss Taylor at
the library in *Mrs Palfrey at the
Claremont* 1971

7 *Blaming* 1976 p 54

8 Robin Grove 'From the Island:
Elizabeth Taylor's Novels'
*Studies in the Literary
Imagination* Volume X1 no. 2
Autumn 1978 p 79

9 undated letter to Ray Russell
probably spring 1938

10 Robert Liddell to Joy Grant
13 April 1987 Grant Papers

11 letter 50 to Ray Russell
13 January 1942

12 letter to Robert Liddell
September 1955 Taylor
Papers

13 letter 350 to Ray Russell
30 January 1944

14 letter 203 to Ray Russell
11 February 1943

15 interview with Phyllis Meras
in the *Providence (Rhode
Island) Sunday Journal* 9 June
1963

16 unpublished PhD by John
Crompton Hull 1992 p183:
the writers Beth, Angel,
Patrick, David and Martha in
A View of the Harbour, *Angel*,
The Soul of Kindness, *The
Wedding Group* 1968 and
Blaming are contrasted with
the painters Bertram, Esmé,
Liz, Harry and Nick, there is a
painter (Frances) in *A Wreath*

of Roses and a writer (Ludo) in
Mrs Palfrey at the Claremont.

17 letter 488 to Ray Russell
18 April 1946

18 letter 197 to Ray Russell
4 February 1943

19 *Palladian* 1946 p 5

20 letter 123 to Ray Russell
13 August 1942

21 letter to Ray Russell c. 1938
Green Notebook p 5

22 Elizabeth Taylor Prologue to
The World of Children 1966
p 12

23 'When I was a Child' *Tricks and
Puzzles* no date Taylor Papers

24 interview by author with
Malcolm Fewtrell 4 April 1995

25 *A Wreath of Roses* p 78

26 letter 545 to Ray Russell 1946

27 letter 86 to Ray Russell
12 May 1942

28 letter 74 to Ray Russell 5 April
1942

29 *Bucks Free Press* 31 January
1936

30 *Palladian* p 8

31 'Girl Reading' *The New Yorker*
29 July 1961, *Good
Housekeeping* April 1962,
A Dedicated Man 1965 p 17

32 'First Death of Her Life'
The New Yorker March 1949,
reprinted *Hester Lilly* 1954
p 109

33 Suzanne Hale letter to Joy
Grant 27 May 1978

34 F Raphael ed. *Bookmarks* 1975
p149

35 *At Mrs Lippincote's* 1945
pp 27–8

36 *Bookmarks* op. cit. p 149

37 letter 361 to Ray Russell
1 March 1944

38 ET to William Maxwell
16 November 1950 *The New
Yorker* Papers

39 *Wilson Library Bulletin* April
1948 p 580

40 *At Mrs Lippincote's* pp 16–17

41 *Angel* p 49

42 *Wilson Library Bulletin* op. cit.

43 letter 389 to Ray Russell
8 May 1944

44 *At Mrs Lippincote's* p 17

45 letter 545 to Ray Russell 1946

46 letter 481 to Ray Russell
7 February 1946

47 *Angel* p 13

48 letter 306 to Ray Russell
October 1943

49 *Abbey School Magazine* 1926 p 6

50 Dorothy Duncan to author
30 April 1997

51 'Beware of the Child': extracts
from the 'Juvenile Diary' of
Elizabeth Taylor p 3 ts. Tulsa

52 *A Game of Hide and Seek*
pp 207–8

53 *Palladian* p 176

54 Suzanne Hale op.cit.

55 *Palladian* p 9

56 ibid. p 13

57 Suzanne Hale op. cit.

58 letter 479 to Ray Russell
15 January 1946

59 letter 541 to Ray Russell late
1945

60 *A Short History of the The Abbey
School 1887–1957* p 12

61 Margaret Short to author
10 April 1997

62 Natalie Copeland to Joy Grant
27 July 1978

63 Suzanne Hale op. cit.
64 *Bookmarks* op. cit. p 150
65 Daphne Roadknight to Joy Grant 21 June 1978
66 Joanna Love to Joy Grant 26 July 1978
67 *Angel* p 8
68 Mary Cumber to author 15 April 1997
69 Joan Watts to Joy Grant 21 March 1978
70 *The Book Club Magazine* November 1951
71 'Juvenile Diary' op. cit. p 4
72 *Palladian* p 115
73 letter 460 to Ray Russell 3 September 1945
74 *Angel* p 7
75 letter 318 to Ray Russell November 1943
76 'Juvenile Diary' op. cit. p 1. But this entry has been touched up by ET: no child would write, at the time, 'we were well primed'.
77 *A Game of Hide and Seek* p 129
78 letter 141 to Ray Russell 8 September 1942
79 letter 541 to Ray Russell late 1945
80 *A Game of Hide and Seek* pp 125, 129
81 *At Mrs Lippincote's* p 107
82 ET to Blanche Knopf 28 March 1947 Texas
83 letter 24 to Ray Russell 4 October 1941
84 *The Abbey School Magazine* 1930
85 Joanna Love op. cit.
86 *The World of Books* interview with Brian Glanville 26 July 1965 BBC Written Archives, Caversham
87 *The Sunday Times* 22 September 1968
88 'A Year I had Forgotten' BBC *Woman's Hour* 24 October 1949 Tulsa
89 jacket of first edition of *At Mrs Lippincote's*
90 'A Year I had Forgotten' op. cit.
91 letter 545 to Ray Russell 1946
92 Margaret Short op. cit.
93 Kay Butler in conversation with Joy Grant 13 April 1978
94 Mary Calfe in telephone conversation with author April 1997
95 Joan Watts op. cit.
96 letter 460 to Ray Russell 3 September 1945
97 letter 541 to Ray Russell 1945
98 *A Game of Hide and Seek* p 16
99 'Juvenile Diary' op. cit. pp 1, 4, 3
100 interview with Daphne Roadknight 15 June 1997
101 *Angel* pp 33–4
102 *The Book Club Magazine* November 1951
103 'A Troubled State of Mind' *The Blush* 1958 p 70
104 *Angel* p 40
105 'A Year I had Forgotten' op. cit.

CHAPTER TWO

1 ET to Blanche Knopf mid-September 1948, Texas
2 This sentence had appeared twenty years earlier, unfortunately in almost the same words, in 'The Idea

of Age' *The New Yorker*
9 February 1952, reprinted in
Hester Lilly p 122. 'Miss A and
Miss M' was published in the
London Magazine October/
November 1971, reprinted
The Devastating Boys p 151.

3 ibid. pp 157, 168, 169, 153

4 letter to Martin Robertson
May 1956 Grant Papers

5 RC Sherriff *No Leading Lady*
1968 p 7

6 *Angel* pp 38, 39, 42

7 'Beware of the Child' op. cit.
p 4

8 Don Potter to Joy Grant 1978

9 letter from Elizabeth Coles to
Virginia Woolf 15 October
1932 *Woolf Studies Annual*
Volume 12 2006

10 cf. Penelope Fitzgerald *The
Knox Brothers* 1977; the author
was the daughter of 'Evoe'
Knox.

11 'Poor Girl' first published in
*Lady Cynthia Asquith's Third
Ghost Book* 1955 reprinted
The Blush p 169

12 ET to Patience Ross
3 February 1975 Huntington

13 letter from Oliver Knox
to Joy Grant 25 February
1978

14 ET to Robert Liddell 1955
Taylor Papers

15 *The Wedding Group* p 5

16 ibid. p 8

17 Eric Gill's notebook,
photocopy of original Tate
Britain Library

18 Fiona MacCarthy *Eric Gill*
1989 p 266

19 ET to Blanche Knopf end
January 1950 Texas

20 letter 84 to Ray Russell 4 May
1942

21 John Rothenstein *Summer's
Lease* 1965 p 184

22 Robert Speaight *The Life of
Eric Gill* 1966 p 211

23 Fiona MacCarthy op.cit. p 237

24 ibid. 1990 edition

25 Nicholas Wheeler Robinson
*A Preliminary Chronicle of North
Dean* 1993 p 34

26 *The Wedding Group* pp 106,
138

27 Fiona MacCarthy op. cit.
p 251

28 Donald Potter to Joy Grant
1978

29 letter 329 to Ray Russell
14 January 1944

30 letter from René Hague to Joy
Grant 19 April 1978

31 author's notes of interview
with Donald Potter 31 January
1997

32 Fiona MacCarthy interview
with Donald Potter 11
September 1987

33 author's notes op. cit.

34 undated letter Donald Potter
to Joy Grant 1978

35 author's notes op. cit.

36 John Lehmann *The Whispering
Gallery* 1955 p 71

37 Donald Potter to Joy Grant
1978

38 letter to Ray Russell Green
Notebook c 1938 p 4

39 Green Notebook p7

40 ET to Francis King 8 June
1969 Texas

41 Bryanston Magazine *Saga* June 1984 p 4

42 *Sunday Telegraph* 22 December 1996

43 Fiona MacCarthy interview with Donald Potter op. cit.

44 letter to Ray Russell Green Notebook c. 1938 p 4

45 HT Adlam interviews with Joy Grant 3 and 23 May 1978

46 *Bucks Free Press* 3 March 1933

47 ibid. 2 March 1934

48 W Somerset Maugham *For Services Rendered* 1932 pp 87, 76

49 *Bucks Free Press* 23 March 1934

50 ibid. 13 April 1934

51 ibid. 20 April 1934

52 ibid. 12 April 1935

53 telephone conversation between Joanna Kingham and the author 14 December 1996

54 letter from ET to Robert Liddell 10 June 1953 *Elizabeth and Ivy* op. cit. p 51

55 Green Notebook p 4

CHAPTER THREE

1 Green Notebook December 1938 p 25

2 ET to Katharine White 13 January 1953 Bryn Mawr

3 *A Game of Hide and Seek* p 97

4 letter to Ray Russell undated Green Notebook p 28

5 letter to Ray Russell 27 March 1942

6 ET to EJ Howard April 1975 Huntington

7 'First Death of Her Life' op. cit. *Hester Lilly* pp 108, 109

8 letter 74 to Ray Russell 5 April 1942

9 *A Game of Hide and Seek* p 97

10 ibid. p 98

11 ET to William Maxwell 21 July 1952 *The New Yorker* Papers

12 letter 545 to Ray Russell undated probably March 1946

13 *Palladian* pp151, 152

14 'First Death of Her Life' op. cit. *Hester Lilly* p 108

15 Josephine Bales interview with Joy Grant 1978

16 Green Notebook pp 11,12

17 Donald Potter interview with author 31 January 1997

18 Green Notebook pp 4, 5

19 *The Devastating Boys* p 133

20 Elizabeth Taylor to Herman Schrijver 11 March 1971 Grant Papers

21 *Bucks Free Press* 13 March 1936

22 ibid. 20 March 1936

23 Daphne Roadknight in conversation with author 18 March 1998

24 John Crompton PhD op. cit.

25 letter to Ray Russell undated c. 1938 Green Notebook p 5

26 1987 letter from Don Potter to Joy Grant, Grant Papers

27 quotation att. to E Arnot Robertson *Three Came Unarmed* 1929 in ET's Commonplace Book (cf. p 36).

28 letter 482 to Ray Russell c. March 1946

29 Denis Healey *The Time of My Life* 1989 pp 34–5

30 *The Times* obituary 3 February 1981

31 letter from René Hague to Joy Grant 19 April 1978 Grant Papers

32 Barbara Wall *René Hague* 1989 p 26

33 Brocard Sewell to the author 17 October 1997

34 letter to Joy Grant 27 February 1989 Grant Papers

35 letter 232 to Ray Russell 28 April 1943

36 undated letter from René Hague to Joy Grant Grant Papers

37 Clifton Reynolds *Valley of Chairs* 1942 p 65

38 letter 161 to Ray Russell 31 October 1942 quoting ibid. p 62

39 *A Game of Hide and Seek* p 47

40 letter 282 to Ray Russell 6 September 1943

41 letter 46 to Ray Russell 5 January 1942

42 HT Adlam interview with Joy Grant 23 May 1978, Grant Papers

43 *At Mrs Lippincote's* p 87

44 ibid. p 120

45 'The Light of Day' first published *Time and Tide* 25 January 1947, *Hester Lilly* p 148

46 'A Year I had Forgotten' op. cit.

47 *The Sleeping Beauty* p 139

48 comment in Ray Russell's handwriting Green Notebook p 1 of copied-out version

49 ibid. p 1

50 ibid. p 3

51 Green Notebook p 29 spring 1939

52 letter 101 to Ray Russell 12 June 1942

53 *At Mrs Lippincote's* p 6

CHAPTER FOUR

1 letter 455 to Ray Russell October 1945

2 letter to Ray Russell Green Notebook p 17 undated

3 *Hester Lilly* p 69

4 *A View of the Harbour* p 26

5 Green Notebook pp 16, 18, 17, 33

6 letter 147 to Ray Russell 25 September 1942

7 letter 328 to Ray Russell 13 December 1943

8 Leonie Caldecott ed. *Women of Our Century* 1984 p 116

9 ET to William Maxwell mid-June 1951 *The New Yorker* Papers

10 René Hague to Joy Grant 19 April 1978 Grant Papers

11 letter 509 to Ray Russell 8 October 1946

12 'Plenty Good Fiesta' *The New Yorker* 14 July 1951 *Hester Lilly* p 186

13 letter to William Maxwell late January 1951 *The New Yorker* Papers

14 Green Notebook pp 23, 25, 28, 33, 52, 45, 47, 50, 53

15 letter 128 to Ray Russell 21 August 1942

16 letter 101 to Ray Rusell 12 June 1942

17   letter 128 to Ray Russell
     21 August 1942
18   *The Times* 30, 29 April
     1941
19   www.btinternet.com/
     ~stalag18a/greece
20   'The Road to Wolfsberg', the
     diary of Sapper Fred Carne
     8 and 29 June 1941,
     www.stalag18a
21   letter 2 to Ray Russell 9 June
     1941
22   letter 3 to Ray Russell
     1 August 1941
23   letter 27 to Ray Russell
     12 October 1941
24   letter 42 to Ray Russell
     8 December 1941
25   letter 32 to Ray Russell
     25 October 1941
26   letter 49 to Ray Russell
     15 January 1942
27   letter 91 to Ray Russell
     22 May 1942
28   letter 95 to Ray Russell
     27 May 1942
29   letter 106 to Ray Russell
     20 June 1942
30   letter 103 to Ray Russell
     5 June 1942
31   letter 112 to Ray Russell
     14 July 1942
32   letter 126 to Ray Russell
     18 August 1942
33   letter 128 to Ray Russell
     21 August 1942
34   conversation with author
     10 February 1998
35   letter 143 to Ray Russell
     14 September 1942
36   letter 101 to Ray Russell
     12 June 1942

37   letter 135 to Ray Russell
     27 August 1942
38   letter 144 to Ray Russell
     17 September 1942
39   letter 150 to Ray Russell
     4 October 1942
40   letter 132 to Ray Russell
     23 August 1942
41   letter 152 to Ray Russell
     6 October 1942
42   letter 150 to Ray Russell
     4 October 1942
43   letter 153 to Ray Russell
     7 October 1942
44   letter 156 to Ray Russell
     17 October 1942
45   letter 164 to Ray Russell
     5 November 1942
46   ms. of *Never and Always*
     Russell Papers p 39
47   ibid. p 75
48   letter 183 to Ray Russell
     10 December 1942
49   *Never and Always* op. cit.
     pp 4, 6
50   letter 174 to Ray Russell
     19 November 1942
51   letter 254 to Ray Russell
     30 June 1943
52   letter 253 to Ray Russell end
     June 1943
53   'Ever So Banal' written
     30 June 1943 published *Kite*
     Spring 1946

CHAPTER FIVE

1   *At Mrs Lippincote's* p 20
2   letter 35 to Ray Russell
    1 November 1941
3   letter 268 to Ray Russell
    11 August 1943

4 letter 255 to Ray Russell
   14 July 1943
5 letter 261 to Ray Russell
   18 July 1943
6 *At Mrs Lippincote's* p 10
7 Barbara Pym notebook end
   November 1975 Bodleian
8 *At Mrs Lippincote's* p 8
9 letter 255 to Ray Russell
   14 July 1943
10 Mollie Panter-Downes *One
    Fine Day* 1947 p 135
11 *Daily Telegraph* obituary
12 letter 198 to Ray Russell
    4 February 1943
13 *Horizon* no. 49 January 1944
    pp 5–6
14 *Horizon* no. 24 December
    1941 p 418
15 letter 238 to Ray Russell
    23 May 1943
16 letter 275 to Ray Russell
    27 August 1943
17 'For Thine is the Power'
    Tribune 31 March 1944 p 18
18 'Mothers' written 1 August
    1943 published *Here Today*
    1945 p 16
19 *At Mrs Lippincote's* p 149
20 Preface to *The World of Children*
    op. cit. p 9
21 Rita Felski quoted in C
    Briganti and K Mezei *Domestic
    Modernism, the Interwar Novel,
    and EH Young* 2006 p 33
22 letter 285 to Ray Russell
    11 September 1943
23 *At Mrs Lippincote's* p 196
24 letter 280 to Ray Russell
    3 September 1943
25 'A Nice Little Actress' written
    17 September 1943 published

Modern Short Stories First Series
ed. Denys Val Baker August
1944 pp 28–33
26 letter 302 to Ray Russell
    17 October 1943
27 letter 301 to Ray Russell
    14 October 1943
28 'Better Not' written October
    1943 *The Adelphi* October
    1944
29 'EM Forster as a Poor Liar'
    unpublished ts. November
    1943 Tulsa
30 letter 328 to Ray Russell
    13 December 1943
31 letter 177 to Ray Russell
    1 December 1942
32 letter 298 to Ray Russell
    30 September 1943
33 letter 238 to Ray Russell
    23 May 1943
34 Commonplace Book op. cit.
35 letter 314 to Ray Russell
    13 November 1943
36 letter 264 to Ray Russell
    August 1 1943, letter 500
    August 1947, letter 491
    14 May 1946
37 *A Game of Hide and Seek*
    p 177
38 letter 321 to Ray Russell
    1 December 1943
39 letter 337 to Ray Russell
    2 January 1944
40 letter 207 to Ray Russell
    22 February 1943
41 'Husbands and Wives' written
    December 1943 published
    Here Today (Reading) Spring
    1945, *New Short Stories* 1945–6
    ed John Singer (Glasgow) and
    Dangerous Calm: The Selected

Stories of Elizabeth Taylor ed.
Lynn Knight 1995 p 279
42 letter 343 to Ray Russell
20 January 1944, letter 41 to
Ray Russell 30 November
1941, letter 72 to Ray Russell
1 April 1942, letter 99 to Ray
Russell 9 June 1942
43 'Better Not' op. cit.
44 Charles Morgan *Reflections in a
Mirror* Second Series 1946
lecture on 'Creative
Imagination'
45 *At Mrs Lippincote's* pp 14, 24
46 *Elizabeth and Ivy* op. cit. p 16
47 *At Mrs Lippincote's* pp 6, 203
48 original manuscript of *At Mrs
Lippincote's* Russell Papers
49 'A Nice Little Actress' op. cit.
50 letter 365 to Ray Russell
17 March 1944
51 entry for Eric Blair in the
Oxford DNB by Bernard Crick
52 review by Bridget Galton in
the *Hampstead and Highgate
Express* 5 October 2006 of
*Orwell in Tribune: Collected
Writings* ed. Paul Anderson
2006
53 'Violet Hour at the Fleece'
written February 1944, ts.
Taylor Papers, published
Dangerous Calm op. cit. pp
333–8
54 'It Makes a Change' written
4 February 1944, published in
The Adelphi October 1945
55 ET to Reginald Moore
10 April 1944 British
Library
56 letter 484 to Ray Russell
19 February 1945

57 letter 358 to Ray Russell
27 February 1944
58 'A Sad Garden' *Modern
Reading* March 1945, *Harper's*
December 1947, *Hester Lilly*
p 132
59 letter 347 to Ray Russell 29
January 1944
60 ts. Reginald Moore Papers
Misc. 1 British Library
61 CV for ET's election to the
PEN Executive Committee
1965 Tulsa
62 letter 373 to Ray Russell
2 April 1944
63 letter 394 to Ray Russell
22 May 1944
64 The poem was called 'Personal
Poem' and begins: 'Each day is
a stone dropped in a well,/Or
crumb devoured by starlings./
What remains of those days/Is
in my mind,/Is why I turn from
this/And move towards that,/
Or look and lift my head and
listen./Dream in the night/And
weep. *The Decachord* May–June
1944 Volume XXI no. 105
65 letter 439 to Ray Russell
27 October 1944

CHAPTER SIX

1 letter 306 to Ray Russell
October 1943
2 letter 442 to Ray Russell
December 1944
3 letter 357 to Ray Russell
25 February 1944. Some of
the phraseology in this letter
anticipates Elizabeth Bowen's
in a May 1944 issue of *Cornhill*

when she said of Ivy Compton-Burnett's characters: 'They speak of what they will do, and what they have done, but are seldom to be watched actually doing it.'

4 *Oxford DNB* 'Ivy Compton-Burnett'

5 letter 437 to Ray Russell 7 October 1944

6 ICB to ET 28 June 1947, quoted in Hilary Spurling *Ivy: The Life of Ivy Compton-Burnett* 1995 edition p 428

7 letter 461 to Ray Russell late August 1945

8 letters 446, 458, 461 to Ray Russell summer 1945

9 letter 458 to Ray Russell late July 1945

10 letter 461 to Ray Russell late August 1945

11 letter 456 to Ray Russell summer 1945

12 letter 545 to Ray Russell undated 1946

13 letter 250 to Ray Russell 24 June 1943

14 *Spectator* 5 October 1945 p 20

15 *New Statesman* 13 October 1945

16 *The Sketch* 17 October 1945 p 218

17 *Manchester Evening News* 11 October 1945 p 2

18 *Yorkshire Post* 12 October 1945

19 *The Queen* 17 October 1945

20 *Spectator* op. cit.

21 *The Sketch* op. cit.

22 *John O'London's Weekly* 5 October 1945 p 13

23 *The Tatler and Bystander* 24 October 1945 p 120

24 *At Mrs Lippincote's* p 173

25 Ernest Boll in *Modern Language Notes* February 1950

26 letter from Peter Davies to ET 11 September 1945 Taylor Papers

27 letter from Peter Davies to ET 17 September 1945 Taylor Papers

28 letter from Peter Davies to ET 27 September 1945 Taylor Papers

29 letter 461 to Ray Russell c. August 1945

30 Jenny Spencer-Smith *Rex Whistler's War* 1994 p 168

31 letter 482 to Ray Russell March 1946

32 *Palladian* pp 166, 20, 29–30

33 H Holt and H.Pym ed. *Barbara Pym Letters* 1984 p 180, 5 June 1946

34 *Palladian* pp 17, 35, 38, 56, 169–70, 179, 180, 192

35 readers' reports 10 and 19 September 1945 Knopf Archive

36 *New York Times* 21 April 1946 p 23

37 *The New Yorker* 13 April 1946

38 letter 500 to Ray Russell August 1946

39 *Never and Always* p 140

40 *A View of the Harbour* pp 27, 63, 176, 23, 35, 58

41 letter 482 to Ray Russell March 1946

42 *A View of the Harbour* pp 103, 176, 198

43 *Housewife* September 1953

44 ET to William Maxwell
16 November 1950 *The New Yorker* Papers
45 'Simone' Writing Today No. 3
Summer 1946, *Hester Lilly*
p 199
46 *The Listener* 3 October 1946
p 450
47 *The Sketch*
48 *The Tatler and Bystander*
25 December 1946 p 437

CHAPTER SEVEN

1 *At Mrs Lippincote's* p 110
2 letter 410 to Ray Russell 7 July
1944
3 James Rattue *High Wycombe Past* 2002 p100
4 H J Massingham *Chiltern Country* 1940 pp 73, 100
5 EM Forster 'The Challenge of Our Times' 1946 *Two Cheers for Democracy* Penguin 1965
p 68
6 ET 'Ivy Compton-Burnett' August 1951 *The Vogue Bedside Book* ed. Josephine Ross 1984
p 211
7 'In and Out the Houses' published *Saturday Evening Post* 14 December 1968 pp 44–50 *The Devastating Boys* pp 98,103
8 Robert Liddell *Some Principles of Fiction* 1953 pp 23, 25, 26
9 ET to EJ Howard 1971 Huntington
10 letter 502 to Ray Russell 30 August 1946
11 letter 505 to Ray Russell 19 September 1946

12 HJ Massingham op. cit. p 3
13 *The Sleeping Beauty* p 114
14 *Elizabeth and Ivy* op. cit. p 85
15 Alison Uttley *Buckinghamshire* 1950 p 11
16 *In a Summer Season* pp 29, 28
17 John Camp *Portrait of Buckinghamshire* 1972 p 89
18 ET to William Maxwell 20 February 1953 *The New Yorker* Papers
19 'Shadows of the World' date unknown *Hester Lilly* p 141
20 *In a Summer Season* 1961
p 23
21 *The Wedding Group* p 8
22 letter from ET to Blanche Knopf 28 March 1947 Texas
23 'Shadows of the World' *Hester Lilly* p 138, 144
24 telephone call from Prudence Rowe-Evans to author 20 November 1997
25 letter 509 to Ray Russell 8 October 1946
26 letter 508 to Ray Russell 19 December 1946
27 unnumbered letter to Ray Russell 24 February 1947
28 letter 510 to Ray Russell January 1948
29 *Blaming* p 14
30 telephone call from Prudence Rowe-Evans id.
31 letter 457 to Ray Russell undated but c. 1949
32 letter to author from Dr Peter Munz 27 October 1997
33 letter to author from Rachael Low 14 November 1997
34 letter to author from Dr Munz op. cit.

35 Maude Eaton *Girl Workers in New Zealand Factories* British Library CSG 681/17

36 *Blaming* p 83

37 letter to author from Janet Holm 30 March 1998

38 interview Barbara Tizard with author 13 April 1997

39 letter from Peter Munz op. cit.

40 *Blaming* pp 79, 85, 86, 141

41 letter 511 to Ray Russell 12 February 1948

42 readers reports on *Palladian* 18 February 1946 Knopf Archive

43 *New York Times* 30 March 1947 p 18

44 *The New Yorker* 8 February 1947

45 1947 letter to Ray Russell

46 letter from ET to Blanche Knopf 4 March 1947 Knopf Archive

47 ET to Blanche Knopf 12 July 1947 Knopf Archive

48 'The Feminine Genius' *Punch* 3 December 1947

49 *The Listener* 16 November 1947

50 *Time and Tide* 15 November 1947

51 *A Wreath of Roses* pp 248, 250, 31

52 *Oxford DNB* entry on Neville Heath

53 letter 509 to Ray Russell 8 October 1946

54 *A Wreath of Roses* pp 42, 2, 3, 1, 45, 222, 82, 61

55 letter from Barbara Pym to Joy Grant 18 November 1978 Grant Papers

56 *A Wreath of Roses* pp 78, 146, 238, 11, 42

57 Niamh Baker *Happily Ever After?: Women's Fiction in Postwar Britain 1945–60* 1989 pp 152, 153

58 Clare Hanson 'Marketing the "Woman Writer"' in Judy Simons and Kate Fulbrook ed. *Writing: a Woman's Business* 1998 p 73

59 letter to Ray Russell 20 October 1947

CHAPTER EIGHT

1 letter 530 to Ray Russell 21 April 1949

2 'The School Concert' *Harper's Bazaar* July 1947, *A View of the Harbour* pp 9–11, 67, 71–6, 131–3; 'The Light of Day' *Time and Tide* 25 January 1947 p 105, *Harper's* (America) December 1947 and *Hester Lilly* p 148

3 'I Live in a World of Make-Believe' *Harper's Bazaar* (USA) September 1948, *Harper's Bazaar* (UK) April 1949, *Hester Lilly* pp 204, 214

4 letter from William Maxwell to ET early November 1958 Taylor Papers

5 'A Red Letter Day' *The New Yorker* 27 November 1948, *Harper's Bazaar* (England) November 1949

6 letter from Peter Davies to ET 14 March 1949 Taylor Papers

7 letter from Katharine White to ET 26 October 1948 Taylor Papers

8 *The New Yorker* 26 February and 4 March 1996 pp 184, 181

9 letter 523 to Ray Russell 1 October 1948

10 letter 493 to Ray Russell June 1946

11 letter 482 to Ray Russell March 1946

12 letter 524 to Ray Russell 17 October 1948

13 *New York Herald Tribune* 11 October 1953

14 'Sisters' op. cit, *The Devastating Boys* p 127

15 *In a Summer Season* p 141

16 letter 515 to Ray Russell April 1948

17 *TLS* 9 April 1949

18 letter 512 to Ray Russell February 1948

19 letter 515 to Ray Russell April 1948

20 letter from Peter Davies to ET 23 June 1948

21 letter 515 to Ray Russell April 1948

22 letter from ET to Blanche Knopf 13 April 1948 Knopf Archive

23 reader's report on *A Wreath of Roses* August 1948 ibid.

24 letter from Peter Davies to ET 23 June 1948 Taylor Papers

25 *Manchester Guardian* 1 April 1949

26 letter 530 to Ray Russell 21 April 1949

27 Richard Church in *John O'London's Weekly* 15 April 1949

28 letter 530 to Ray Russell 21 April 1949

29 *The Wedding Group* p 161

30 *New Statesman and Nation* 9 April 1949

31 letter 537 to Ray Russell April 1949

32 *Tribune* 29 April 1949

33 interview with Elizabeth Bowen *New York Times* 6 March 1949

34 *The Tatler and Bystander* 6 April 1949 p 24

35 letter from ET to Elizabeth Bowen 24 February 1949 Texas

36 letter from ET to Elizabeth Bowen March 1949 Texas

37 letter 537 to Ray Russell April 1949

38 interview with Elizabeth Bowen op. cit.

39 ET to Blanche Knopf 14 October 1948 Texas

40 *The Times* obituary 27 July 1992

41 letter from Robert Liddell to Joy Grant 27 June 1978 Grant Papers

42 letter to Ray Russell 13 August 1948 Russell Papers

43 letter from Robert Liddell to Hilary Spurling 21 February 1977 Spurling Papers

44 letter from Robert Liddell to Hilary Spurling 29 August 1983 Spurling Papers

45 *Elizabeth and Ivy* op. cit. p 17

46 letter from Robert Liddell to Joy Grant 6 November 1978 Grant Papers

47 letter to Hilary Spurling 14 August 1973 Spurling Papers

48 *Elizabeth and Ivy* op. cit. p 55

49 Robert Liddell to Hilary Spurling 25 July 1979 Spurling Papers

50 ET to Robert Liddell autumn 1955 Taylor Papers

51 letter 519 to Ray Russell 14 July 1948

52 Robert Liddell's talk at PEN op. cit.

53 *Elizabeth and Ivy* op. cit. p 64

54 ET 'Ivy Compton-Burnett' *The Vogue Bedside Book* op. cit. pp 211, 214

55 letter 554 to Ray Russell early 1959

56 June and Neville Braybrooke *Olivia Manning* 2004 p 204

57 *A Game of Hide and Seek* pp 1, 12, 51, 164, 12

58 letter from David Cecil to ET 26 February 1951 Taylor Papers

59 *A Game of Hide and Seek* pp 61, 8

60 Richard Dyer *Brief Encounter* 1993 pp 31, 40, 32

61 ET to Blanche Knopf 23 February 1951 Knopf Archive,

62 letter from ET to Elizabeth Bowen November 1949 Texas

63 *Angel* p96

64 *A View of the Harbour* pp 35–6

65 interview with Elizabeth Bowen *New York Times* op. cit.

66 *Current Biography* 1948 p 613

CHAPTER NINE

1 *A Game of Hide and Seek* p 222

2 'After Hours of Suffering' *Vogue* (America) July 1949 p 65

3 *Hester Lilly* p 136

4 'Nods and Becks and Wreathèd Smiles' *The New Yorker* 19 November 1949 *Hester Lilly* pp 127, 128

5 letter from Brandt & Brandt to Herbert Weinstock 8 May 1950 Knopf Archive

6 reader's report on *A Game of Hide and Seek* May 1950 Knopf Archive

7 letter from Blanche Knopf to ET 26 May 1950 Knopf Archive

8 letter from Peter Davies to ET 23 June 1948 Taylor Papers

9 letter from ET to Blanche Knopf 8 June 1950 Knopf Archive

10 letter from Elizabeth Bowen to ET 18 June 1950 Taylor Papers

11 letter from ET to Elizabeth Bowen 21 June 1950 Bowen Papers Texas

12 Even the smallest note about proofs or mis-spellings survives in both the Knopf Archive at Texas and among *The New Yorker* Papers in the New York Public Library, but when there is a dispute or misunderstanding (anything that the lawyers could potentially be involved in?) the correspondence is missing.

13 Blanche Knopf to Brandt & Brandt 13 June 1950 Knopf Archive

14 ET to William Maxwell 1 September 1950 *The New Yorker* Papers

15 Harriet O'Donovan Sheehy *Guardian* obituary 26 August 2000

16 William Maxwell to ET 7 March 1956 Taylor Papers

17 G Plimpton ed. *Writers at Work, Paris Review Interviews* 1987 p 66

18 Anne M Wyatt-Brown *Barbara Pym: A Critical Biography* 1992 p 8

19 letter from William Maxwell to John Taylor 10 December 1975 Taylor Papers; 'The Rose, The Mauve, The White' *The New Yorker* 22 June 1957, *The Blush* p 95

20 ET to Barbara Pym October 1952

21 The whole of the first section, pp1–46, appeared in *The New Yorker* on 19 August 1950.

22 'Gravement Endommagé' *The New Yorker* 7 October 1950, *Hester Lilly* p 114

23 ET to William Maxwell 16 August 1950 *The New Yorker* Papers

24 'The Idea of Age' was published in *The New Yorker* on 9 February 1952 and in *Hester Lilly*.

25 *Books of Today* February 1951

26 *The Observer* 1 February 1951

27 Richard Church in *John O'London's Weekly* 2 March 1951

28 letter from Robert Liddell to Barbara Pym 8 April 1951, Pym Papers Bodleian

29 *World Review* April 1951

30 William Maxwell to ET 3 December 1952 Taylor Papers

31 *New York Herald Tribune* 11 October 1953, repeated in almost the same words in *John O' London's Weekly* 15 January 1954

32 *Elizabeth and Ivy* op. cit. p 39

33 unpublished piece about Ivy Compton-Burnett written c. 1971 p 2 Tulsa

34 William Maxwell to ET 9 April 1951 *The New Yorker* Papers

35 ET to William Maxwell 12 April 1951 ibid.

36 letter from ET to Elizabeth Bowen 12 February 1951 Bowen Papers, Texas

37 Elizabeth Jane Howard to Joanna Kingham 29 September 1985 Taylor Papers

38 ET to Blanche Knopf 23 February 1951 Knopf Archive

39 Blanche Knopf to ET 4 April 1951 ibid.

40 ET to Bill Maxwell 21 June 1951 *The New Yorker* Papers

41 *Housewife* September 1953

42 'Oasis of Gaiety' *The New Yorker* 18 August 1951, *Hester Lilly* pp 176, 175

43 ET to Katharine White 13 December 1957 Bryn Mawr

44 'A Responsibility' *Dangerous Calm* op. cit. p 331

45 William Maxwell to ET 26 July 1951 Taylor Papers

46 *The Sleeping Beauty* pp 1, 171, 187, 209

47 ET to Patience Ross 26 November 1953 Taylor Papers

48 William Maxwell to ET 3 December 1952 Taylor Papers

49 Susannah Clapp introduction to *The Sleeping Beauty* Virago 1982 p xi

50 Olivia Manning 'The Facile Feminine Pen' *Harper's Bazaar* (UK) August 1952

51 ET to Patience Ross August 1952 Taylor Papers

52 Herbert Weinstock to Patience Ross 10 December 1952 Knopf Archive

53 ET to William Maxwell 20 February 1953 Grant Papers

54 Willliam Maxwell to ET 3 December 1952 Taylor Papers

55 ET to William Maxwell 7 December 1952 Grant Papers

56 ET to Katharine White 13 January 1952 Bryn Mawr

57 handwritten copy of letter from ET to Patience Ross mid-January 1953 Taylor Papers

58 ET to Patience Ross 18 June 1953 Taylor Papers

59 Katharine White to ET 23 April 1953 Bryn Mawr

60 ET to Patience Ross 11 February 1953 Taylor Papers

61 ET to Barbara Pym 3 November 1952 Bodleian

62 *Daily Telegraph* 20 March 1953

63 *Daily Mail* 29 March 1953

64 *The Listener* 2 April 1953

65 Robert Liddell to Barbara Pym 31 May 1953 Bodleian

66 ibid. 23 July 1953 Bodleian

67 *New Statesman* 4 April 1953

68 ET to Katharine White 15 March 1953 Bryn Mawr

69 ET to William Maxwell 26 August 1953 Grant Papers

70 *New York Times* 13 September 1953

71 *New Republic* 2 November 1953 p 25

72 *The Sleeping Beauty* p 159

73 ET to William Maxwell October 1953 Grant Papers

74 JB Priestley in a review of *Hester Lilly* in *The Sunday Times* 7 November 1954

75 interview with Brian Glanville for *The World of Books* op. cit. This part of the interview was not in fact broadcast.

76 AL Barker introduction to *Hester Lilly* Virago 1990 pp xi, xiii

77 John Wiltshire *Recreating Jane Austen* 2001 p 129

78 DW Harding *Regulated Hatred* 1998 pp 11, 12, originally *Scrutiny* 7 1940

79 Wiltshire op.cit. p 129

CHAPTER TEN

1 letter 345 to Ray Russell
   25 January 1944
2 William Maxwell to ET
   28 January 1954 *The New
   Yorker* Papers
3 ET to William Maxwell
   20 November 1952
4 ET to Patience Ross 22
   September 1953 Taylor Papers
5 *Hester Lilly* p 54
6 ET to Patience Ross 3
   February 1953 Taylor Papers
7 'Spry Old Character' *The New
   Yorker* 7 March 1953, *Hester
   Lilly* pp 90, 94, 106
8 'Swan-Moving' *The New Yorker*
   26 December 1953, *Hester Lilly*
   pp 153, 156
9 'Goodbye, Goodbye' *The New
   Yorker* 14 August 1954, *Woman
   and Beauty* May 1955, *The
   Blush* pp 155, 161
10 William Maxwell to ET 9 June
   1954
11 Charles Poore in the *New York
   Times* 23 September 1954
12 Dan Wickenden *New York
   Herald Tribune* 26 September
   1954
13 'Taking Mother Out' *Harper's
   Bazaar* March 1950, *Hester
   Lilly* pp79–82
14 William Maxwell to ET August
   1954 Taylor Papers
15 *Elizabeth and Ivy* op. cit. p 32
16 ET to William Maxwell 10 May
   1951 *The New Yorker* Papers
17 ET to Elinor Bellingham
   Smith, undated ?late 1950s,
   Taylor Papers
18 ET to William Maxwell
   7 December 1952 Grant
   Papers
19 *Blaming* pp 123-4
20 John Moynihan *Restless Lives:
   The Bohemian World of Rodrigo
   and Elinor Moynihan* 2002
   p 123
21 L Marks and T Van den Bergh
   *Ruth Ellis – A Case of Diminished
   Responsibility* 1977 reprinted
   1990 pp 74, 65
22 letter to author from a
   Shrewsbury contemporary
   23 February 1997
23 letter to the *Evening Standard*
   7 July 1955 quoted in
   J Goodman and P Pringle *The
   Trial of Ruth Ellis* 1974 p 134
24 *In a Summer Season* pp 39, 29,
   38
25 entry for Ruth Ellis in the
   Oxford DNB
26 *In a Summer Season* p 31
27 conversation between Jean
   Bourne and author
   15 December 1996
28 ET to Patience Ross 20 May
   1955 Taylor Papers
29 Robert Hancock *Ruth Ellis:
   The Last Woman to be Hanged*
   1963 reprinted 1996 pp 94,
   104
30 *Elizabeth and Ivy* op. cit. p 57
31 notes on letters from ET to
   Ivy Compton-Burnett 1970,
   Spurling Papers
32 *In a Summer Season* p 60
33 Elizabeth Bowen to ET
   14 May 1955 Taylor Papers
34 'A Memoir' unpublished ts.
   1973 Tulsa

35 Elizabeth Bowen to ET 14 May and 29 June 1955 Taylor Papers
36 ibid. 29 October 1954
37 letter 466 to Ray Russell 25 September 1945
38 ET to Patience Ross 20 May 1955 Taylor Papers
39 ET to Barbara Pym late September 1955 Bodleian
40 'Hare Park' *The New Yorker* 14 April 1956, *Cornhill* Summer 1956, *The Blush*; 'The Ambush' *The New Yorker* 2 June 1956, *Woman's Own*, *The Blush*
41 *Elizabeth and Ivy* op.cit. p 66
42 ET to Robert Liddell September 1955 Taylor Papers
43 'Setting a Scene' *Cornhill* Autumn 1965 p 69
44 *Angel* pp 55, 93, 14
45 Eileen Bigland *Marie Corelli* 1953 p 73
46 *Angel* pp 51, 50
47 Amanda McKittrick Ros *Delina Delaney* p 44
48 ET to Robert Liddell April 1956 Taylor Papers
49 *A Game of Hide and Seek* p 116
50 ET to William Maxwell 12 May 1960 Grant Papers
51 Claire Tomalin *Sunday Times* 19 February 1984
52 Preface to *Angel* Virago 1984 pp vi–vii
53 *Angel* p 54
54 *TLS* 7 June 2006 'English Taylor's Relentless Englishness' Trev Broughton
55 *The Independent* 1 September 2008

56 WR Geddes *Nine Dayak Nights* 1957 p ix
57 ibid. p 32
58 Heather Sutton in interview with author 24 November 1997
59 *Blaming* pp 129, 142
60 Robert Liddell to Barbara Pym 28 November 1978 Bodleian
61 *Blaming* pp 163–4
62 *A Wreath of Roses* p 148
63 *Blaming* pp 166, 167, 169, 171, 174, 188

CHAPTER ELEVEN

1 ET to Robert Liddell in 1959 *Elizabeth and Ivy* op. cit. p 16
2 ET to Katharine White 13 December 1957 Bryn Mawr
3 ET to William Maxwell 5 November 1952, Grant Papers
4 ET to William Maxwell 20 November 1952 *The New Yorker* Papers
5 back of letter from Peter Davies to ET 4 March 1953 Taylor Papers
6 *Elizabeth and Ivy* op.cit. pp 73, 74, 75
7 *At Mrs Lippincote's* p 33
8 *The Sleeping Beauty* p 34
9 ET to William Maxwell 17 March 1956
10 conversation between Mrs Martin Robertson and Joy Grant April 1978 Grant Papers
11 letter 271 to Ray Russell 18 August 1943

12 ET to Renny Taylor April 1956
    Taylor Papers
13 *Elizabeth and Ivy* op.cit. p 60
14 Scrapbook, Taylor Papers
15 *Elizabeth and Ivy* op. cit. p 59
16 ET to Robert Liddell April
    1956 Taylor Papers
17 'The Letter-Writers' *The New
    Yorker* 31 May 1958, *Cornhill*
    Summer 1958, *The Blush*
    pp 40, 41, 51
18 *Elizabeth and Ivy* op.cit. p 68
19 'In a Different Light'
    A Dedicated Man p 78
20 *Elizabeth and Ivy* op.cit. pp 68,
    69
21 'The Voices' *The New Yorker*
    20 July 1963, *Cornhill* Spring
    1964, *A Dedicated Man* p 186
22 Robert Liddell to Francis King
    4 May 1959, Texas
23 *Elizabeth and Ivy* op.cit. pp 73,
    74
24 ET to Robert Liddell early
    1959 Taylor Papers
25 *At Mrs Lippincote's* p 42
26 *Evening Standard* 4 June
    1957
27 *Spectator* 14 June 1957
28 ed. Z Leader *The Letters of
    Kingsley Amis* 2000, letter to the
    Spectator 19 November 1983
29 *Time* 9 September 1957
30 *The Commonweal* 25 October
    1957
31 ET to Patience Ross 5 June
    1957 Taylor Papers
32 'The Rose, The Mauve, The
    White' *The New Yorker* 22 June
    1957, *Woman's Own* (date
    unknown), *The Blush* pp103,
    106, 95

33 William Strunk Jr and EB
    White *The Elements of Style*
    1959 pp 2, 4
34 William Maxwell to ET mid-
    August 1958, Taylor Papers
35 ET to William Maxwell
    17 August 1958, Grant Papers
36 ET to William Maxwell
    11 August 1958, *The New
    Yorker* Papers
37 'The Blush' *The New Yorker*
    17 August 1957, *The Blush*
    pp 27, 33, 32
38 ET to William Maxwell 7 July
    1957 *The New Yorker* Papers
39 *Bucks Free Press* 1 May 1976
40 postcard dated 31 June 1956
    Russell Papers
41 'A Troubled State of Mind'
    Vogue (USA) as 'Where Can It
    End?' 1 November 1958,
    Cornhill Spring 1958, *The
    Blush* p62
42 'Perhaps a Family Failing' *The
    New Yorker* 5 July 1958, *The
    Blush* p 143
43 'Summer Schools' *The New
    Yorker* 6 September 1958, *The
    Blush* p 117
44 *The Listener* 13 November
    1958
45 *Elizabeth and Ivy* op.cit. p 72
46 *In a Summer Season* pp 31, 28,
    21, 24, 21, 56, 105, 25, 141,
    152, 124, 90
47 Introduction by Susannah
    Clapp to the Virago edition of
    In a Summer Season p vi
48 'The Prerogative of Love' *The
    New Yorker* 23 July 1960,
    Harper's Bazaar (UK) June
    1961, *The Blush* pp 36, 37

49 *At Mrs Lippincote's* p 56
50 *Elizabeth and Ivy* op.cit. p 66
51 *London Magazine* November 1958 pp 13–15
52 *New Statesman* 20 December 1958
53 ET to Robert Liddell early 1959 Taylor Papers
54 WL Webb in the *Manchester Guardian* 25 November 1958

CHAPTER TWELVE

1 letter to Patience Ross July/August 1965 Taylor Papers
2 *TLS* 12 May 1961
3 ET to William Maxwell 11 August 1958 *The New Yorker* Papers
4 ET to Patience Ross 21 August 1963 Taylor Papers
5 ET to Robert Liddell 1959 Taylor Papers
6 Robert Liddell ts. of talk at the PEN Club 11 March 1987, Grant Papers; Robert Liddell to Barbara Pym 1957, Bodleian
7 ET to Barbara Pym 7 February 1959 Bodleian
8 'The Little Girl ts. Tulsa
9 ET to William Maxwell, Grant Papers 7 December 1958
10 'Setting a Scene' *Cornhill* Autumn 1965 p 71
11 'The Thames Spread Out', *The New Yorker* 19 December 1959, *Argosy* May 1960 *A Dedicated Man* pp 51, 63, 59
12 *Elizabeth and Ivy* op.cit. p 110
13 'A Dedicated Man' *The New Yorker* 4 June 1960 *Cornhill*

Autumn 1960, *A Dedicated Man* p 125
14 'The Benefactress' *The New Yorker* 5 December 1959, *Cornhill* Spring 1960, *A Dedicated Man* pp 94, 102
15 21 September 1959 telegram *The New Yorker* Papers
16 ET to Robert Liddell 1960 Taylor Papers
17 *Elizabeth and Ivy* op.cit. pp 96, 85, 93, 96
18 Herman Schrijver to ET 7 December 1965 Grant Papers
19 Francis King to the author 20 January 1997
20 Mary Ellen Chase *New York Herald Tribune* 12 February 1961
21 Norman Shrapnel in the *Guardian* 28 April 1961
22 Richard Mayne *New Statesman* 28 April 1961
23 John Weightman on *The Critics* 30 April 1961Tulsa
24 'Girl Reading' *A Dedicated Man* p 27
25 'Setting a Scene' *Cornhill* Autumn 1965 p 70
26 William Maxwell to ET 31 May 1961 *The New Yorker* Papers
27 'In a Different Light' (first called 'A Feeling of Affection') *The New Yorker* 28 October 1961, *Cornhill* Winter 1961/2, *A Dedicated Man* pp 76, 79, 89
28 *The Soul of Kindness* pp 207, 113
29 *New Statesman* 25 September 1964
30 *Spectator* 25 September 1964

31 *New Statesman* op.cit.
32 *Observer* 27 June 1965
33 Peter Davies to ET 5 March 1951 Taylor Papers
34 *Manchester Guardian* 16 December 1958
35 Elizabeth Jane Howard *Slipstream: A Memoir* 2002 p 326
36 'As If I Should Care'/ 'Façade Collapsing' *The New Yorker* 19 May 1962, *A Dedicated Man*
37 ET to Patience Ross 1 February 1957 Taylor Papers
38 'Mice and Birds and Boy' *The New Yorker* 9 February 1963, *Cornhill* Summer 1963, *A Dedicated Man* pp174, 176
39 'Mr Wharton' *The New Yorker* 8 June 1963, *A Dedicated Man*
40 ET to William Maxwell August 1959 *The New Yorker* Papers
41 Robert Liddell to Francis King 20 May 1962 Texas
42 ET to Katharine White 14 July 1961 Bryn Mawr
43 'Crêpes Flambées' in *The Devastating Boys* p183
44 William Maxwell to Carl Brandt 16 May 1966 *The New Yorker* Papers
45 'In the Sun' *The New Yorker* 16 April 1964, *Argosy* August 1964, *A Dedicated Man* pp 188, 197, 195
46 ET to Barbara Pym 12 March 1968 Bodleian
47 ET to William Maxwell 22 November 1966 *The New Yorker* Papers

48 Oliver Knox to Joy Grant 25 February 1978 Grant Papers
49 *The Times* 7 April 1960
50 *The Listener* 24 September 1964
51 *TLS* 24 September 1964
52 Elizabeth Bowen to ET 28 June 1964 Taylor Papers
53 ET to Elizabeth Bowen February 1964 Texas
54 postcard from ET to Herman Schrijver April 1964 Grant Papers
55 *Elizabeth and Ivy* op.cit. p 108
56 'Hôtel du Commerce' *Cornhill* November 1965, *The Devastating Boys* p 142
57 Carl Brandt to William Maxwell 30 November 1964 *The New Yorker* Papers
58 'Tall Boy' *The New Yorker* 31 December 1966, *The Devastating Boys* pp 71, 67
59 ET to Robert Liddell, two undated letters mid-1960s, Taylor Papers
60 William Maxwell to ET 17 May 1966 Taylor Papers
61 ET to William Maxwell late May 1966 Grant Papers
62 EB White *Charlotte's Web* 1952 Penguin 1975 p 175
63 ET to William Maxwell October 1957 *The New Yorker* Papers
64 'Have You Met Elizabeth Taylor?' Stella Dobson on *Woman's Hour* 22 March 1956, Tulsa
65 *Mossy Trotter* 1967 p 23

66 Bill Maxwell to Carl Brandt 27 October 1965 *The New Yorker* Papers
67 *Saturday Evening Post* 14 December 1968, *The Devastating Boys*
68 'The Fly-Paper' *Cornhill* Spring 1969, *The Devastating Boys* p 181
69 Paul Theroux *Encounter* September 1972 p 71
70 Norah Smallwood to ET 24 June 1971 Chatto & Windus files, Reading
71 Janice Elliott *New Statesman* 3 May 1968
72 Brigid Brophy *London Magazine* April 1968
73 Angus Wilson 'In the Jane Austen tradition' *Observer* 28 April 1968
74 Paul Scott *The Times* 27 April 1968

CHAPTER THIRTEEN

1 *At Mrs Lippincote's* p 110
2 'Summer Schools' *The Blush* p 117
3 'Last Laugh', unpublished ts. of a short story by Dorothy Whipple, Whipple Papers, Private Collection
4 *Mrs Palfrey at the Claremont* p 2
5 Herman Schrijver to ET 17 August 1971 Grant Papers
6 Introduction to *Mrs Palfrey at the Claremont* Virago 1982 p viii
7 Elizabeth Bowen to ET 13 September 1971 Taylor Papers
8 *Daily Telegraph* 31 October 1998
9 ET to William Maxwell c. 1969 *The New Yorker* Papers
10 William Maxwell to Carl Brandt March 1969 *The New Yorker* Papers
11 Preface by Paul Bailey to *The Devastating Boys* Virago pp xi–xii
12 Richard Gordon *Fifty Years a Fisherman* 1985 pp 90, 91, 94
13 *The Times* 22 November 1971
14 John Gross in conversation with the author 11 October 2006
15 *TLS* 27 August 1971 p 1017
16 ET to Herman Schrijver 27 November 1971 Grant Papers
17 letter from Susan Hill to Joy Grant 1 October 1979 Grant Papers
18 *The Times* 22 November 1971
19 ET to Elizabeth Jane Howard 14 June 1972 Huntington
20 'The Blossoming' *The Saturday Story Book* 32 1972, *Dangerous Calm* op.cit. p 302
21 'The Wrong Order' *London Magazine* April/May 1973, *Winter's Tales* 19 1973, *Dangerous Calm* op. cit. pp 303, 304, 315, 321, 320
22 ET to Norah Smallwood 11 January 1972 Chatto & Windus files, Reading
23 *Book World* 30 April 1972
24 *New York Times* Book Review 23 April 1972
25 *TLS* 9 June 1972

26 ET to Joanna Kingham April 1971 Taylor Papers
27 ET to Elizabeth Jane Howard 26 June 1972 Huntington
28 Robert Liddell to Barbara Pym 4 October 1972 Bodleian
29 ET to Francis King September 1972 Texas
30 ET to Janet Fitzgerald 1 September 1972 Grant Papers
31 ET to Joanna Kingham 26 July 1972 Taylor Papers
32 ET to Elizabeth Jane Howard mid-July 1972 Huntington
33 'Madame Olga' *McCall's* August 1973 pp 109, 56
34 ET to Francis King September 1972 Texas
35 'The Ghost Story' undated ms. Tulsa
36 ET to Janet Fitzgerald 29 March 1973 Grant Papers
37 'A Memoir' p11, undated ts. Tulsa
38 *Blaming* pp 58, 84, 46
39 ET to Janet Fitzgerald 29 March 1973 Grant Papers
40 'How Do You Spell Wednesday' ts. Tulsa
41 Ann Thwaite ed. *Allsorts* 5 1972 p 96
42 unpublished ts. 'The Etiquette of Modern Society' Tulsa
43 Elizabeth Jane Howard to ET 24 April 1975 Taylor Papers
44 ET to Elizabeth Jane Howard June 1975 Huntington
45 ET to Patience Ross 30 July 1975 Taylor Papers
46 ET to Patience Ross Huntington undated
47 ET to Elizabeth Jane Howard undated Huntington
48 Katharine White to ET 25 June 1975 Taylor Papers
49 ET to Patience Ross 7 July 1975 Huntington
50 ET to Patience Ross 29 August 1975 Huntington
51 ET to Elizabeth Jane Howard mid-October 1975 Huntington
52 Elizabeth Jane Howard to ET 29 October 1975 Taylor Papers
53 Kingsley Amis to ET 30 October 1975 Taylor Papers
54 *A View of the Harbour* p 262
55 Taylor Papers
56 Homer *Iliad VI*
57 *At Mrs Lippincote's* p 186
58 Joanna Kingham to Elizabeth Jane Howard 28 November 1975 Taylor Papers
59 John Taylor to the Secretary of PEN 29 December 1975 PEN Archive Tulsa
60 Kingsley Amis *Memoirs* 1991 p 296
61 Patience Ross to John Taylor 25 November 1975 Taylor Papers
62 Robert Liddell to Barbara Pym 21 January 1977 Pym Papers Bodleian
63 *Bucks Free Press* 23 June 2006
64 *Catalogue of English Literature (Comprising Printed Books, Autograph Letters and Manuscripts)* sold at Sotheby's, London on 21 and 22 July 1983, lot 528; quotation from Susannah Clapp introduction to *The Sleeping Beauty* p vi

CHAPTER FOURTEEN

1   letter 455 to Ray Russell
    October 1945
2   Rosemary Dinnage in the *TLS*
    10 September 1976
3   CP Snow *Financial Times*
    23 September 1976
4   Kingsley Amis review of
    Blaming, *Observer*
    12 September 1976
5   quoted Reading *Evening Post*
    8 December 1976
6   Francis King *Spectator*
    25 February 1984
7   Paul Bailey *New Statesman*
    10 August 1973
8   AN Wilson *Evening Standard* in
    1995
9   Richard Ford Introduction *The
    Essential Tales of Chekhov* 1999
    pp vii, xiv
10 Anita Brookner review of *The
    Blush, Spectator* 29 November
    1986
11 Kingsley Amis *Memoirs* op. cit.
    p 296
12 Jonathan Keates *Spectator*
    3 April 1999
13 Philip Hensher 'The Other
    Liz Taylor' *Daily Telegraph*
    1 April 2006
14 *Atlantic Monthly* September
    2007
15 NH Reeve *Writers and their
    Work: Elizabeth Taylor*
    2008
16 Robert Liddell 'The Novels
    of Elizabeth Taylor' *A Review of
    English Literature* Volume 1
    No. 2 April 1960 p 61
17 Alison Light *Forever England*
    1991 p 21
18 Rosemary Dinnage op. cit.
19 Philip Hensher op. cit.
20 Anne Tyler *The Washington Post*
    21 August 1983
21 Kingsley Amis letter to the
    Spectator 19 November 1983
22 Elizabeth Jane Howard
    introduction to *The Wedding
    Group* 1985 p x
23 Paul Bailey introduction to
    Mrs Palfrey at the Claremont
    1982 p x

INDEX

INDEX

INDEX

INDEX